The Beaches of O'ahu

The Beaches of O'ahu

John R. K. Clark

A KOLOWALU BOOK
University of Hawaii Press
Honolulu

Title page photograph of Mākaha Beach by Christine A. Takata

Library of Congress Cataloging in Publication Data

Clark, John R K   1946–
  The Beaches of O'ahu.

  (A Kolowalu book)
  Bibliography: p.
  Includes index.
  1. Beaches—Hawaii—Oahu. 2. Oahu—
Description and travel. I. Title.
GB458.8.C59   919.69'3'044   77–8244
ISBN 0–8248–0510–0 pbk.

To my parents
Alice Lee and George V. Clark

Contents

Maps

Preface

The idea for this book surfaced in May 1972 while I was still a lifeguard with the City and County of Honolulu. I spent the last year of my two years in the lifeguard service at Sandy Beach where my partner Daryl Picadura and I participated in numerous rescues during each of our working weeks. When you grow up in the islands, you know that the ocean can be dangerous as well as pleasurable. But it was not until I worked as a lifeguard that I realized just how many beach-related catastrophes are caused by ignorance. Visitors, military personnel, and even our own local residents are all too often totally ignorant of the power and dangers of the sea. This situation results in many critical, and some fatal, incidents all along O'ahu's shoreline.

I decided to write a water safety guide that would describe in detail not only the dangers of every beach on O'ahu, but that would also note the locations of all available emergency facilities, such as lifeguard towers, emergency phones, hospitals, and fire stations, so that help could be found quickly day or night. My aim was to produce a simple, easy-to-use guide that would familiarize beach-goers with potential ocean hazards and that would also provide ready reference to available emergency assistance.

In the course of compiling my water safety material, I became very involved with the variety of names by which O'ahu's different beaches are known. I conceived the idea of incorporating a brief history of each beach or shoreline area that would include explanations and origins of the various place names. This fit in with my ongoing studies in Hawaiiana, and I felt that the historical narratives would be of interest and would also pro-vide some color to the important, but cut-and-dried, water safety information. I spent over three years compiling the shoreline histories and still continue to add to my personal notes whenever possible. My pamphlet developed into a book.

During the course of my research, I interviewed over three hundred individuals either in person, by telephone, or by mail. Much of what I was told is oral history passed from person to person and has never before appeared in print. This is especially true of the old Hawaiian shoreline place names. My intention in documenting this information is not only to record it before it is lost for good, but also to provide a historical basis and stimulus for further research. With this end in mind I would like to invite any serious student of Hawaiiana who wishes to pursue any of the information in this book to contact me personally. There is still a great deal of historical information about O'ahu's shoreline areas, especially in the minds of many of our older, long-time residents, that has yet to be recorded.

Specific information about each of O'ahu's beaches is presented in a section that comprises the bulk of the book. To make it easier to locate a particular beach, I divided the island into geographical districts. Beginning with Kaloko Beach, known also as Queen's or Alan Davis beach, near the Hawai'i Kai golf course, and pro-ceeding in a clockwise manner, I have listed every beach along O'ahu's shoreline.

District maps and maps locating the individual beaches are provided to help readers find their way to a specific beach.

For each beach, I have provided a history of its naming, water and shore conditions, and other information I thought of interest. In addition, specific information on available emergency facilities, comfort stations, lifeguard service, and public access, among others, has been provided in tabular format. A key to interpreting the abbreviations precedes the entire beaches section.

My training and service as a lifeguard have no doubt influenced my approach to the contents of this book. I found that I could not provide the beaches information alone without prefacing it with some information that I believe everyone should have before hitting the beach. I hope that everyone will take the time to read through this section, entitled "General Information."

Acknowledgments

During the course of my research for *The Beaches of O'ahu* I probably interviewed over three hundred individuals either personally, by mail, or by telephone. It would be impossible for me to acknowledge all of them in print. To all of them I extend my warmest *mahalo*. There is a small group, however, whose contributions have been of major importance to the success of this book, and I would like to recognize them personally: Jose Angel, Janyce Blair, Emily Kainanui and Henry Blanchard, Aileen and Timothy Brown, E. H. Bryan, Jr., Camille Clark, Peter Cole, Agnes Conrad, Alan S. Davis, Hattie Domingo, Ellen Fullard-Leo, J. Atherton Gilman, Jean Grace, June Gutmanis, Henrietta and James R. Holt, Mr. and Mrs. Daniel Hookala, Herbert A. Kamakeeaina, Sr., Aloha Kaeo, Wally Kaokai, Peter Kau, Rachel Lee, Makahiwa Lua, Louis Mahoe, J. Cline Mann, Caroline and Alika Neill, Ida Nihipali, Roy Niino, Rose Pfund, and Harry B. Soria, Jr.

Pronunciation of Hawaiian

Increasingly, in Hawai'i, concern is being voiced at the mispronunciation of Hawaiian words, the place names in particular. In this book, I have supplied the diacritics necessary to the correct pronunciation of the place names. The following guides (adapted from the *Hawaiian Dictionary*) are offered as an additional aid.

Consonants

p, k	about as in English but with less aspiration.
h, l, m, n	about as in English.
w	after *i* and *e* usually like *v;* after *u* and *o* usually like *w;* initially and after *a* like *v* or *w*.
'	a glottal stop, similar to the sound between the *oh'*s in English *oh-oh*.

Vowels

Unstressed

a	like *a* in above
e	like *e* in bet
i	like *y* in city
o	like *o* in sole
u	like *oo* in moon

Stressed

(Vowels marked with macrons are somewhat longer than other vowels.)

a, ā	like *a* in far
e	like *e* in bet
ē	like *ay* in play
i, ī	like *ee* in see
o, ō	like *o* in sole
u, ū	like *oo* in moon

Diphthongs

(These are always stressed on the first member, but the two members are not as closely joined as in English.)

ei, eu, oi, ou, ai, ae, ao, au

Common Hawaiian Words Used in the Text

ahupua‘a. Land division usually extending from the mountain to the sea.

‘Ewa. Place name west of Honolulu used as a direction term.

haole. White person; formerly it was used to indicate any foreigner.

heiau. Pre-Christian place of worship; some *heiau* were elaborately constructed stone platforms, other simple earthen terraces.

hukilau. A seine; the method of fishing with the seine.

imu. Underground oven.

kahuna. Priest, minister, sorcerer.

kama‘āina. Native-born; lit., land child.

kapu. Taboo, prohibition.

konohiki. Headman of an *ahupua‘a* under the chief; also land or fishing rights under control of the *konohiki*.

kuleana. A small piece of property within an *ahupua‘a*.

kupua. Demigod, especially a supernatural being possessing several forms.

lae. Cape, point, promontory.

lānai. Porch, veranda.

limu. A general name for all kinds of plants living underwater, both fresh and salt; a common term for seaweed.

lū‘au. Young taro tops, especially as cooked with chicken or octopus; Hawaiian feast, named after the taro tops always served at one.

makai. Toward the sea, in the direction of the sea.

mauka. Inland, upland, toward the mountains.

menehune. Legendary race of small people who worked at night, building fish ponds, roads, temples.

mo‘o. Lizard, reptile of any kind.

muliwai. Pool near the mouth of a stream, as behind a sandbar, often enlarged by ocean water left by high tide.

‘opihi. Limpet.

paniolo. Cowboy (probably from the Spanish español).

papa. A flat section of ocean bottom, such as a shelf or reef.

Pele. The goddess of the volcano.

wana. A sea urchin.

General Information

Dangerous Water Conditions

Many of our beaches on Oʻahu are protected by coral reefs, so strong currents are not a serious problem to inshore swimming. In some places, however, such as Yokohama Bay, Mākaha, Sandy Beach, Makapuʻu, Sunset, and Waimea Bay, to name a few, the beaches are not sheltered from the open ocean and the surf comes straight in, unobstructed, often causing very treacherous water conditions. Some of the water hazards to be encountered in such areas are:

Shorebreaks

Places where waves break close to shore or directly on it are known as shorebreaks. The ocean swells that hit these beaches generally pass abruptly from a deep bottom to a very shallow one, causing the waves to rise quickly in height and to break with considerable downward force. Shorebreaks usually are very dangerous swimming areas, a fact substantiated by the numerous rescues and injuries that happen each month at places like Sandy Beach and Makapuʻu. Even so, these places are popular recreational beaches because most people enjoy being tossed and rolled around by the big waves, and because, for more experienced swimmers, some shorebreaks provide excellent waves for bodysurfing.

One of the most important points for a swimmer to know, when playing in a shorebreak, is how to go out safely through the surf, to the quieter waters beyond. The trick is, simply, to take a big breath of air and to dive *under* each incoming wave. Many people, especially among our out-of-state visitors, will turn their backs to the cresting waves or will attempt to jump through or over them. This approach may work for waist-high waves or smaller ones, but all too often in the high waves of our Hawaiian surf it invites disaster. The swimmer, receiving the entire force of the wave upon his back, shoulders, and head, is pounded against the bottom and then tumbled and tossed about, often with complete loss of wind, control, and sense of direction. If he's lucky, he comes up with nothing worse than a nose full of salt water and a scoured skin.

Shorebreaks should be approached with a great deal of caution, even by swimmers who think they are experts.

Backwash

After a wave has washed up on the shore, the water it has brought must flow down the beach again as it returns to the sea. Backwash is simply the returning water from the spent wave. Trouble for a swimmer can develop if the backwash gains speed because the beach is steep. When this happens, the rush of the returning water can be almost as forceful as that of an incoming wave. A strong backwash is especially dangerous to small children and elderly people playing near the shore's edge. It can easily sweep them off their feet and carry them out into the surf. All beaches that have a steep slope should be considered dangerous, especially at or near high tide, when some of the bigger waves can rush up to and over the top of the slope. The higher a wave goes up the beach, the greater will be the force of its backwash. Smart people on a beach will keep themselves and their children beyond the reach of *all* waves.

1

Tourists stand in anticipation of being bowled over by the whitewater in Waimea Bay's dangerous shorebreak. This type of play in the ocean during winter surf months has resulted in many drownings on the North Shore.

Rip Currents

Rip currents are flowing, riverlike movements of water that run from shallow areas near shore out to sea. They are a major cause of the near and actual drownings that occur every year. The formation of a rip current is a very simple process. Waves generally come in sets, one after another, with a short lull between sets. After the first wave of a set rolls up on the shore, its mass of water washes down the beach back into the ocean, but the approach of the second incoming wave prevents the entire backwash from dispersing completely. After three or four waves of a set have come in, a substantial volume of water is being contained inshore by the waves still coming in. This build-up, or imbalance, begins to flow sideways along the shore until it finds a lower level in the ocean bottom. In other words, the water seeks a point of release, which will allow it to flow seaward. The point of release may be an actual channel in the reef, a trough gouged in the sand, or other similar bottom conditions. The result of such a build-up of water under such circumstances is a rip current flowing swiftly and steadily out to sea.

Rip currents occasionally create undertows where high surf occurs in shorebreak areas, such as Yokohama Bay and Sandy Beach. An undertow occurs just where the waves are breaking, when the build-up of water on the beach can find no other path seaward than to flow out through the incoming surf. When a wave breaks on the outgoing rip, the rip is forced to go under the wave. This is an undertow, but it lasts only as long as is needed for the wave to break and to pass over. A swimmer trapped in one will feel as if he is being pulled underwater by the current. Once the wave is gone the rip immediately comes to the surface and flows seaward again. Undertows, then, are not the terrible things they are thought to be, that drag hapless swimmers down into the depths and sweep them for miles underwater out to sea. Nonetheless, they are still very dangerous, especially to a struggling swimmer who is trying to keep his head above water. A few seconds underwater may seem like an eternity to a frightened swimmer, and may well draw him into it if he yields to panic.

Rip currents can be recognized by their effect on incoming waves and by the general direction of their movement. Strong rips will tend to flatten waves, and generally they will be heading out to sea. In places where a lot of seaweed is floating close to shore, or where the surf is churning up the sandy bottom, rip currents are easily seen. They resemble small rivers of seaweed or of sand, flowing away from shore.

If you ever get caught in a rip current, don't fight it. Just ride along with the current until it loses its power, which usually happens not far offshore, or try to ease out of it by swimming to one side, at an angle to the beach. The disastrous mistake that almost every inexperienced swimmer makes is in trying to swim back to shore, against the rip, in his determination to return to his point of departure from the beach. This is about as effective as swimming upstream in a rushing river, and often will tire a swimmer to the point of complete exhaustion. This is the major reason why rip currents are a leading cause of near drownings and actual drownings. If you get swept away from a beach, just remember that it will be easier for you to walk back along the nice safe shore than to swim against the tug of that merciless rip.

Tsunami or "Tidal Waves"

Tsunami, or seismic sea waves, frequently are called "tidal waves" because as they move up a river or over the land they resemble the bore tidal floods that occur daily in the mouth of the Amazon River, the Bay of Fundy, and other such funnel-like areas. Tsunami, though, have nothing to do with tides. They are set in motion by great disturbances, such as earthquakes, volcanic eruptions, landslides, nuclear explosions, and other such occurrences. Most tsunami occurring naturally are generated in the oceanic trenches around the borders of the Pacific Ocean, the most active areas being along the Pacific coast of Japan, the Kurile-Kamchatka chain, the Aleutian Island arc, and along the coast of Central and South America.

One of the worst tsunami in modern history occurred early in the morning of April 1, 1946, when a violent earthquake disturbed the northern slope of the Aleutian Trench. Minutes after the earthquake occurred, waves more than 100 feet high smashed the lighthouse at Scotch Cap, Unimak Island, in the Aleutians, killing five people. The first wave struck Hawai'i less than five hours later, having traveled across the north Pacific Ocean at the rate of 435 miles per hour. This wave, and the several that followed it, battered exposed island shores, and reached heights of fifty-five feet in some places. When the destructive waves subsided, 159 persons were dead and 163 injured; 488 homes had been demolished and 936 damaged; and property damage was estimated at $25 million. This tsunami, the most destructive natural disaster in Hawai'i's recorded history, was the last one ever to take the islands by surprise. Since then a seismic sea wave warning system has been established. Fortunately, the Pacific Ocean is so large that waves moving even at high speeds take several hours to cross it, thereby giving the system enough time to warn coastal inhabitants of approaching tsunami.

When the possibility exists of a tsunami reaching Hawai'i's islands, the public will be informed by the sounding of the Attention Alert Signal sirens. This particular signal is a steady one-minute tone on the sirens, followed by one minute of silence, and then a repetition of blast and silence for as long a time as may be necessary. As soon as you hear this signal, you should turn on a radio or television set immediately, and tune it to any station for essential Civ-Alert emergency information and instructions. The initial signals will be sounded not only on the coastal sirens, but on all other sirens as well. This is meant to alert boat owners who do not live near the ocean, and also to alert people with relatives or friends living in threatened areas who are not capable of removing themselves from places in jeopardy. The warning will be broadcast by Civ-Alert, as well as by police and fire department mobile units, and by Civil Air Patrol aerial units. The warning will state the expected time of arrival of the first wave.

Do not take chances! When a tsunami warning is given, move *immediately* out of coastal areas that are subject to possible inundation. Maps defining inundation areas on O'ahu are found in the front pages of the O'ahu telephone directory. But you should be aware that the limits of inundation indicated on the maps may be exceeded if a tsunami is generated by a local earthquake. In such an event, moreover, the siren warning may not have time to function. Therefore, any violent earthquake, one that forces you to hold onto something to keep from falling down, should be considered a natural tsunami warning. Immediately evacuate all low-lying areas. If you are in a house, take emergency supplies with you, lock the house, and leave quickly. If you live in an area not mapped in the telephone directory, just remember that an elevation of fifty feet above sea level has been set arbitrarily as ground safe from any likely wave.

Remember also these additional points:

1. A tsunami is not a single wave. It is a series of waves. Stay out of the danger areas until an "All Clear" signal is issued by a competent authority. An "All Clear" signal will *not* be given by the sirens.

2. Never go down to the beach to watch for a tsunami. If you can see the approaching wave, you will be too close to escape from it when it sweeps ashore.

3. Approaching tsunami sometimes are heralded by a sudden noticeable rise or fall of coastal water. This is nature's tsunami warning and should be heeded, instantly.

4. The Pacific Tsunami Warning Center does not issue false alarms. When a warning is issued, a tsunami exists. The tsunami of May 1960 killed sixty-one people in Hilo who thought it was "just another false alarm," and did not run when they should have.

The warning sirens are tested throughout the state on the first working Monday of every month, at 11:00 A.M., to make certain that each siren is operating properly. While the signals are sounding, Civ-Alert announces over all broadcasting stations that a test is underway and explains what is taking place. The entire test lasts only a few minutes. You should listen to them every once in a while just to keep yourself informed.

Dangerous Marine Animals

Jellyfish

There are many kinds of jellyfish in Hawaiian waters, but probably the one most familiar to islanders is the Portuguese man-of-war, *Physalia*. The man-of-war is easily recognized by its translucent, crested, blue "bubble," usually less than six inches long, that floats on the surface of the water. Seafarers of old found a resemblance between this crested bubble and sailing ships of their time, so the creature was called the Portuguese man-of-war. The crest on the gas-filled bubble is used as a sail of sorts, and it can be raised, lowered, or curved to help determine direction. The man-of-war, drifting with the winds and currents, has retractable tentacles that are trailed underwater to snare its food. Each tentacle contains thousands of poison-filled nematocysts that sting and paralyze the entrapped prey.

The man-of-war usually is not a problem on O'ahu's swimming beaches unless there is a strong onshore wind. When such a wind arises, the creatures are blown inshore, where they become a menace to swimmers. The tentacles are capable of delivering a severe sting, causing a burning pain and, quite often, reddened welts. Places so affected should be rubbed immediately, and gently, with clean, wet sand. This treatment will remove any pieces of tentacle still clinging to the victim without exposing the helping hand to stinging. Then the afflicted areas, after being rinsed free of sand, can be washed with freshwater or with a solution of household ammonia or baking soda. Man-of-war stings, like those of certain insects, can cause acute reactions in some people who are allergic to the poisons, so if any extreme symptoms are observed—such as shock, severe swelling, cramps, trouble in breathing, convulsions, vomiting, or anything else unusual—professional help should be sought AT ONCE. Take the suffering person to the nearest physician or hospital.

In addition to the Portuguese man-of-war, the umbrella- or bell-shaped jellyfishes also are found in our waters. In calm or protected places, these jellyfish move under their own power by contractions of the bell, but they, too, depend mainly upon winds and currents. Some of these jellyfish also have stinging tentacles, so contact with all of them should be avoided as much as possible. Even in their smallest stages, when they are almost invisible, they can be bothersome. Swimmers who develop unbearable itching, allergic reactions, and other harmful responses should be taken to a physician as soon as possible.

Coral

Coral is found in abundance throughout Hawaiian waters and accounts for a good portion of the abrasions and lacerations incurred by swimmers, surfers, and divers. Coral cuts, no matter how small, should always be treated and watched carefully, because they are very susceptible to infection and are extraordinarily slow to heal. For cases of severe cuts, where you are required to give first aid, immediately apply direct pressure to involved arteries in order to stop the bleeding. If you are in deep water, take the injured swimmer to shore or to a protected place as quickly as possible. Profuse bleeding in the water may attract sharks.

Eels

Eels are found in almost every reef in Hawai'i. They live in holes, crevices, and under coral heads, where they feed mainly on fish and crabs. Generally, they leave their hiding places only because the prospects of food are better elsewhere or because they have been disturbed. Eels usually are not aggressive unless they are confronted and threatened, so it is best to leave them alone. They have powerful jaws and many sharp teeth, and they can be vicious when they do attack.

Sharks

Sharks are not a problem at Hawai'i's beaches and do not pose any threat to the ordinary swimmer. Generally they are found in the open ocean, and come near shore only where the water is deep and lacks a protecting reef. Sharks in Hawaiian waters are well fed by the natural abundance of reef and pelagic fish, so they do not need to hunt for other kinds of food, as is the case in other parts of the world. In Hawai'i, usually a shark will approach a swimmer only out of simple curiosity and, after it has looked, it will move on. The chief exception to this rule of passing interest is well known to many local divers: sharks are attracted to fish blood, as well as to animal blood, and many a string of fish has been seized by a cruising shark. For this reason, most divers keep a long line between themselves and the catch they've speared.

If you should meet a shark face-to-face, the most important point to remember is not to panic. Avoid creating any commotion, and restrain yourself from making a wild, frenzied sprint toward shore. Although sharks are attracted by the scent of blood or food, as well as by bright or contrasting colors, they are drawn from far greater distances by low-frequency vibrations such as those produced by a wounded fish or by a swimmer thrashing about erratically. Keep the shark in view at all times, and swim smoothly and steadily to safely. Although sharks have been driven off by yelling, and blowing bubbles underwater, and even by charging them aggressively, probably your safest course is an immediate and quiet retreat.

Sea Urchins

Sea urchins, common in all Hawaiian waters, are covered with sharp, brittle, needlelike spines that protect the animals within from predators. They are found in almost all types of underwater terrain, but usually are living in, upon, or close to rocks and coral. If they are stepped on or even brushed against, the tips of the spines easily break off and are embedded in the skin, causing more discomfort than anything else. The fragile slivers are not easily removed, even with a needle, but they will dissolve after a week or so if left alone. The punctured places should be checked occasionally, in any event, to make sure that no infection develops. A common folk remedy in Hawai'i is to urinate on the afflicted part. As strange or distasteful as this may sound, it is effective sometimes. The uric acid hastens the dissolution of the bothersome spines.

Beach Equipment

Skin Diving Equipment

The inshore reef waters that surround the Hawaiian Islands contain some of the most beautiful fish and underwater terrain that can be found anywhere in the world. With the aid of a few basic pieces of skin diving equipment, underwater exploration is easily available all year round to any competent swimmer. The following points are guidelines to help you select the proper equipment.

Face Mask

The human eye is not adapted for accurate or lengthy viewing underwater, an obvious fact to anyone who has ever opened his eyes in either fresh or salt water. The face mask provides a constant layer of air between the eyes and a transparent lens, thereby allowing the wearer to see things clearly underwater. The only distortion that remains is in size and distance: objects appear to be slightly larger, and distances slightly closer, than they actually are.

There are numerous variations in face mask design, but the essential features to look for are a soft, flexible, face-fitting skirt; an adjustable, well-anchored headstrap with a double band in the rear; and a shatter-proof or tempered lens that is secured by a metal band.

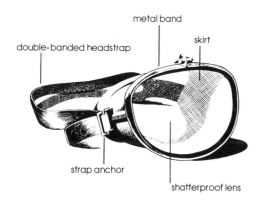

metal band

double-banded headstrap

skirt

strap anchor

shatterproof lens

The shatterproof lens costs more than an ordinary one, but a mask without it is a potential hazard. If a diver is wearing a non-shatterproof product and accidentally receives a hard blow to the lens, the entire glass plate may shatter inward, lacerating the face and possibly the eyes of the unsuspecting wearer. The risk is not worth the savings.

To insure that the face mask you have selected is the proper size and fit for your facial features, perform this simple test. Hold the mask against your face without securing the head strap. Inhale deeply through your nose and hold your breath. The vacuum created inside the mask will cause it to adhere to your face if there are no leaks. If the mask does not stick tightly or simply falls off, it will undoubtedly leak in the water. Try different sizes or styles of masks until the test is successful for you.

Snorkel

The snorkel is a simple device that allows the skin diver to continue normal breathing while lying or swimming face down on the ocean's surface. There are many designs, but basically the snorkel is a J-shaped tube made of hard plastic, rubber, or similar material. One end is placed in the mouth, while the opposite end sticks up above the water, to provide the user with a continuous supply of air. When the diver submerges, water will fill the tube, but the water can be expelled by blowing sharply into the mouthpiece upon resurfacing. The same action is used for the occasional wave or chop that splashes water into the snorkel while the swimmer is maneuvering on the surface.

Select a light, simply designed snorkel that has an easy-to-grip mouthpiece. Avoid any arrangements in

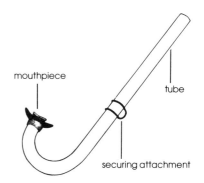

mouthpiece

tube

securing attachment

which the snorkel is built into the mask. In these combinations there is no way to expel the water except by lifting the mask away from the face. If the entire mask suddenly fills with water, and the diver panics and does not think to rip it away from his face, a critical situation immediately arises. Also avoid snorkels that have a ball-and-socket arrangement to prevent water from entering the tube. These, too, can create a panic situation if the ball plugs the tube just as the diver is inhaling or if the ball gets stuck in its sealing position.

A good snorkel is a simple, energy-conserving device. It allows you to focus your attention upon objects underwater without the interruption and effort of lifting your head for a breath of air.

Fins

A fin is simply a man-made extension of the foot that provides more surface area for gaining easier and swifter propulsion in the water. Fins are made in numerous variations of total blade area, curvature, outline, and flexibility, but basically there are two types that concern the average skin diver: those with the closed heel, or "shoe-fins," and those with the open heel. Shoe fins offer maximum protection against sharp coral and rocks because they cover the entire foot. Generally they are more comfortable to the novice diver because usually the rubber is softer and more flexible. This characteristic also reduces the possibility of cramps in foot muscles that are not used to supporting a fin. Open heel fins do not afford as much protection; they generally have stiffer ribs, and sometimes an additional center rib as well, which increases the thrust potential considerably. This variety usually is preferred by bodysurfers and by more experienced divers.

Comfort is a major consideration in selecting a pair of fins. If the fins are too tight or too heavy for your feet, they may cause muscle cramps. If they are too loose, they may cause blisters and be ineffectual for propulsion. Determining your individual needs and estimating the supporting strength of your lower leg muscles (preferably by testing yourself with someone else's fins) will help you to select a reasonably comfortable pair before you actually use them in the water.

The final factor to consider is whether or not the fins you are interested in will float by themselves. If you plan

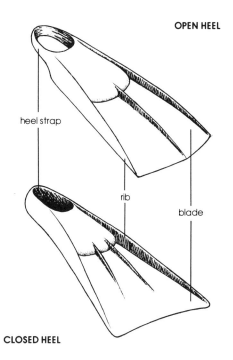

OPEN HEEL

heel strap

rib

blade

CLOSED HEEL

to bodysurf as well as skin dive with the same pair of fins, you will be much better off with the floating type. Fins are often ripped off the bodysurfer's feet by a churning wave, and a floating fin is much easier to find than one lying on the bottom.

The key words to remember in selecting all components of your skin diving gear are safety, comfort, and simplicity. The more complex your equipment is, the more chances you have for trouble. Comfort speaks for itself. If your gear causes you discomfort, the pleasure of your experience is lessened, if not lost. And, of course, safety cannot be overemphasized. Be sure to select proper equipment that will not endanger you in any way.

Flotation Gear

Flotation gear is a general name for any inflatable device, such as an air mattress, rubber raft, inner tube, beach ball, ring buoy, plastic boat, or other contraption, that can support the weight of a child or an adult upon the surface of the water. Such inflatable items come in all sizes and shapes and are used primarily by children as water toys and beach playthings. Many people do not realize that flotation gear give a false sense of security and can be extremely dangerous for any weak person or for someone who cannot swim. If a child, for example, tips his raft over, or punctures his air mattress, or falls through the center of his inner tube, and he cannot swim or float in water over his head, a critical and possibly fatal situation immediately arises. This is why it is imperative for parents to supervise closely any children who cannot swim, especially if they are playing with flotation devices. Adults should also be fully aware of their own capabilities before using any kind of flotation gear.

Many parents of nonswimming children feel that their youngsters are safe if they are using their playthings in calm, shallow water, but all too often this foolish trust proves to be dangerous. A sharp gust of wind can easily whisk a child on an air mattress into deep water or, even more commonly, may blow a beach ball away from him into deep water. Without thinking, the child will chase the ball into water beyond his limits and, as soon as he realizes he has gone in too far, he will panic.

Flotation gear should be used with a great deal of caution on the part of everyone. In addition to flotation devices, the same caution should be applied to surfboards and other kinds of water craft that do not require life vests. They can be as dangerous as leaking boats.

Wave-Riding Sports

Hawai'i is known throughout the world for surfing and canoe riding, and few visitors or residents in the islands are unfamiliar with these popular pastimes. There are, however, some other wave-riding sports practiced by islanders that are not as widely known.

Bodysurfing

Bodysurfing is the art of riding a wave in which a swimmer uses only his body for riding and maneuvering. Two basic techniques in bodysurfing have been developed. In the first, and perhaps the older, style, the swimmer presses both arms against his sides and rides on the shoulder of the wave just ahead of the breaking white water. This method generally is used in big offshore breaks, such as occur outside Makapu'u Beach, where the rides are long and often bumpy, and therefore require a tight, streamlined body. This older style, however, is not as effective in other kinds of surf, such as shorebreaks, of the sort that occur off Sandy Beach, where the waves are extremely steep and fast, and break in very shallow water. These waves require a technique in which the rider keeps either one or both of his arms out in front of him, and uses them in addition to his body as a means of controlling his speed, direction, and

position on the wavefront. This method gives the rider more than a fighting chance in catching the fast shorebreaks, and allows him a degree of adaptability in riding them that is not possible with the more streamlined technique. Most of the better bodysurfers in the islands are adept in both styles and sometimes will use both, as necessary, while riding the same wave.

Almost all bodysurfers wear fins now, to give them the extra thrust and propulsion so often needed to catch a wave. The most popular types are the open heel fins with permanent, unadjustable heel straps, but for bodysurfing perhaps the most necessary characteristic of any fin is its ability to float. This quality is important because fins all too often are ripped off the foot by the rough water.

In addition to fins, some bodysurfers also use handboards, a comparatively recent innovation. A handboard, as its name implies, is simply a small board that is strapped to the palm of either hand. Usually it is homemade, fashioned of wood or surfboard foam, and shaped somewhat in an exaggerated outline of a hand with the fingers extended and joined, wide and rounded in the back, and pointed in the front. Handboard users feel that the board gives them a slight advantage in speed and planing ability, but this point has not been proved satisfactorily to most free bodysurfers who regard the handboard as more of a hindrance than a help.

The effectiveness of handboards aside, the most important thing to realize is that they are potentially dangerous. If a churning wave thrusts your hand into your face, or into any other part of your body, or into someone else alongside you, the board may do some damage. Therefore, handboards should be used with caution.

Paipo Board Surfing

In the days of old, Hawaiians referred to bodysurfing as *kaha* (or *kaha nalu*) and *pae* (or *paepo'o*). During the early 1900s, the term *paepo'o* was commonly used in Waikīkī, and it meant riding a wave with only the body. After World War II, this particular word took on an alternate definition, referring to bodysurfing with a small board. The pronunciation of the original word, *paepo'o,* was altered, and now even the spelling is changed to paipo. Today "to paipo" means to go bodysurfing with a "bellyboard." The board itself is called a paipo board.

Paipo board surfing is an intermediate development between bodysurfing and surfboard riding. The paipo board is small (3 to 4 feet long), thin (about ¼ inch thick), and usually made of plywood that is protected by paint or some other waterproofing. The shapes and sizes vary according to individual preferences. Because paipos usually are ridden in a prone position, some spectators call them "bellyboards." The paipo board rider has much more speed and freedom of movement than does a bodysurfer and often catches much longer rides. Some paipo riders prefer to kneel on their boards, a technique that reduces their speed but allows them maximum maneuverability in the critical sections of the wave. The big outside breaks at Makapu'u attract some of the best paipo riders on O'ahu, and it is well worth the drive to watch them perform on a good day.

A variation of paipo board riding is "mat surfing." Instead of a board, the rider surfs on a small, air-filled, canvas mattress. However, several shortcomings have kept mat surfing from gaining widespread popularity. The mats are very buoyant, which makes them hard to take out through incoming surf; they are reluctant to go in any direction other than straight toward shore; and finally, they deflate when punctured. In spite of these drawbacks, mat surfing still remains a very enjoyable sport.

Sand Sliding

"Sand sliding" is the art of riding the shallow water of a wave as it is receding over the sand. After a wave washes up on a beach and the greater part of it returns to the ocean, a thin layer of water is left trailing over the sand. It is this layer that is used in sand sliding. At first, sand sliders used only their bodies in this daring sport. As the wave receded, the rider would run behind it and, at the right moment, would throw himself flat upon the seemingly waterless sand. The thin layer of water still present, however, was enough to support him, and his momentum carried him skimming over the beach, riding along on his lower chest and stomach while he held his arms close to his side. As might be imagined, the key to successful sand sliding was, and still is, perfect timing. If the rider dives too early, while the water is yet too deep, he simply sinks to a stop. If he dives too late, he misses the fleeting moment entirely—and ends his attempt in an abrupt, belly-scraping halt.

The older style of the sport, that of using only the body, is rarely seen anymore. In recent years the paipo board has been put to this use also. The rider runs after the receding wave, drops his board in front of him, jumps upon it, and goes skimming over the thin cushion of water.

Another variation is to use an air-filled bag instead of a board. The rider grasps a corner of wet air-filled cotton bag in each hand and holds it in front of him, runs after the wave, falls across the bag at the right moment, and slides along, his body supported entirely by the bag. The original bags were military mattress covers. Sometimes even plain sheets were used. In recent years, bags designed specifically for the sport, usually called "bellybags," have been put on the retail market.

All three forms of "sand sliding" look easy, but in fact they take quite a bit of practice and coordination. All are fun, though, and they also provide good exercise because they require the rider to run in wet sand.

A young sand slider skims over the beach at Bellows Field Beach Park while other youthful enthusiasts surf and body-surf in the small waves offshore.

Emergency Facilities

Emergency Phones

At present, in 1977, fifty-nine emergency telephones are located around the coast of O'ahu in beach areas that are heavily used for recreational purposes. Each phone is housed in a bright yellow metal box, with a big red EMERGENCY stenciled across the door of the box. The telephones are placed either right on the beach or near the comfort station in a beach park. Orange directional signs, showing the location of each phone, are posted on the main roads passing the beach areas. The phones are free, they are in operation twenty-four hours a day, and they can be used by following the simple instructions posted within each box.

Everyone should be familiar with the standard operating procedure:

1. Lift handset and wait for operator. (Coins are not necessary.)
2. Give operator station number shown on door.
3. Give operator information as to type of emergency.
4. Answer operator's questions.
5. Be calm; speak slowly and clearly.
6. Do not hang up until the operator tells you to do so.

The emergency phones have been installed specifically for public use. If ever you have a legitimate emergency of any kind, such as a possible drowning, need for a search and rescue mission, a fire, a missing person, boat trouble, or if you need an ambulance or a police officer, use one of these emergency phones. It is a direct line to the Honolulu Fire Department's Central Alarm Bureau, where dispatchers handle calls for help with other direct lines to the police, ambulance services, and rescue units. You should know exactly where to find the nearest emergency phone whenever you go to a beach, and especially before you enter the water.

Lifeguard Service

Long before 1900, visitors from the mainland were coming to Hawai'i in steadily increasing numbers. Before World War I, Waikīkī was well established among residents (and a few tourists) as the swimming, canoeing, and surfing center of the islands. When the need for an organized lifeguard service at Waikīkī became apparent, local surfers and beachboys from the Waikīkī area formed a group of volunteers. In spite of the efforts of these volunteers, however, the need for professional, full-time guards was evident. In 1912, the territorial legislature enacted a law providing for two lifeguards working under the Board of Harbor Commissioners. In 1917, the number was increased to four.

In 1935, Walter Napoleon took over the Territorial Beach Patrol, the official name of the lifeguard service at that time, and the headquarters was moved from its original home at the Moana Hotel to its present quarters in the Natatorium. Even though the guard service had been operating as an official organization for over twenty years, Napoleon still had only a handful of guards, John D. Kaupiko, Sam Steamboat, "Solo" Mahoe, Alfred Kaluau, and "Diamond" Martin. During these years some citizens were very concerned about the critical lack of professional lifeguards in Waikīkī. Drownings and rescues were nearly always front-page material in the newspapers; and the problems of water safety, especially among tourists, were causes for some alarm. But the lifeguard force was never enlarged.

During World War II, all of the official lifeguards became involved in the war effort and were no longer available for their beach patrols. Between 1941 and 1945, whenever possible, temporary lifeguards were recruited from among the available island men capable of performing those duties.

After the war, the four guards and their captain who served as the beach patrol simply could not provide the protection demanded by the fast-growing tourist and resident populations on O'ahu, so a City and County

volunteer service was organized by Police Chief Arthur Tarbell and Richard Bearse. Several months after the volunteers went to work in 1947, the Board of Parks announced civil service examinations for two lifeguard captains to supervise the volunteers and to act as special police to enforce the rules and regulations pertaining to the parks and beaches. In 1949, the lifeguard service, until then under the Board of Harbor Commissioners, was transferred to the Department of Parks and Recreation. This uniting of the State with the City and County guards was the beginning of our present lifeguard staff. Bill Smith, one of Hawai'i's outstanding competitive swimmers and a gold medalist in swimming at the 1948 Olympics in London, was the first captain of the new organization.

Before 1968, there were no full-time lifeguards on duty at O'ahu's public beaches except for Waikīkī and Ala Moana. Since then beaches at Hanauma Bay, Sandy Beach, Makapu'u, Kailua, Waimea Bay, and Mākaha also have been designated as permanent stations, with lifeguards on duty daily all the year round. Most of the other City and County towers on our beaches are manned throughout the entire summer by assistant lifeguards, and during the rest of the year only on weekends and holidays, depending upon the availability of the part-time assistants. When no lifeguards are on duty, or in areas where there are no guards at all, the Honolulu Fire Department's shoreline engine companies and its two Search and Rescue companies are called whenever professional help is needed. In many instances, however, rescues are made by other swimmers, surfers, or bodysurfers in an area. This was the case for many years at Makapu'u, for example, where the regular bodysurfers from Waimānalo, and even the park keepers, made numerous rescues before City and County lifeguards were assigned to this beach.

When you go to a guarded beach, remember the following points:

1. All City and County lifeguards are commissioned as special police officers. As such they have the same duties as the state parks police and as our regular police officers in enforcing city ordinances and state laws applying to their specific areas. The public must remember, however, that the first responsibility of lifeguards is to protect the lives of the swimmers on their assigned

beaches, and they should be left alone to perform this job unless a genuine emergency of another kind requires their assistance elsewhere.

2. The ultimate responsibility for the safety of all children lies with their parents or guardians. Lifeguards are not babysitters and cannot be expected to watch over unsupervised children as if they were their only charges. They are responsible for the welfare of everyone in their beach area.

3. All lifeguards are trained in first aid and are equipped with first-aid kits. The guards in Waikīkī and Ala Moana also carry two-way radios, so in addition to being able to supply immediate aid for medical emergencies, they also have a direct line to lifeguard headquarters for additional help. All country stations are situated near an emergency phone, so these guards also have access to a direct emergency line.

4. Lifeguards are put on a beach for your protection. If you are not familiar with an area, ask the guards to advise you in picking a safe place to swim. Remember that they are professional watermen and lifesavers. Follow their suggestions.

Search and Rescue Companies, Honolulu Fire Department

In January 1934, the Honolulu Fire Department acquired a 1923 Model "T" Ford truck that had been discarded first by the United States Post Office Department and then by the Hawai'i National Guard. In the fire department's shop, the truck was completely dismantled, the body was scrapped, and the engine was thoroughly overhauled. Then the body of an old condemned hose-wagon was installed on the chassis, and the entire reconstituted truck was given several coats of standard red fire engine paint and named "Rescue Wagon." On April 16, 1934, it responded from its home in the McCully Station to its first call at Ala Wai Boulevard and McCully Street, where an automobile had crashed through the bridge's guard rail and plunged into the canal. This was the beginning of the Search and Rescue division of the Honolulu Fire Department.

The original Rescue I apparatus remained at the McCully Station, where it was manned by the laddermen on duty, as they were needed. This was the situation un-

til 1960, when finally the rescuemen were reorganized as a separate unit apart from the firefighting units.

In 1964, Rescue I was moved from McCully to its present home in the Pāwa'a Station, and in the same year Rescue II was put into commission at the Kalihi-Kai Station. Today these Search and Rescue units are among the finest in the nation. They are equipped with appliances to handle practically every conceivable emergency situation, from dogs stuck in cesspools to people trapped on cliffs in almost inaccessible valleys. The rescuemen themselves are capable physically and technologically of meeting all kinds of emergencies. Their basic training, in addition to two years of firefighting experience, includes learning to remove victims pinned in car wrecks, mountain rescue operations, and certification in advanced first aid, life saving, cardiopulmonary resuscitation, and SCUBA diving. Each unit also maintains a continuous retraining program in each phase of its mission.

An important addition to the Search and Rescue units came in 1968 when the Honolulu Fire Department acquired a helicopter. This apparatus has proved its worth many times over in both mountain and sea rescue missions.

A good precentage of each year's approximately 1,500 calls for the rescue squads are due to emergencies that arise out of aquatic recreational activities. You should exercise maximum good judgment and discretion in whatever you and your family do. Otherwise someone may have to risk his life to help you. Several members of these rescue squads have been killed or seriously injured in the line of duty.

United States Coast Guard

Until 1939, Hawai'i was a section command under the Twelfth Coast Guard District in San Francisco. When the lighthouse service was merged with the Coast Guard in July of that year, the additional functions and responsibilities justified the creation of the Fourteenth Coast Guard District. Today this vast district extends from Pago Pago, American Samoa, some 900 miles south of the equator, to the northernmost island of Japan, and then eastward to Hawai'i. Its headquarters is in Honolulu.

The primary mission of the Coast Guard in Hawai'i is search and rescue, which is managed by the Rescue Co-ordination Center. In a normal year, many overdue sea-craft are sought; disabled ships are assisted; and sinkings, grounded vessels, and other marine accidents are investigated. In addition the Coast Guard undertakes medical evacuations of sick people from outlying islands and from ships at sea. Generally, the Coast Guard covers the deep-water, offshore emergencies, while the Fire Search and Rescue units handle the shallow water, near-shore situations.

Besides its many local responsibilities, such as operating all the lighthouses in Hawai'i, the Coast Guard also maintains pollution patrols by both air and water craft in order to detect discharges of fuel oil and other pollutants and hazardous material. The Honolulu office maintains a trained strike force on O'ahu capable of combating oil spills ranging in size from a small harbor mishap to a massive offshore discharge. When needed, the strike force and its equipment can be flown to any of the Hawaiian islands.

If you should encounter any type of oil spill, pollutant, or hazard in the ocean, the Coast Guard should be notified.

Beach Thefts

A major problem at many of O'ahu's beaches is thefts from cars. Many people, especially tourists, lose thousands of dollars every year in cash, cameras, jewelry, and other personal items of value. The thieves operating in the beach areas are often very professional and can break into a locked car or car trunk, loot it, and be gone within a few minutes. Beach-goers, especially tourists, should bring with them only what is necessary and should never leave anything of value in the car even if it is locked. Automobiles from car rental agencies are prime targets.

The Honolulu Police Department is well aware of this problem and details officers in casual clothes to assist the regular beat men in patrolling the particularly hard-hit areas. These protective efforts, however, do not deter the thieves in spite of the large number of arrests that are made every year. The business is much too lucrative. Any valuables that are not going to be personally carried should be left in the hotel or at home.

The Beaches of O'ahu

Explanation of Key Symbols

F: Facilities—A list of all facilities and site improvements, such as concessions, restrooms, picnic tables, and parking areas, on the beach or within the beach park. Comfort stations are buildings that include showers with the restroom facilities.

LG: Lifeguard—Whether or not lifeguard service is provided, who provides the service (such as the City and County of Honolulu), and if it is provided, what the general schedule is. The specific hours that lifeguard towers are manned changes occasionally, so this information is not included but may be easily obtained by calling lifeguard headquarters.

EP: Emergency Phone—The location of the nearest City and County emergency telephone. Not all beaches are convenient to emergency phones. Where other sources of assistance are much closer, no emergency phones have been listed. A general description of O'ahu's emergency phone system and its use may be found in the General Information section of this book.

PP: Pay Phone—The general location of the nearest public telephone.

FS: The location of the nearest City and County fire station; the location of military fire stations is also noted if the beach is part of a military installation. All fire stations serve as emergency first aid centers; it should be noted, however, that fire stations may be temporarily unoccupied when the fire companies are out on a call.

H: Hospital—The location of the nearest hospital with an emergency room open twenty-four hours a day. In some areas other medical facilities may be closer than the hospital indicated, but they have not been listed because they do not offer continuous emergency service. Kaiser Medical Center, 1677 Ala Moana Boulevard, in Waikīkī, is primarily for individuals who subscribe to the hospital's medical plan, but Kaiser will accept all emergencies brought to its facility.

SS: Service Station—The general location of the nearest service station for automobiles; specific station names, addresses, gasoline brand names, and hours of operation are not given.

WA: Water Activities—The primary water activities, such as surfing, diving, or fishing, commonly practiced at the particular beach; beachcombing is also noted for some areas.

WC: Water Conditions—A concise description of the various and hazardous ocean conditions which may be encountered; also descriptions of geographical features of the beach or park areas that are of interest from a water safety standpoint, such as the presence of streams, deep channels, or sea cliffs.

PA: Public Access—Public access to the majority of O'ahu's beaches is unlimited, especially at public beaches and beach parks. Beaches fronted by private property are public property up to the existing vegetation line; in these areas public rights-of-way that provide the primary access routes are noted. All exceptions and situations of limited access are also noted.

AI: Additional Information—Any additional information of interest or pertinence to the particular area.

The Districts of Oʻahu

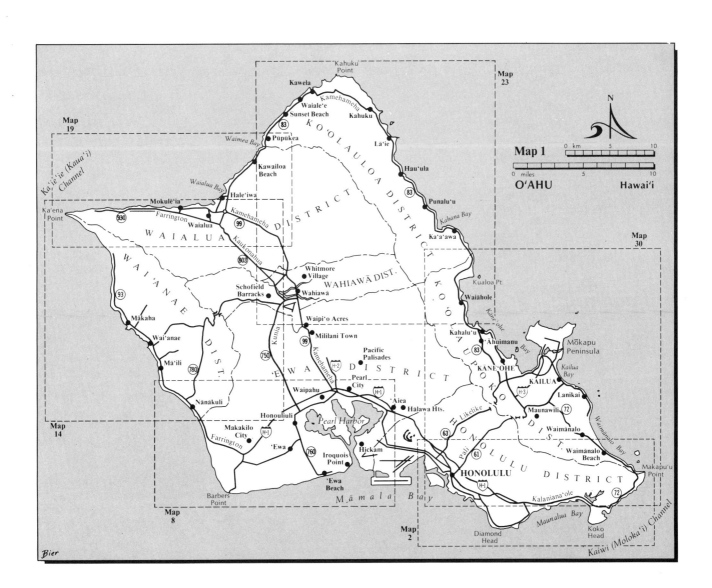

The Beaches of Honolulu District

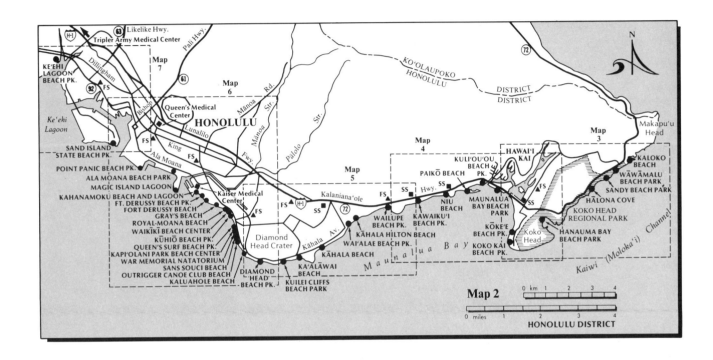

Map 2

HONOLULU DISTRICT

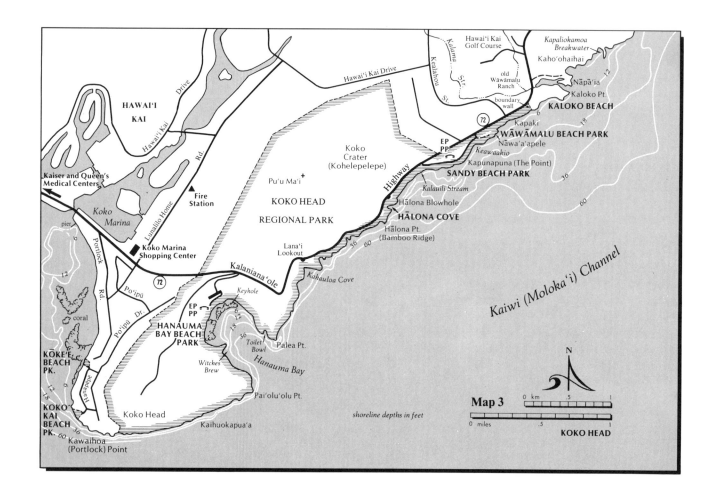

Kaloko Beach

(also Queen's or Alan Davis beach)

8800 Kalaniana'ole Highway (near Hawaii Kai golf course)

 F: none; roadside parking along Kalaniana'ole Highway
LG: none
EP: Sandy Beach, Koko Head Regional Park, 8800 Kalaniana'ole Highway
PP: Sandy Beach, Koko Head Regional Park, 8800 Kalaniana'ole Highway
FS: 515 Lunalilo Home Road, Hawai'i Kai
 H: Kaiser Medical Center, 1677 Ala Moana Boulevard; Queen's Medical Center, 1301 Punchbowl Street
SS: Koko Marina Shopping Center, Hawai'i Kai, 7120 Kalaniana'ole Highway
WA: beachcombing; diving only for experienced divers; pole fishing; throw-netting

WC: unpredictable and unsafe all year; entire shoreline made of lava rock; strong currents; dangerous entry into ocean
PA: shoreline access only from adjoining Wāwāmalu Beach Park, part of Koko Head Regional Park

Kaloko Beach takes its name from the nearby lava point that forms a natural boundary between the eastern end of the rough sand beach and the ocean. At its western extremity, this beach is separated from Wāwāmalu Beach Park by the crumbling remnants of an old retaining wall that once marked the border of Wāwāmalu Ranch. In recent years this particular area has been called Queen's Beach. This new name, first applied during the late 1930s by Hawaiian throw-net fishermen, now includes not only the beach itself but also a projected resort development in Kealakīpapa Valley. To the shorecasters, the divers, and the other fishermen who make up the majority of the people who use the beach nowadays, Kaloko is known simply as "Alan Davis."

In 1932, Alan Sanford Davis, a well-known corporation official in the islands, and for many years before his death in 1975 the head trustee of the Campbell Estate, obtained a thirty-year lease from the Bishop Estate for the land extending from Kamehame Gap to Makapu'u Bluff. He built a beautiful home near the mouth of Kalama Stream, on the land known as Napaia. He called his holdings Wāwāmalu Ranch, because Wāwāmalu, "shady valley," was the name of a former Hawaiian village in this region.

On April 1, 1946, one of the most destructive tsunami ever to hit the Hawaiian Islands destroyed the Wāwāmalu ranchhouse and several other neighboring buildings. On that morning, fortunately, all members of the Davis family were awake, preparing to leave for school or work. Mr. Davis had just finished shaving when he heard water rustling against the sisal fence in his yard. He realized immediately that something was wrong and suspected a tsunami. His suspicions proved to be correct. The *paniolo* on the ranch drove his wife and baby up to Makapu'u Gap, and Mr. Davis followed in another car with his young daughter, Nancy. Then, between the third and fourth waves, Mr. Davis returned alone to his home, to make sure that everyone had vacated the area, to try and save the family's pets, and to salvage his personal belongings. The interior of the house was already a shambles and, as he was picking his way through the interior, the next wave struck. He was so startled that he grabbed the object nearest him, a painting hanging on the wall, and ran for the road, wading knee-deep through turbulent water. Soon after this wave receded, Mr. Davis once again reached the safety of the gap. He and his family watched the next wave totally demolish their house and roll up almost the entire length of Kealakīpapa Valley. Fearing that the succeeding waves might wash up the entire length of the valley and spill through the gap into Makapu'u Beach, the whole group drove up to the lighthouse at the very top of Makapu'u Bluff.

The only possession that Mr. Davis saved that day hangs now in the Davis' home—a painting of a large, breaking wave. Other household items were found later, as far away as Hanauma Bay, and some were uncovered recently by Kaiser-Aetna crews working in Kalama Valley, more than a mile away. Island-wide surveys of the devastated areas determined that some of the highest waves of the entire set of tsunami had hit this region of O'ahu. Today the only evidence left of the former ranch home are several sections of a concrete wall that once closed off part of a saltwater pond to form a swimming pool. Similar pools can still be seen today at residences along Kaiko'o and Black Point roads, near Diamond Head. Probably this natural pond at the mouth of Kalama Stream gave Kaloko, "the pond," its name. However, to most divers and fishermen the region is still known as "Alan Davis."

Kaloko Beach is a rather short and rough stretch of shore hemmed in on the land side by scrubby vegetation and on the ocean side by a rocky lava shelf. Although many tidal pools have been formed in this lava, none is big enough for wading, and there are no coves or inlets big enough for swimming. The only access to the open ocean is across the sharp lava and through the often pounding surf, so recreational swimming here is impossible. In addition, the end-of-the-island currents here can be very powerful. The region attracts fishermen because it provides good places for "throw-netting," surfcasting, and diving for experienced watermen. The only public access to the beach is from the end that borders Wāwāmalu Beach Park.

Wāwāmalu Beach Park
(part of Koko Head Regional Park)
8800 Kalaniana'ole Highway (across from Hawai'i Kai golf course)

F: none; roadside parking along Kalaniana'ole Highway
LG: none
EP: Sandy Beach, Koko Head Regional Park, 8800 Kalaniana'ole Highway
PP: Sandy Beach, Koko Head Regional Park, 8800 Kalaniana'ole Highway
FS: 515 Lunalilo Home Road, Hawai'i Kai
H: Kaiser Medical Center, 1677 Ala Moana Boulevard; Queen's Medical Center, 1301 Punchbowl Street
SS: Koko Marina Shopping Center, Hawai'i Kai, 7120 Kalaniana'ole Highway
WA: beachcombing; diving only for experienced divers; pole

fishing; board surfing; paipo board surfing; throw-netting
WC: unpredictable and unsafe all year; strong currents
PA: unlimited

Before 1800 the area to the rear of Sandy Beach and Wāwāmalu Beach Park was a fairly well-populated Hawaiian community of fishermen and farmers, living in a village called Wāwāmalu, or "shady valley." The name recalls a time when the nearby valleys were heavily wooded, and is preserved on the bridge spanning Kalama Stream near the entrance to the Hawai'i Kai golf course. The plains now occupied by the golf course were known to Hawaiians as Ke Kula o ka Mau'u Wai. Here, between Kealakīpapa and Kalama valleys, the *uhi* (yam) and the *'uala* (sweet potato) were cultivated.

During the early 1800s, whaling was a very important and expanding industry in New England. In 1819, after word had spread of the discovery of rich sperm whale grounds in the Arctic Ocean and off Japan, whalers from New England entered the Pacific. Soon Honolulu and Lahaina became ports for outfitting and provisioning the ships and for giving the sailors some rest and relaxation. Food staples that were available locally, such as potatoes and yams, were gathered from places like Wāwāmalu for sale to the whalers. In order to take aboard the Wāwāmalu produce, the ships anchored in the lee of Koko Head, outside of Haha'ione Valley, where they took aboard such provisions. The demand for fresh vegetables and meat from the islands founded some very profitable businesses in Hawai'i. The businesses were further stimulated, at least temporarily, by the Gold Rush of 1849 in California. In addition to supplying the whalers, local firms also shipped staples to the west coast of the mainland. By 1870, the entire whaling enterprise had ceased completely in Hawai'i. The development of San Francisco as a port, coupled with the completing of the transcontinental railway, eliminated the need for ships to sail around the Horn to take whale oil and bone to the East Coast.

By the beginning of this century, the Hawaiian community had all but disappeared from the famous Wāwāmalu potato-growing area, although much evidence of a once-thriving village had been left behind in the form of fishing shrines, *heiau,* pig pens, house foundations, canoe shelters, and so on. The devastating tsunami of April 1, 1946, wiped out almost all these traces of the former inhabitants and left the region still more barren and desertlike. Wāwāmalu was also a home of the *pua-pilo,* the Hawaiian caper, a shrub which thrives in rocky shoreline areas. It has large creamy white flowers, with many stamens, that open in the evening, giving off a rich fragrance. Since the tsunami, no traces of the plant can be found.

Wāwāmalu Beach Park, between Kaloko and Sandy beaches, is one of the three main sections of Koko Head Regional Park. Its entire length is bordered by Kalaniana'ole Highway on one side and on the ocean side by a rough lava shelf. The sandy beach lying between the road and the ocean is good for sunbathing, but swimming in the sea is dangerous. Because there is no protective fringing reef offshore, the currents can be strong at times. Moreover, access to the water is difficult over the sharp rocks on the shore. Wāwāmalu is still a popular area, however, because it is reached so easily, simply by pulling off the highway. The beach often picks up the weekend and holiday overflow of sunbathers from nearby Sandy Beach. Wāwāmalu Beach Park has a much-frequented surfing spot originally known as "Irma's," in honor of Irma's Lunchwagon that served patrons in this area for many years.

Sandy Beach Park
(part of Koko Head Regional Park)
8800 Kalaniana'ole Highway (near Hālona Blowhole)

 F: 2 comfort stations; 2 lifeguard towers; 186 parking stalls
LG: daily service provided by City and County
EP: next to park comfort station
PP: next to park comfort station
 H: Kaiser Medical Center, 1677 Ala Moana Boulevard; Queen's Medical Center, 1301 Punchbowl Street
FS: 515 Lunalilo Home Road, Hawai'i Kai
SS: Koko Marina Shopping Center, Hawai'i Kai, 7120 Kalaniana'ole Highway
WA: beachcombing; diving only for experienced divers; board surfing; bodysurfing (excellent shorebreak for experienced bodysurfers); paipo board surfing; swimming
WC: unpredictable and unsafe all year; strong currents; exceptionally hazardous rip currents around "The Point," the lava rock area fronting comfort station; dangerous shorebreak

24

Sandy Beach. Tourists and local bodysurfers catch a wave in the famous and often dangerous Sandy Beach shorebreak. Sandy is the most popular beach among Oʻahu's beach-going youth because of its good bodysurfing waves and its proximity to both the Honolulu and Waimānalo Kailua sides of the island.

PA: unlimited
AI: flag warning system used by lifeguards: green = safe; red = dangerous; yellow = variable intermediate conditions

Sandy Beach is one of the three main swimming beaches included within Koko Head Regional Park. It lies at the base of Koko Crater, or Kohelepelepe, as the mountain was known to the Hawaiians. In the legends told of Pele, it was said that a sister of the fire goddess, attempting to distract Kamapuaʻa, a handsome demigod, from his pursuit of Pele, threw her own vagina to this spot, where he followed it. Kohelepelepe meaning labia minor, refers (with Hawaiian directness) to the resemblance between the natural shape of the crater (when viewed from a distance) and this part of the female anatomy.

Sandy Beach and the entire Blowhole area were not accessible by automobile until October 1931, when the newly constructed coastal road following the cliffs from Hanauma Bay was opened to the public. Formerly the only access to this region was over a foot trail used primarily by fishermen, most of them members of the former Honolulu Japanese Casting Club. Because this was the only extensive sand beach along this rocky coast, it was called simply "the sand beach by the Blowhole." Later it became known as Sand Beach, and finally as Sandy Beach, or just plain Sandy. With the opening of the new road in 1931 the beach attracted

25

many sightseers and campers, along with the fishermen, but very few swimmers. Residents, being very conscious of the power of the ocean there, stayed away from the often treacherous shorebreak and strong rip currents. During the Second World War, however, many servicemen who were ignorant of the dangers of our island waters attempted to swim at Sandy, often with tragic results. By July of 1944, so many men had drowned there that Sandy was placed off limits to all military personnel. During the 1950s, O'ahu's youths began to find their way to Sandy, and learned how to bodysurf in the turbulent shorebreak. By the 1960s, the beach had become just as popular as Makapu'u with the island bodysurfing community. In 1968, when the City's Parks and Recreation department improved the area and installed a comfort station, Sandy became one of the most popular gathering places for O'ahu's beach-going youth.

The beach itself is about 1200 feet long and is fairly wide with a sloping foreshore. The bottom immediately offshore, a mixture of patches of sand, lava, and reef, drops off abruptly to an average depth of eight to ten feet. This quick change in depth creates the very steep and hard-breaking waves that pound in Sandy's shorebreak. On a big day the surf erodes the sand to form a steep foreshore, which in turn produces a strong, forceful backwash. This backwash is especially dangerous to children and elderly swimmers who, often caught off guard while playing at the water's edge, are swept into the dangerous shorebreak. The backwash also creates powerful rip currents that are an additional hazard to unknowing swimmers. The lifeguards at Sandy Beach make more rescues in the course of a year than do the guards at any other beach in Hawai'i except Makapu'u. The popularity of Sandy Beach has created a major problem. There are always so many experienced bodysurfers in the water who make riding the waves look so easy that tourists and residents unfamiliar with the beach continually misjudge the real dangers. For this reason, a flag warning system has been devised: red for very dangerous water conditions; green for safe; and yellow for all intermediate conditions. Since February 1971, lifeguards have been stationed at Sandy daily, all the year around. Newcomers to the beach should consult the lifeguards before entering the water.

Besides the shorebreak, Sandy has one other very

hazardous area, which is called "The Point." Formerly known as Kapunapuna, this jut of rough lava is located immediately in front of the comfort station. Bodysurfing in this area can be very dangerous, especially when the tide is low. Over the years, the rocks here have caused numerous injuries, even to experienced watermen. Just to the left of The Point is the small cove of Keawaakio, popular with many swimmers who wish to avoid the pounding shorebreak on the Blowhole side of the beach. The relative calmness and safety of this area, however, is misleading. A very strong rip current that is almost impossible to swim against runs out of this cove. Most swimmers swept out of Keawaakio have to swim entirely around The Point in order to get back on shore. Those who panic at the helplessness and at the speed with which they are being carried out sometimes try to come in over The Point. Usually these swimmers are battered against the rocks, ending up bruised and cut, occasionally very seriously. When the surf is big the hazards around The Point and in the shorebreak make Sandy one of the most dangerous beaches on the island, but for experienced shorebreak bodysurfers the waves have no equal, anywhere.

Hālona Cove

(part of Koko Head Regional Park)
8800 Kalaniana'ole Highway (next to Hālona Blowhole)

F: none; parking area available at Hālona Blowhole lookout
LG: none; summon from Sandy Beach
EP: Sandy Beach, Koko Head Regional Park, 8800 Kalaniana'ole Highway
PP: Sandy Beach, Koko Head Regional Park, 8800 Kalaniana'ole Highway
FS: 515 Lunalilo Home Road, Hawai'i Kai
H: Kaiser Medical Center, 1677 Ala Moana Boulevard; Queen's Medical Center, 1301 Punchbowl Street
SS: Koko Marina Shopping Center, Hawai'i Kai, 7120 Kalanianaole Highway
WA: diving; pole fishing; swimming
WC: unpredictable and unsafe all year; cove turbulent with large surf activity; dangerous rip currents at mouth of cove
PA: unlimited; follow trail down cliffs from Hālona Blowhole lookout parking lot

Hālona Cove. Sunbathers and swimmers enjoy the isolation of this tiny pocket beach on a calm day. A portion of the Hālona Blowhole lookout can be seen at the top of the cliff.

AI: popular entry point for novice divers; this cove adjoins popular pole fishing point called "Bamboo Ridge"

Hālona Cove is a tiny sand beach situated between the cliffs that form the lookout over the famous Blowhole on one side and Hālona Point on the other. The cove is a favorite place for sunbathers and adventurous picnickers who wish to get away from the crowds at nearby Sandy Beach. The only way to reach the cove is to hike down the cliffs or, only on a calm day, to follow the wave-cut terrace that edges the ocean from the Blowhole. Inshore swimming in the area is safe on calm days, but is extremely dangerous when the waves are rough. Heavy surf makes the entire cove very turbulent and creates strong rip currents that sweep seaward into the large cave that has been hollowed out beneath the Blowhole. These very waves that stir up the cove are also the ones that cause the Blowhole to spout. A surge moves into the cave with such tremendous power that it forces a compressed rush of air and water up into the chimney, where the mixture erupts through the narrow hole onto the lava terrace above. Contrary to popular

27

belief, the Blowhole chimney is not a funnel-shaped shaft that drops straight down into the sea cave beneath it. In reality, it is a narrow vertical tunnel, with two L-shaped steps. People who have been swept into the spouting hole do not fall through it, into the sea below, but rather are trapped on one of those steps in the shaft, where it is almost impossible to reach them. If they do succeed in reaching the ocean their chances of escaping are almost nonexistent because of the rapid succession of oncoming waves, each of which seems determined to push victims back into the cavern. There is only one recorded case of a person having been washed through the chimney and surviving the experience. The Blowhole terrace, and the waters outside of Hālona Cove, are places to be very cautious, although, unfortunately, many curious visitors are not.

Hālona means the "peering place." The steep lava sea cliffs here provide a convenient view into the ocean's depths as well as of the Blowhole's activity. The name also suggests the fact that this coast of O'ahu is one of the best places to watch the humpback and sperm whales that winter yearly in island waters, to mate and bear their young. The whales are seen frequently in the offshore waters from December to April.

Hālona Point has long been one of the favorite grounds of O'ahu's shoreline fishermen. It is commonly known to many islanders as "Bamboo Ridge" because of the multitudes of bamboo fishing poles that line the perimeter of the point on a good day. Until the coastal road opened in 1931, these fishermen back-packed all of their equipment in and, of course, carried their catches out in the same way.

In 1929 a group of fishermen founded the former Honolulu Japanese Casting Club, the forerunner of today's many casting clubs. In spite of their caution in fishing off the rocky lava ledges that are found along O'ahu's coastline, every year a number of their members and fellow fishermen were swept away and lost in heavy surf. In 1935 members of the club began a community service project to erect concrete warning markers at dangerous spots around the island. Each marker had the Japanese character *abunai,* or "danger," carved on two of its sides. The markers usually were placed at a spot where a fisherman had lost his life; they can still be seen along the coast in Nānākuli and Ka'ena as well as in the Koko Head area.

In addition to setting up the warning markers, the members of the Honolulu Japanese Casting Club pooled their money and sent away to Japan for a carved statue of O-Jizosan, the guardian god for people at all dangerous waterways and coastlines. When the statue arrived it was placed on top of Hālona Point, overlooking the ridge and cove below. With the outbreak of World War II, however, O-Jizosan's head was broken off, because he was a god of "the enemy," and eventually his body was demolished entirely. The postwar cost of replacing the statue was too prohibitive for the club members, so they decided to have his figure carved into a large stone. This was done, and today O-Jizosan stands again in place, watching over fishermen and swimmers near Hālona.

In spite of such precautions, the dangerous cliff areas around O'ahu continue to take the lives of fishermen, 'opihi pickers, and an occasional unwary tourist. Also, the Koko Head area in recent years has attracted a large number of novice SCUBA divers, because it offers relatively easy access to deep waters. These divers, who all too often are not prepared to contend with the difficult conditions and currents that frequently occur in those waters, occasionally fall victim to the ocean. The entire shoreline from Hālona Blowhole to Koko Head should be approached with a great deal of respect and caution.

Hanauma Bay Beach Park
(part of Koko Head Regional Park)
7455 Kalaniana'ole Highway

- F: 3 comfort stations (beach area); 4 restrooms (upper lookout area); 1 pavilion/caretaker's residence; 1 grass volleyball court; 2 lifeguard towers; 141 parking stalls; cooking stands and tables; 1 food concession in pavilion area
- LG: daily service provided by City and County
- EP: in lower park (beach area)
- PP: in lower park (beach area)
- FS: 515 Lunalilo Home Road, Hawai'i Kai
- H: Kaiser Medical Center, 1677 Ala Moana Boulevard; Queen's Medical Center, 1301 Punchbowl Street
- SS: Koko Marina Shopping Center, Hawai'i Kai, 7120 Kalaniana'ole Highway
- WA: diving; snorkeling; occasional board surfing on inner reef during big swell at high tide; swimming

Eric M. Nishida

Hanauma Bay. A portion of Hanauma Bay's shoreline viewed from Koko Head Ridge. The sandy opening in the middle of the reef is the Keyhole, the most frequented swimming area in the bay. The narrow sea terrace at the foot of the steep cliffs leads out to another popular feature, the Toilet Bowl. Hanauma Bay, a sealife conservation district, is utilized extensively by snorkelers and SCUBA divers, and is one of the foremost swimming, picnicking, and scenic areas on O'ahu.

WC: safe all year inside fringing reef; currents in outer bay are dangerous when surf is big; walking access to outer points of bay along wave-cut lava terraces are also dangerous when surf is big, especially at high tide
PA: unlimited
AI: entire bay is marine conservation area; an ideal place for novice snorkelers; underwater trails marked on ocean floor of bay (signs and information board in beach area provide regulations and details)

Hanauma Bay has long been one of the most popular recreational swimming and picnic places on O'ahu, among tourists and residents alike. It is a beautiful bay lying within a pair of volcanic craters that have been breached by the ocean. The curved beach at the bay's head is not very wide, but it is about 2,000 feet long and complements the entire park area very nicely. In addition to the usual beach park facilities, the City and County has provided a pavilion with a snack bar, living quarters for a full-time, resident park superintendent, and seven-day-a-week, year-round lifeguard service.

Hanauma means either "curved bay" or "handwrestling bay." The sport of *uma* was performed with two players. Kneeling, the opponents faced each other, grasped right hands with their elbows planted on the ground, and each man attempted to force the other's hand to the earth. Hanauma was a noted playground for O'ahu's ruling families and this fact, coupled with the natural shape of the bay, gives support to both interpretations of the name.

Hanauma Beach is protected by a shallow fringing reef that lies just offshore. Wave energy and currents from the outer bay are expended on the edge of this reef, leaving the inner waters very calm and safe for swimming during all kinds of surf conditions beyond the reef. Several good-sized sand pockets within the reef attract the greater number of recreational swimmers. The largest and most popular of these pockets is the *kīpuka,* or the "Keyhole," as it is more commonly known. A *kīpuka* is a deep place in a shoal, and this one, when seen from the cliffs above, does resemble a keyhole. One of the few danger spots within the inshore reef is the small channel, near the center of the bay, that was dredged to received the trans-Pacific telephone cable. Occasionally there are strong rip currents in this area, running into the bay through the reef.

The left point of the bay is called Palea, "brushed aside," and the right is Pai'olu'olu, "lift gently." The reasons for these names are forgotten now, but probably they refer to the wave action at each point when the surf is big. The waves that break on the shallow underwater shelf at Palea are dissipated very quickly in the deeper water within the shelf: in effect, they are "brushed aside." In complete contrast, the heavy surf that breaks on Pai'olu'olu washes up the sloping cliff there almost like a wave coming up on a beach. Reaching heights of forty to fifty feet above the level of the ocean, at times the white water almost seems to be advancing and receding in slow motion. One can very easily imagine that these waves have been "lifted gently."

On each side of the bay there is a wave-cut terrace a few feet above sea level that runs out toward each point. The terrace extending toward Pai'olu'olu on the right ends in a half cove called the "Witches' Brew." When the surf is rough, the water in this cove is extremely turbulent. The predominant trade wind swells induce a swirling current in the water which, of course, gave rise

to the name Witches' Brew. The terrace on the opposite side of the bay, heading out to Palea, ends at a small inlet called the "Toilet Bowl." At the head of this inlet is a small pool that is separated from the sea by a natural rock wall. At the base of this wall is an opening through which water passes freely, although slowly. The swells that surge into the inlet cause the water in the pool to rise and fall in almost an exact imitation of that in a flushing and filling toilet bowl.

Picturesque though these names may be, the two places play a very important part in the water safety of Hanauma Bay. The majority of the drownings and critical incidents that occur in the bay happen either in or near the Witches' Brew or the Toilet Bowl. Scuba divers and free divers swim in these areas and use the terraces leading out to them to enter and leave the waters of the inner bay. Occasionally people are washed off the ledges by unexpected waves. This happens most frequently when high tides and heavy surf occur simultaneously. The distances to both points from the beach are great, making it imperative for each area to have a distinguishing name. This insures that the lifeguards or the fire department rescue personnel do not waste valuable time in going to the wrong place. For this reason the popular names, Witches' Brew, Toilet Bowl, and even the Keyhole, all have important roles in the safety procedures at Hanauma Bay. These common new names are much more widely known and used than are the older Hawaiian terms.

Hanauma's popularity among O'ahu's royalty as a resort area was due not only to its beauty and isolation but also to its excellent fishing. The bay is said to have been the favorite fishing grounds of Kamehameha V, as it was well into the twentieth century for divers, throw-netters, and shore-casters drawn there from all over O'ahu. In 1967, however, the entire bay was set aside by law as an underwater park and conservation area. The present regulations state that it is "unlawful for any person to hook, spear, seine, capture, kill, destroy, alter, deface, possess or remove any fish, crustacea, mollusk, sea shells, coral or any other animal life, or any sand or any geologic features, from the Conservation District. Possession by any person of fishing gear, including, but not limited to hook and line, rods, reels, seines and spears, crowbar and noxious chemicals, within the Conservation District shall be deemed to be prima facie evidence of violation of this regulation.'' Since the establishment of the Conservation District the numbers of marine creatures in the bay have increased tremendously, and the fish, no longer victims of the hunt, have become relatively tame. For this reason, the bay attracts snorkelers and novice SCUBA divers, in addition to the throngs of sunbathers and picnickers who are content to stay on the beach.

Koko Kai Beach Park
10 Hanapepe Place

 F: none; undeveloped half-acre lot; roadside parking
LG: none
EP: Maunalua Bay Beach Park

PP: Koko Marina Shopping Center, Hawai'i Kai, 7120 Kalaniana'ole Highway
 FS: 515 Lunalilo Home Road, Hawai'i Kai
  H: Kaiser Medical Center, 1677 Ala Moana Boulevard; Queen's Medical Center, 1301 Punchbowl Street
 SS: Koko Marina Shopping Center, Hawai'i Kai, 7120 Kalaniana'ole Highway
WA: surfing; bodysurfing; diving; pole fishing; area frequented primarily by surfers who ride the surfing break called ''China Wall'' offshore of Portlock Point
WC: the waters fronting the park are deep and unprotected from the open ocean; there are often very powerful and dangerous currents, especially when the surf is big. At certain times of the year an extremely treacherous offshore current runs in the opposite direction of the usual westerly currents; it is known as the ''Molokai Express'' and has caused many mishaps to surfers and divers in the area. Big surf surging over the wave-cut terraces below the park also poses a danger to sun bathers, fishermen, and spectators
PA: unlimited; the ocean edge of this minipark is composed

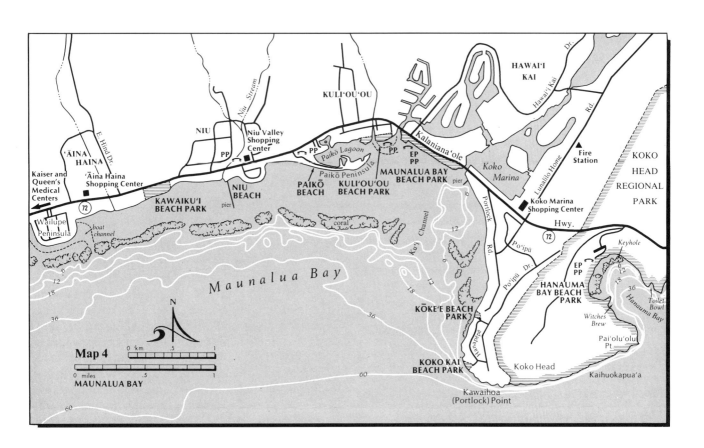

31

entirely of low sea cliffs and wave-cut terraces; the only access to the ocean is gained by climbing down the cliffs or by following the public right-of-way near the intersection of Moloaʻa Street and Hanapepe Loop

AI: undoubtedly one of the most beautiful views of Maunalua Bay and the Koʻolau Mountain Range. See text for Maunalua Bay Beach Park for explanation of Koko.

Kōkeʻe Beach Park

158 Kōkeʻe Place

 F: none; undeveloped half-acre lot
LG: none
EP: Maunalua Bay Beach Park
PP: Koko Marina Shopping Center, Hawaiʻi Kai, 7120 Kalanianaʻole Highway
FS: 515 Lunalilo Home Road, Hawaiʻi Kai
 H: Kaiser Medical Center, 1677 Ala Moana Boulevard; Queen's Medical Center, 1301 Punchbowl Street
SS: Koko Marina Shopping Center, Hawaiʻi Kai, 7120 Kalanianaʻole Highway
WA: surfing; diving; pole fishing; area frequented primarily by surfers to gain access to the smaller surfing breaks between the outer point and shore
WC: occasionally powerful currents when the surf is big; low sea cliffs make up the minipark's shoreline
PA: unlimited; ocean reached by climbing down the low sea cliffs
AI: many of the streets in this area of Hawaiʻi Kai are named after geographical areas on the island of Kauaʻi. Kōkeʻe Beach Park was simply named after the street on which it is located. Kōkeʻe is located in the Waimea district of Kauaʻi

Maunalua Bay Beach Park

(formerly called Kuʻi)
6505 Kalanianaʻole Highway

 F: 1 comfort station; 1 boat ramp; unmarked parking available in park area
LG: none
EP: located in park area
PP: located in park area
FS: 515 Lunalilo Home Road, Hawaiʻi Kai
 H: Kaiser Medical Center, 1677 Ala Moana Boulevard; Queen's Medical Center, 1301 Punchbowl Street

SS: Koko Marina Shopping Center, Hawaiʻi Kai, 7120 Kalanianaʻole Highway
WA: crabbing; pole fishing; board surfing (offshore); swimming; throw-netting
WC: safe all year; shallow ocean bottom made up of coral reef and mud flats; dangerous drop at bottom end of park into deep boat channel
PA: unlimited
AI: entire park area is man-made, created by deposition of dredged material from bay bottom; given to City and County by Henry J. Kaiser in 1960

Maunalua means "two mountains." The name comes from this land division's two most prominent peaks, at Koko Head (Kuamoʻokāne) and the summit of Koko Crater (Puʻu Maʻi). In later years the name Maunalua was extended to the large bay that stretches from Portlock Point to Black Point. The prominence of the name Koko in this region comes from a former canoe landing that was situated on the shore near what is now Portlock Road. A Hawaiian legend tells how the ground there came to be red. A chief and chiefess of the nearby district of Waiʻalae had a daughter whom they gave up in adoption. When the girl reached maturity, she went one day to the home of her real parents to visit with them. They were not there when she arrived. While waiting for them to return, she picked a stalk of sugarcane and ate it. Then she went out to the point now called Koko Head and swam in the sea. The unfortunate maiden did not realize that her parents had a shark god whose duty was to kill anyone who molested the foodplants they had cultivated. While she was swimming, the shark attacked her, and the blood from her wounds spurted upon the land. From that time on, this place was called *koko,* or "blood."

Captain Cook's voyage of 1778–1779 had demonstrated that European traders could make great profits by purchasing furs from the Indians along the northwestern coast of America and then selling them to merchants in China. In London several ships were sent out to engage in what would eventually be called the "China Trade." In the Pacific the winds that carried those merchants vessels to and from the Orient were known as the "Trade Winds" and are still so called. The two British trading vessels that anchored in the lee of Koko Head in May 1786 were the *Queen Charlotte,* commanded by Captain George Dixon, and the *King George,* commanded by Captain Nathaniel Portlock. They had stopped to take on food, water, and other provisions for their long voyage westward to Canton, China. Before leaving with the supplies he had obtained form nearby Kuli'ou'ou Valley, Captain Portlock named this anchorage "King George's Bay," and called Diamond Head "Point Rose." His names did not endure, but today Lae o Kawaihoa is known as Portlock Point.

In the ensuing years Maunalua Bay was used extensively by other foreign vessels. During the 1820s, whalers from New England began frequenting Hawai'i, and Honolulu soon became a center for their operations. The newly discovered sperm whaling grounds in the Arctic and off the coasts of Japan brought numerous whalers to the Hawaiian Islands to be outfitted and provisioned. Pigs, sweet potatoes, and yams were among the local products in constant demand. Ships often anchored in the quiet waters of Maunalua Bay, while their crews went ashore to pick up fresh produce grown in the valleys nearby.

During these fur trapping and whaling days, attempts were made to take Hawaiians to the mainland as sailors, workers, and also as boatmen on the Columbia and Snake rivers, but generally the cold and dry climates of the continent did not agree with them. The endeavor was abandoned eventually, but there are still places on the mainland where the Hawaiians left an imprint. One of these is a mountain range in southwestern Idaho named after two Hawaiians who were killed there by Indians: the mountains are called the Owyhees, which was as close as most *haole* of the time could come to spelling Hawai'i.

Maunalua Bay Beach Park was developed by Henry J. Kaiser. In January 1960 the newly finished park along Kalaniana'ole Highway was turned over to the City and County of Honolulu. It consisted of 535,000 square feet of new land created with coral and other dredged material from the bay bottom that were pumped into low places along the existing shoreline. Kaiser also cleared a channel for small boats through the shallow coral flats in the bay.

Inland from the beach park is a large body of water that was formerly an enormous fishpond known as Kuapā. At one time it covered 523 acres and its longest wall extended 5,000 feet. Today most of this pond has been filled in, and the remaining waterways are called Koko Marina. Ku'i Channel, leading from the ocean into the marina, borders the eastern end of Maunalua Bay Beach Park. The access channel to the public boat ramp fronts the entire seaward shoreline of the beach park. The presence of these deep channels around almost the entire *makai* edge of the park is potentially very dangerous, especially for nonswimmers and little children. The water is often murky and sometimes distinguishing where the shallow coral reef drops into the boat channels is difficult to do.

The beach park has little to offer the recreational swimmer. Both the beach and the offshore bottom are primarily coral and mud flats. The biggest attraction of the park, beside its picnic areas, is the public boat ramp, the only one between Kailua and Waikīkī.

Kuli'ou'ou Beach Park

(borders Paikō Lagoon)
96 Bay Street

  F: 1 comfort station; 1 basketball court; 1 softball field; children's play apparatus; picnic facilities; 25 parking stalls
 LG: none
 EP: Maunalua Bay Beach Park
 PP: in park
 FS: 515 Lunalilo Home Road, Hawai'i Kai
  H: Kaiser Medical Center, 1677 Ala Moana Boulevard; Queen's Medical Center, 1301 Punchbowl Street
 SS: Koko Marina Shopping Center, Hawai'i Kai, 7120 Kalaniana'ole Highway or Niu Valley Shopping Center, 5730 Kalaniana'ole Highway
 WA: crabbing; pole fishing; swimming; throw-netting
 WC: safe all year; shallow ocean bottom made up of coral reef and mud flats
 PA: unlimited

Kuli'ou'ou means "sounding knee." The name refers to a knee drum that was tied to the knee and played while performing the hula. The reason this area was named Kuli'ou'ou is now unknown.

Kuli'ou'ou is probably best known in contemporary times as the site of a cave, Ka Lapa o Māua. Its location was reported to the Bishop Museum in 1938 and subsequent excavations unearthed many precontact artifacts such as adzes and fishhooks. Facing Koko Head, Ka Lapa o Māua is situated about 100 feet above sea level in the bluff between Niu and Kuli'ou'ou valleys. With the widespread growth of residential communities in the ensuing decades, many other caves utilized by the Hawaiians have been located not only in Kuli'ou'ou, but in most of the rocky mountain sides from 'Āina Haina to Hawai'i Kai.

The shoreline fronting Kuli'ou'ou Beach Park is composed primarily of mud flats and rocks. These conditions make recreational swimming very uninviting. The park is popular with fishermen and picnickers.

Paikō Beach

(borders length of Paikō Drive, Kuli'ou'ou, off Kalaniana'ole Highway)

  F: none; parking area available on Paikō Drive
LG: none
EP: Maunalua Bay Beach Park
PP: entrance to Paikō Drive
FS: 515 Lunalilo Home Road, Hawai'i Kai
  H: Kaiser Medical Center, 1677 Ala Moana Boulevard; Queen's Medical Center, 1301 Punchbowl Street
SS: Niu Valley Shopping Center, Kalaniana'ole Highway
WA: crabbing; diving and swimming only in offshore reef areas; board surfing
WC: safe all year; shallow inshore areas made up of coral reef and mud flats which are exposed at low tide; narrow sand beach disappears almost completely at high tide
PA: 1 public right-of-way next to 218 Paikō Drive
AI: Paikō Lagoon is designated as a state bird sanctuary

The island of Pico, one of the Azores, consists mainly of the lofty, 7,613-foot mountain for which the island was named, *pico* meaning hill in Portuguese. From that island, a young man who had been christened Manuel found his way into the Pacific as a whaler and eventually jumped ship in Hawai'i. He took his family name from his home island. Thus Manuel Pico became one of the 400 or 500 Portuguese whalers who settled in Hawai'i before the first group of contract laborers arrived. The majority of the Portuguese people who migrated to the Hawaiian Islands came between 1878 and 1899. The first group came from Funchal, the capital of Madeira, in September 1878.

When Pico first arrived in Hawai'i, he encountered some difficulty with his last name. *Piko* in Hawaiian, pronounced the same as *pico* in Portuguese, means umbilical cord and figuratively also refers to the genitals. The Hawaiians felt very uneasy about calling this man Piko, so they altered his name to the inoffensive Paikō. Pico accepted this variation and used it officially; his last will and testament, for example, was made out for Manuel Paikō.

In 1877 Paikō was appointed Superintendent of Roads on Maui. His professional ventures, however, centered a good deal on acquiring land, not only on Maui, but on Kaua'i and O'ahu as well. In 1874 he leased 400 acres of Crown Land in Kuli'ou'ou-Iki, and in later years he purchased some of this property. He made his home there until he died on April 8, 1890. His will, now in the Hawai'i State Archives, stated specifically that the land was to be sold or auctioned, if ever there were no direct heirs, and the resulting money was to be given to the Roman Catholic church, the designated residual legatee. Manuel and his wife, the former Domitila Kuawaa, had only one child, Joseph, who in turn had only one child, Joseph, Jr. When Joseph Paikō, Jr., died childless in 1947, his will, following his grandfather's wishes, provided that the majority of the estate was to be held in trust for St. Francis Hospital until the fiftieth anniversary of his death. A substantial provision also was made for his widow until her death.

One of the better-remembered personal attitudes of later members of the Paikō family was the ferocity with which they guarded their fishing rights at Kuli'ou'ou-Iki. The old Hawaiian laws, following the ways of the former *ahupua'a* land divisions, included offshore fishing rights as part of an acquired beach-front property. After annexation of the islands by the United States in 1898, the Organic Act recognized this tradition, but stipulated that holders had to register their fishing rights with the territory's Attorney General by 1905. The Paikō family registered their rights, which extended from the beach to the reef and thereafter guarded them jealously. Their area was an excellent mullet- and torch-fishing ground. Stories of gun shots heard on good torching nights were not uncommon.

Paikō Beach, fronting the length of Paikō Drive, is a very narrow strip of coarse, dirty sand and pebbles. At high tide, the beach disappears almost completely under water. The shallow coral and mud flats just offshore extend out more than a hundred yards toward the reef, making this a very poor place for recreational swimming. The beach at Paikō is frequented primarily by net and torch fishermen and by surfers, all of whom must wade through the rocky, muddy shallows to reach the cleaner, deeper areas near the reef.

The tip of Paikō Peninsula sometimes is called "Stubenberg's Island," for Arthur F. Stubenberg who owned the land from 1948 to 1973. It is also known to many of the local residents on the drive as "Sand Point," a name descriptive of the tidal land the area comprises. Stubenberg's Island, or Sand Point, impounds a natural lagoon between Paikō Drive and the Kuliʻouʻou-Iki shoreline. On March 30, 1974, Paikō Lagoon was officially declared a wildlife sanctuary by the State's Department of Land and Natural Resources, primarily in an effort to save several endangered species of Hawaiian shoreline birds. No fish or wildlife of any kind may be removed from the area.

Niu Beach

(fronting Niu Valley at Niu Peninsula off Kalanianaʻole Highway)

F: none; roadside parking along Kalanianaʻole Highway
LG: none
EP: Maunalua Bay Beach Park
PP: Niu Valley Shopping Center, 5730 Kalanianaʻole Highway
FS: 5046 Kalanianaʻole Highway, Wailupe
H: Kaiser Medical Center, 1677 Ala Moana Boulevard; Queen's Medical Center, 1301 Punchbowl Street
SS: Niu Valley Shopping Center, 5730 Kalanianaʻole Highway
WA: offshore diving; pole fishing; board surfing; swimming; throw-netting
WC: safe all year; shallow inshore ocean bottom made up of coral reef; narrow beach area

PA: 1 public right-of-way along Niu Stream, Kalanianaʻole Highway

The same bottom and shoreline conditions found at Paikō are also found along the entire coastline through Niu and ʻĀina Haina to Wailupe. In Niu, however, the shoreline residents solved the problem of a swimming area by constructing a long, narrow pier over the mud flats to a sand pocket in the cleaner offshore waters, but use of this facility is restricted to the subdivision's residents and their guests.

Kawaikuʻi Beach Park

(formerly ʻĀina Haina Beach Park)
5475 Kalanianaʻole Highway

F: 1 comfort station; picnic facilities; 33 parking stalls; 1 pavilion
LG: none
EP: Wailupe Beach Park
PP: ʻĀina Haina Shopping Center, 5140 Kalanianaʻole Highway
FS: Wailupe, 5046 Kalanianaʻole Highway
H: Kaiser Medical Center, 1677 Ala Moana Boulevard; Queen's Medical Center, 1301 Punchbowl Street
SS: ʻĀina Haina Shopping Center, 5140 Kalanianaʻole Highway
WA: offshore diving; pole fishing; board surfing; swimming; throw-netting
WC: safe all year; shallow ocean bottom made up of coral reef and mud flats
PA: unlimited

Kawaikuʻi Beach Park is located at the eastern end of the ʻĀina Haina shoreline. Kawaikuʻi is the name of a freshwater spring that was near the park's *makai* Koko Head boundary. Kawaikuʻi means "the united water." There are two explanations for the name. The spring was at the ocean's edge so the fresh and salt waters naturally merged together or "united." Kawaikuʻi was also where travelers, as well as residents and fishermen of Wailupe Valley, came for their drinking water. People washed their clothes upon flat rocks near the spring. The congregating of people at the spring for whatever reason adds another context for the name Kawaikuʻi. In former times, the area was noted for its *limu ʻeleʻele,* a very sen-

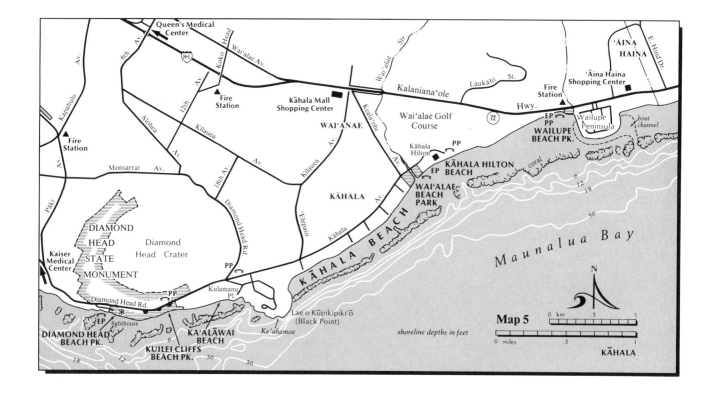

sitive type of seaweed that grows only in certain areas where freshwater mingles with saltwater.

The ocean bottom fronting the park is shallow and comprised primarily of coral and mud flats. The area is frequented by fishermen and occasionally by surfers who ride the breaks in the offshore reef.

Wailupe Beach Park

5045 Kalaniana'ole Highway

F: 1 comfort station; picnic facilities; 20 parking stalls
LG: none
EP: in park
PP: in park
FS: 5046 Kalaniana'ole Highway, Wailupe
H: Kaiser Medical Center, 1677 Ala Moana Boulevard; Queen's Medical Center, 1301 Punchbowl Street
SS: 'Āina Haina Shopping Center, 5140 Kalaniana'ole Highway

WA: offshore diving; pole fishing; board surfing; swimming; throw-netting (inshore)
WC: safe all year; shallow ocean bottom made up of coral reef and mud flats; dangerous drop into deep boat channel surrounding adjoining Wailupe Circle
PA: unlimited

The large valley to the rear of the beach park was formerly known as Wailupe Valley. Some 2,090 acres of the valley were purchased in 1924 by Robert Hind and for the following twenty-two years the acquisition was the site of the Hind-Clarke Dairy.

After World War II, the rapid growth of Honolulu toward Koko Head made the land too valuable to maintain as dairy range. In November 1946, Robert Hind, Ltd., sold the Hind-Clarke Dairy operation to Creameries of America. In 1947, Wailupe Valley became the subdivision project known as 'Āina Haina, literally "Hind's Land." 'Āina Haina has remained the valley's name to this day.

Shortly after work on 'Āina Haina began, the

Hawaiian Dredging Company began filling in the old Wailupe fishpond on the shoreline. More than one-half-million cubic yards of coral were pumped into the pond, the fill coming primarily from dredging operations that created the boat channel around the pond. The final result was the now exclusive Wailupe Peninsula residential area.

Wailupe Beach Park is located on the western side of Wailupe Peninsula. Like the rest of the 'Āina Haina area, the ocean bottom fronting the park is primarily shallow coral and mud flats. The primary danger is the Wailupe boat channel offshore from the park. The drop into the channel is deep and abrupt from the shallow inshore bottom, a dangerous situation for wading children or any nonswimmer.

Kāhala Hilton Beach

5000 Kahala Avenue

 F: showers; restrooms; changing areas; concessions (food and beverage, beach equipment)
LG: private service provided by hotel
EP: Wai'alae Beach Park, 4925 Kāhala Avenue
PP: on hotel grounds
FS: 971 Koko Head Avenue, Kaimukī
 H: Kaiser Medical Center, 1677 Ala Moana Boulevard; Queen's Medical Center, 1301 Punchbowl Street
SS: Kāhala Mall Shopping Center, 4211 Wai'alae Avenue
WA: diving; sailing; snorkeling; occasional board surfing (offshore) during big surf; swimming
WC: safe all year; deep swimming area fronting beach; surrounding area is shallow coral reef
PA: accessible from the adjoining shoreline
 AI: 800 foot-long sand beach and small offshore island created from former shoreline; completed in 1963

The Kāhala Hilton Hotel opened in January 1964. During development of the site in 1963, both the saltwater lagoon and the beach-front swimming area were dredged out of the coral flats that form the shoreline. The small offshore island also was constructed during that period. The 800-foot-long sand beach fronting the hotel was created by importing 18,000 cubic yards of sand from Moloka'i. Unfortunately the beach experiences continual erosion, so the sand must be replenished regularly.

The dredged swimming area that runs the length of the sand beach is always calm and provides a very safe swimming spot. The hotel also stations its own lifeguards in the area, for the additional protection of guests.

Kāhala is the name of a deepwater fish, the amberjack, which formerly frequented the offshore waters of Maunalua Bay. The hotel chose its name not for the fish but for that of the residential area nearby.

Wai'alae Beach Park

4925 Kāhala Avenue

 F: 1 comfort station; cooking stands and tables; 42 parking stalls
LG: none
EP: in park
PP: in park
FS: 971 Koko Head Avenue, Kaimukī
 H: Kaiser Medical Center, 1677 Ala Moana Boulevard; Queen's Medical Center, 1301 Punchbowl Street
SS: Kāhala Mall Shopping Center, 4211 Wai'alae Avenue
WA: crabbing; offshore diving; pole fishing; board surfing; swimming; throw-netting
WC: safe all year; shallow ocean bottom made up of coral reef; sand-bottom channel runs out to reef for swimming; freshwater canal divides park in half (dangerous for little children); ocean occasionally murky from canal runoff
PA: unlimited

Wai'alae means "water of the mudhen" and is said to refer to a spring that once flowed in the area. According to tradition, the spring once supplied water for the ruling chief of O'ahu. The lower parts of the land division of Wai'alae were very barren and hot. During the reign of Kamehameha III, the king while on a tour around the island asked an old couple living in Wai'alae where he could get some water to drink. The ancestors of this couple had been the guardians of the spring. They told the king that the only reason they stayed there was to carry out their duty and to reveal the location of the water hole only to him. The spring was kept hidden, sealed by a large stone slab covered by *pōhuehue*, the beach morning glory, a strong vine found in sandy beach areas. The location of the spring has been lost now for many years.

Wai'alae Beach Park is bisected by Wai'alae Stream, which empties into the ocean here. The stream has carved a wide, sand-bottom channel through the offshore reef, but there is little sand in the park area itself. The shoreline is made up mostly of rubble and pebbles broken off from the offshore coral flats. The primary danger in the area is the deep stream canal in the park area, which is a natural attraction and hazard for little children. Swimming is safe, but rather poor because of the numerous coral shoals and shallow water. The park is used primarily by picnickers and fishermen.

Kāhala Beach

(shoreline fronting the length of Kāhala Avenue from Black Point to Wai'alae Beach Park)

F: none; roadside parking along Kāhala Avenue
LG: none
EP: Wai'alae Beach Park, 4925 Kāhala Avenue
PP: Fort Ruger Park, 3906 Kāhala Avenue; Wai'alae Beach Park, 4925 Kāhala Avenue
FS: 971 Koko Head Avenue, Kaimukī
H: Kaiser Medical Center, 1677 Ala Moana Boulevard; Queen's Medical Center, 1301 Punchbowl Street
SS: Kāhala Mall Shopping Center, 4211 Wai'alae Avenue
WA: diving; pole fishing; snorkeling; board surfing; swimming; throw-netting
WC: safe all year; shallow inshore reef with occasional sand pockets for swimming; narrow sand beach
PA: 6 public rights-of-way along Kāhala Avenue; also accessible by following beach from Wai'alae Beach Park

Kū'ula-kai, the Hawaiian god of fishermen, lived on Maui. Legend tells us that he charged his son 'Ai'ai to travel about the islands and establish fishing stations *(ko'a)* and shrines *(kū'ula),* and also to teach the people all the techniques concerned with fishing, such as net-weaving, pond-building, proper worshiping, and all other related subjects. Always the first fish of each variety they caught was to be marked and dedicated to Kū'ula. After the offering had been made, the fishermen were free of all obligations for that particular type of fish.

Armed with his father's great knowledge, 'Ai'ai trav-

eled around Maui and then to Kaho'olawe, Lāna'i, Moloka'i, and O'ahu. Here he landed first at Makapu'u, where he raised up a *pōhaku i'a,* or fish stone, called Mālei. Then he established fishing stations at Kawaihoa, Maunalua, Wai'alae, and Kāhalai'a.

It is this legendary reference that establishes the commonly accepted meaning of the place name Kāhala. The full name *kāhalai'a* means ''the amberjack fish.'' Another possible definition of the name that is associated with the ocean comes from the Hawaiian historian David Malo, who wrote that *kāhala* was a method of catching sharks with a hook and then using a net of very strong cord to ensnare them. Advocates of this interpretation point out that Lae o Kūpikipiki'ō (Black Point), which adjoins the Kāhala area, has long been known among local fishermen as a shark ground. Regardless of these older meanings, Kāhala today is synonymous with affluence because it is the name of one of Honolulu's more exclusive residential areas.

Kāhala Beach is a long and narrow stretch of sand that runs in a relatively straight line from Wai'alae Beach Park to Black Point. Because of the shallowness of the offshore fringing reef, the waters here are not especially good for swimming, but occasional sand pockets along its length do provide spots where people can swim and wade. These pockets are very safe because of the protective reef and afford ideal conditions for novice snorkelers. The Waikīkī end of the beach attracts surfers and fishermen: an offshore break offers a fair surfing spot and the inshore waters are good squid grounds. Six public rights-of-way allow access to the beach for those who do not reside along this shoreline.

Ka'alāwai Beach

(situated between Kuilei Cliffs Beach Park and Black Point)

F: none; parking area available on Kulamanu Street
LG: none
EP: Diamond Head Beach Park, at foot of Beach Road
PP: Fort Ruger Park, 3906 Kāhala Avenue
FS: 971 Koko Head Avenue, Kaimukī
H: Kaiser Medical Center, 1677 Ala Moana Boulevard; Queen's Medical Center, 1301 Punchbowl Street

SS: Monsarrat Avenue
WA: diving; pole fishing; snorkeling; board surfing; body-
    surfing; swimming; throw-netting
WC: safe all year; inshore areas protected by fringing reef;
    many surfing breaks outside of reef
PA: public right-of-way at end of Kulamanu Place; access
    possible from Kuilei Cliffs Beach Park

When Diamond Head was still an active volcano, a lava flow from a late eruption extended into the ocean, crossed the offshore reef, and formed the southernmost tip of Oʻahu. Hawaiians called this promontory Lae o Kūpiki-pikiʻō, "point of raging sea." Now it is more commonly known as Black Point, a descriptive name referring to the color of the rough dark lava. The Waiʻalae and Waikīkī sides of the point are separated by a small cove that was called Keʻahamoe. Located just west of the Black Point blowhole, Keʻahamoe was a place much frequented by fishermen as well as by gatherers of *limu* and shellfish. The highest part of Black Point, fortified during World War II, is called Pāpū Circle, *pāpū* appropriately meaning "fort."

In 1906, George Carter and James Wilder made an amateur archaeological survey along the beach at Kaʻalāwai. They discovered some foundation stones of what they determined to be a *heiau*. In the same area, they also found several freshwater springs bubbling up in the sea near the water's edge. They noticed that thirsty horses could easily located the springs. Kaʻalāwai means "the watery rock," and probably refers to these springs surfacing at the western inshore edge of Black Point. The freshwater would have been a natural assembly point for both people and animals, because the surrounding country was very dry and barren. The spring waters of Kaʻalāwai can still be located among the partially submerged lava rocks. A small wading area marks one spot.

Kaʻalāwai played an important role in Hawaiian history. In 1893, Queen Liliʻuokalani, the last royal ruler of Hawaiʻi, was deposed and the Hawaiian monarchy replaced by a republic, much to the distress of many loyal residents. Toward the end of the year in 1894, Robert Wilcox and Samuel Nowlein, along with other royalists, plotted to overthrow the republic and restore the queen to her throne. During a number of clandestine meetings, some held at George Lycurgus' home at Sans Souci in Waikīkī, the royalists decided to smuggle into Oʻahu a shipment of arms and ammunition from San Francisco. The contraband cargo was landed and cached on Rabbit Island, near Makapuʻu Point, then later was secretly transported and buried in the sands of Kaʻalāwai, near Henry Bertelmann's home. In spite of the royalists' efforts, the Wilcox Insurrection, as the attempt was later labeled, failed. During a skirmish on the beach in front of Bertelmann's home between the small band of revolutionists and a force of police, one or two policemen were wounded and a royalist, Charles Carter, was killed. The republic's officials suppressed the rebellion and arrested and imprisoned all of the insurrection's ringleaders.

One of the most outstanding establishments at Kaʻalāwai today is the huge estate owned by Doris Duke (Cromwell), the wealthy tobacco heiress. In 1932, she erected her palatial home, "Shangri-La," on the Waikīkī side of Black Point. The luxurious mansion was designed and furnished in Persian-Islamic style. A natural bay at the foot of her property was converted into a small boat harbor by the addition of a breakwater and other associated structures. The anchorage, used only for a short period in the early thirties, has not been employed since for its original purpose. The harbor has become a very popular swimming area among the children from Kaʻalāwai and nearby Kaimukī, and usually is referred to simply as "Duke's" or "Cromwell's."

In the past the ocean waters off Kaʻalāwai were famous fishing grounds for mullet. When the *ʻanae-holo,* the sea-going mullet, made their yearly journey from Pearl Habor around Diamond Head and up the east coast of Oʻahu to Lāʻie, they would swim past Kaʻalāwai by the thousands. Such schools could be seen as recently as the later 1950s and early 1960s, but on a much smaller scale. Today they have almost disappeared.

Before Black Point was formed, Kaʻalāwai and Kāhala were parts of a single beach, so the features of both are similar. Kaʻalāwai Beach is also narrow and made of white sand, but it is wider than Kāhala. It is well protected by the fringing reef and has several small sandy pockets ideal for swimming and snorkeling. The reef here, however, unlike the one off Kāhala, has several wide channels throughout its length which attract many surfers. The most popular spot is called "Brown's" and is located directly offshore from the Francis Ii Brown estate, "'Āinamalu.'' On days when the surf is up on the south shore, the outside reef at Brown's forms some of the best big waves on this side of Oʻahu. The beach is still frequented by *limu*-pickers, throw-net fishermen, and skin divers. The only public access is from Kulamanu Place or through Kuilei Cliffs Beach Park.

Kuilei Cliffs Beach Park
Diamond Head Road

 F: parking available at 3 parking area lookouts; upper park landscaped, otherwise undeveloped
LG: none
EP: Diamond Head Beach Park, at the foot of Beach Road
PP: easternmost lookout
FS: 381 Kapahulu Avenue, Waikīkī
 H: Kaiser Medical Center, 1677 Ala Moana Boulevard; Queen's Medical Center, 1301 Punchbowl Street
SS: Monsarrat Avenue
WA: diving; snorkeling; board surfing; swimming
WC: inshore waters safe all year; occasional strong currents along shore during large surf; shoreline rocky with several sand pockets for swimming
PA: unlimited; follow trails down cliffs to beach below; easiest access from end of Beach Road near Diamond Head Lighthouse
AI: middle lookout has a monument dedicated to Amelia Earhart; lookouts are favorite places from which to watch ending moments of the Trans-Pacific Yacht race and the Molokaʻi-to-Oʻahu canoe race

The verb *kui* means "to string together pierced objects," such as shells or flowers in a *lei,* or fish on a line. Kuilei, the name of the fishing grounds fronting the beach park, means "*lei* stringing," but now the reason why the area was given this identity is unknown.

The beach park consists of eleven acres of landscaped but otherwise undeveloped land. Located at the base of the southern slopes of Diamond Head, the Kuilei Cliffs stand between the lighthouse and the first of the homes at Kaʻalāwai Beach. The only direct accesses to the beach in the park area are the narrow trails leading down the cliffs from Diamond Head Road. The alter-native to descending the cliffs is to follow the shoreline from either Kaʻalāwai Beach at the east or Beach Road, the remnant of a wagon track that once ran along the shoreline to Kaʻalāwai, at the west. During the 1950s and early 1960s, the relative seclusion of Kuilei Beach attracted nude sunbathers and members of Honolulu's homosexual community, many of whom lived in nearby Waikīkī. Here these two groups were not bothered by curious or unsympathetic beach-goers, and they swam and sunbathed without harassment. With the growth of Oʻahu's surfing community, however, many of Waikī-kī's surfers who were looking for new, uncrowded surfing spots began to frequent Kuilei. Nudists and homosexuals lost the seclusion of the beach and the majority of them moved off to other places. The nudists' problem was solved with the development of a nudist park on private property in Kahuku. Homosexuals, in the light of the more tolerant attitudes of contemporary society, re-established themselves at Queen's Surf in Kapiʻolani Beach Park.

The sand beach at Kuilei Cliffs Beach Park is winding and narrow, and has many outcroppings of coral reef along its length. Although the water is deep enough for swimming, the offshore bottom is made up of coral flats and shoals that discourage most recreational swimmers. The absence of a protective reef offshore makes this an ideal surfing area, because board riders do not have to contend with raised rocks. This situation also creates occasional strong along-shore currents that pull steadily toward Waikīkī. Surfers are well aware of these currents, which often carry their boards toward the lighthouse when the surf is big. Other than its occasional use by sunbathers and fishermen, Kuilei Beach is frequented primarily by surfers. One of its main attractions for them is the fact that the offshore water is seldom flat, no matter what the time of year may be. It is a rare day that finds the surf at Diamond Head without ridable waves, even though they may be small or poorly formed.

For the general public, Kuilei Cliffs Beach Park is little more than the three drive-in lookouts beside Diamond Head Road, high above the beach itself. They provide an excellent view not only of the surfers below, but also of the entire panorama of sea and sky, all the way to Molokaʻi and beyond. The lookouts are favorite gathering places each year for watching the finishing minutes of both the Trans-Pacific Yacht Race and the Moloka'i-to-O'ahu canoe race.

The middle lookout, the largest of the three, is also the site of a memorial to Amelia Earhart. She was the first woman to fly across the Atlantic Ocean; the first woman to fly solo across the continental United States; and in 1935, she became the first person to fly alone from Hawai'i to North America. Four years later, in July of 1939, she attempted to fly from New Guinea to Howland Island, on her way to Hawai'i. Miss Earhart's plane failed to reach Howland Island, and presumably she was lost at sea. The monument above Kuilei Cliffs honors her great courage and adventurous spirit.

Diamond Head Beach Park

Beach Road

F: none
LG: none
EP: foot of Beach Road
PP: easternmost lookout in Kuilei Cliffs Beach Park
FS: 381 Kapahulu Avenue, Waikīkī
H: Kaiser Medical Center, 1677 Ala Moana Boulevard; Queen's Medical Center, 1301 Punchbowl Street
SS: Monsarrat Avenue
WA: diving; board surfing; swimming
WC: inshore waters safe almost all year; occasionally strong currents along shore during large surf; shoreline primarily rocky; no sand pockets for swimmers
PA: unlimited; use Beach Road

Diamond Head is probably the most famous landmark in the islands. Situated on the eastern edge of Waikīkī, this dormant volcano's crater dominates the entire shoreline of O'ahu from Maunalua Bay to 'Ewa. British sailors exploring the slopes of the mountain in 1825 found a number of sparkling stones which later were shown to be crystals of calcite. Believing their discoveries to be valuable, they called their field of fortune "Diamond Hill." In time the Hawaiian versions of the English words "diamond" and "hill" led to "Kaimana Hila," but to the old Hawaiians the mountain was either Lē'ahi or Lae'ahi. Because the original meaning of the name is obscure, the correct spelling and translation have never been agreed upon by students of Hawaiiana. One interpretation says that Lē'ahi is a contraction of the two words *lei* (a wreath) and *'ahi* (fire), the two words combining to mean "wreath of fire" (possibly because of signal beacons that were lighted on special occasions). The other popular interpretation is that Lē'ahi is a contraction of *lae* (a cape or promontory) and *'ahi* (the yellow-fin tuna), the combination meaning "point of the *'ahi* fish." This second explanation seems to be the more probable of the two. When Diamond Head was an active volcano, the shape of the crater was determined in part by *ka moa'e,* the trade winds. Blowing from the northeast, they prevented the building up of the rim on the Kāhala side of the mountain and in turn helped to raise the high peak and edges on the Waikīkī side. From the east this highest section of the crater's rim, rising 760 feet above the level of the sea, does strongly resemble the crest of the *'ahi* fish. The resemblance is mentioned also in the legend of Hi'iaka, Pele's youngest sister. It is interesting to note that Hawaiians gave the name *'ahi* to the yellow-fin tuna because they associated it with heat and therefore with fire. When, while trolling in their wooden canoes, they hooked one of these fish, the *'ahi* ran out with the line so hard and so fast that the *mo'o,* the gunwale strakes, actually smoked from the heat of friction. For this reason, and probably because Hawaiians also used the heat of friction from "fire sticks" to start their cooking fires, the fish were named *'ahi.* The mountain must also have been used as a reference point in locating a deep-sea fishing grounds for *'ahi* the *ko'a lawai'a 'ahi.* It would be very much in character with the Hawaiians' love of using words with double meaning for them to have named this mountain Lae'ahi, thereby giving their respect both to the fish and to fire.

Diamond Head was purchased in 1904 by the federal government for $3,300. Fort Ruger and a number of gun emplacements for coast artillery defenses were established there before 1941. Following the attack on Pearl Harbor, it was heavily fortified against further attack on O'ahu. Many of the gun emplacements, pill boxes, fox holes, and lengths of barbed wire still remain. Today Diamond Head houses the headquarters for both the State Civil Defense and the Federal Aviation Agency. Several sections of the huge crater's floor are used by the Hawai'i National Guard, and on special

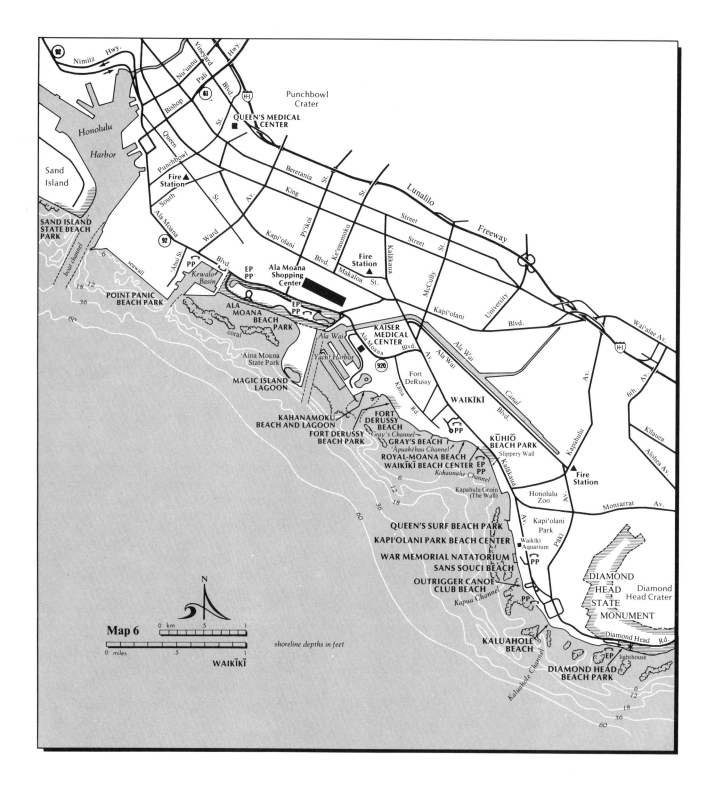

Nimitz Hwy.

Honolulu Harbor

Sand Island

SAND ISLAND STATE BEACH PARK

POINT PANIC BEACH PARK

Nu'uanu
Pali Blvd.
Vineyard Hwy.
Bishop
Queen
Punchbowl St.
South St.
Ala Moana

Queen's Medical Center

Fire Station

Ward Ave.
Ahui St.
Ala Moana Blvd.
Kewalo Basin

PP
EP PP

ALA MOANA BEACH PARK
'Aina Moana State Park
coral
Yacht Harbor

MAGIC ISLAND LAGOON

KAHANAMOKU BEACH AND LAGOON

FORT DERUSSY BEACH PARK

FORT DERUSSY BEACH
GRAY'S BEACH
ROYAL-MOANA BEACH
WAIKĪKĪ BEACH CENTER

Gray's Channel
'Āpuakēhau Channel
Kikaunahe Channel

Kapahulu Groin (The Wall)

QUEEN'S SURF BEACH PARK
KAPI'OLANI PARK BEACH CENTER
WAR MEMORIAL NATATORIUM
SANS SOUCI BEACH
OUTRIGGER CANOE CLUB BEACH

Kapua Channel

KALUAHOLE BEACH

Kaluahole Channel

DIAMOND HEAD BEACH PARK

Punchbowl Crater

Beretania St.
King St.
Kapi'olani Blvd.

Pi'ikoi St.
Ke'eaumoku St.
Makaloa St.

Ala Moana Shopping Center

Fire Station

EP PP
EP PP

KAISER MEDICAL CENTER

Ala Moana Blvd.
Ala Wai Blvd.
Kalia Rd.

Fort DeRussy

WAIKĪKĪ

PP

KŪHIŌ BEACH PARK
Slippery Wall

Kalākaua Ave.
Kapahulu Ave.

Honolulu Zoo

Waikīkī Aquarium

PP

PP

Lunalilo Freeway

Kalākaua St.
McCully St.
University Ave.
Kapi'olani Blvd.

Ala Wai Canal

Kapi'olani Park

Monsarrat Ave.
Pākī Ave.

Wai'alae Av.
6th Av.
Kīlauea Av.
Alohea Av.

Fire Station

DIAMOND HEAD STATE MONUMENT

Diamond Head Crater

Diamond Head Rd.
EP lighthouse

DIAMOND HEAD BEACH PARK

shoreline depths in feet

N

Map 6

0 km   .5   1

0 miles   .5   1

WAIKĪKĪ

occasions by the general public for large festivals, but the major portion of the land is undeveloped. These unused areas, covered primarily with *kiawe* and *koa-haole* trees, are a natural sanctuary for many birds that frequent the lowlands of the south shore. The *pueo,* the Hawaiian owl, made its home here when Diamond Head was still considered to mark the edge of town; and it could be seen, as late as the 1950s, circling the area in search of food. As Honolulu grew, advancing from Waikīkī toward Koko Head, the owls left Diamond Head for the wilderness of remoter mountains.

Diamond Head Beach Park is the name of two acres of undeveloped cliff and shoreline lying between the lighthouse and Beach Road. The narrow beach is almost completely edged by coral reef and rock, and provides few possibilities for pleasurable swimming. The waters here are used almost entirely by divers who fish in the broken offshore reef. When the ocean is rough, the along-shore currents can be quite strong. Better swimming areas can be found farther along the beach, at Ka-ʻalāwai.

Kaluahole Beach
(also Tongg's or Diamond Head Beach)
eastern end of Kalākaua Avenue

F: none
LG: none
EP: Kūhiō Beach Park, Monsarrat at Kalākaua avenues
PP: Kapiʻolani Regional Park, 2745 Kalākaua Avenue
FS: 381 Kapahulu Avenue, Waikīkī
 H: Kaiser Medical Center, 1677 Ala Moana Boulevard; Queen's Medical Center, 1301 Punchbowl Street
SS: Monsarrat or Kapahulu avenues
WA: diving; snorkeling; board surfing; swimming
WC: safe all year; entire shoreline is composed of seawalls at the water's edge; small sandy beach and channel provide only swimming area; well protected
PA: 1 public right-of-way located next to 3837 Kalākaua Avenue

ʻAiʻai, the son of Kūʻula-kai, the Hawaiian god of fishermen, was commanded by his father to travel throughout the islands of Hawaiʻi and teach the people all the ways of fishing and to establish fishing stations and shrines along the islands' shorelines. After ʻAiʻai established a station at Kāhalaiʻa on Oʻahu, he traveled on to Kaʻalāwai, where he placed a brown and white rock in the ocean. In this rock was a cavern that soon filled with the *āholehole* fish, so it was appropriately named Kaluahole, the *āhole* cavern. The old land division of Kaluahole included both Kaʻalāwai and Kuilei, but in recent years the Kaluahole shoreline usually has been placed between Beach Road and the boundary of Kapua (approximately the ʻewa intersection of Diamond Head Road and Hibiscus Drive).

The reef fronting the shoreline where Kaluahole and Kapua meet was the scene of two interesting shipwrecks. In 1878, the steamer *Estbank* went aground here. It was salvaged by a prominent island family, who used some of the rewards to construct an estate which they named Estbank. Thirty-five years later, in 1913, the bark *S. C. Allen* went aground on the same reef during a storm. Owned by K. Matsumoto, the *Allen* was a lumber carrier for Lewers and Cooke Company, Ltd. Although all of her cargo was salvaged, and most of her timbers, her heavy winch was left to rust on the reef, where the bulk of it remains to this day. Surfers, naturally enough, called the nearby surfing break "The Winch."

During the later 1800s and early 1900s many luxurious homes were constructed along the shoreline of eastern Waikīkī and at the foot of Diamond Head. The beautiful sand beach at Kapua and Kaluahole was said to have been the best in that whole area. Early home owners, who often had built their mansions too close to the water, put up groins to protect their property. Storm surf was often heavy, and the beach began to erode because of the imposition of these man-made structures. When erosion really became a major problem, substantial seawalls were built at the water's edge and then the beach disappeared completely. Today the shorelines of Kapua and Kaluahole are fronted almost totally by high retaining walls. Ironically enough, most of the sand that remains from this once beautiful beach is contained *behind* the seawalls throughout the entire area. It will never see light again because it has been covered by imported top soil or macadamized parking lots for high-rise buildings. Other than the small beach at Kaluahole, at the very end of Kalākaua Avenue, the only beach along this entire shoreline is the one in front of the

Kaluahole Beach. Looking east along the high sea walls that dominate this section of shoreline at the foot of Diamond Head. Only this tiny beach remains of a once wide sand beach that fronted this now exclusive residential area.

Outrigger Canoe Club. The o.c.c. is the only private facility in the entire area to restore the natural beach.

In March 1946, Ruddy Fah Tongg, a well-known island businessman, purchased a piece of property at the end of Kalākaua Avenue at the rear of the small sand beach of Kaluahole. Two of his sons, Mike and Ronnie, were avid surfers and, together with other enthusiastic kids in the neighborhood, they surfed in the numerous breaks among the offshore reefs. The Tongg's home soon became a gathering point for many local surfers. Some of the best wave riders on Oʻahu in the later 1950s, such as Paul Strauch, Jr., Robbie Estes, and Eric Romanchek, spent much of their time in the surf here. The offshore breaks soon were known among islanders as "Tongg's." Although the Tongg family moved to ʻĀina Haina in 1961, the beach and the surf in Kaluahole are still referred to as "Tongg's" by the surfing community.

Kaluahole Beach, the only one in the immediate area with sand, is a very short and narrow pocket. It provides only minimal sunbathing space. The wide Kaluahole Channel, however, which comes all the way in to the beach through the offshore reef, is an ideal swimming area in an otherwise poor location. There are no particular inshore water hazards. Convenient public access to the area does not exist, because the entire shoreline here is privately owned.

Waikīkī Beach

Waikīkī is located in the former Kona district of Oʻahu. Kona was the name Hawaiians gave to the leeward districts not only of Oʻahu, but also of Hawaiʻi, Kauaʻi, Molokaʻi, and Niʻihau. In 1859 the Kona district on Oʻahu was officially named the Honolulu district, and was so drawn as to encompass all the lands from Maunalua through Moanalua.

Waikīkī, with its splendid waves for surfing and wide sand beaches, was a natural focal point for recreation in Kona. Its proximity to the commercial center of Honolulu and its harbor encouraged the development and popularity of "The Beach." Throughout the late 1800s, Waikīkī attracted not only foreigners but also residents as well. Many of Oʻahu's affluent *haole* families, along with members of the Hawaiian ruling families, built comfortable seaside houses. By 1901 the first large tourist hotel, the Moana, had opened for business, the fame of Waikīkī as "a favorite watering-place" (to quote a local publication) having spread nation-wide with annexation.

The name Waikīkī is most commonly translated as "spouting water," probably in reference to the duck ponds, taro lands, and swamps that filled most of the area between the present shoreline and Mōʻiliʻili. The Mānoa and Pālolo streams flowed directly into those marshy lowlands, often causing widespread flooding during heavy rains. In January 1922, an extensive project was launched to transform Waikīkī into a dry, attractive, and livable area. The Waikīkī Reclamation Project included not only dredging the Ala Wai Canal, but also draining and filling hundreds of acres of swampland to make a new tract for residential purposes. Tons of coral fill wiped out the former duck ponds and bullrushes, and the new canal channeled the

mountain streams into the ocean away from the Waikīkī area. The inland features of Waikīkī were changed completely. The way was paved for the growth that followed and for the high-rise construction that still continues.

Waikīkī Beach includes all of the two-mile stretch of shoreline from the Outrigger Canoe Club to Kahanamoku Lagoon. This former barrier beach is almost entirely artificial now, having been "improved" with imported sand and with groins and seawalls constructed along most of its length. Alterations of the shoreline, which date back to the early 1900s, resulted primarily from attempts to reduce beach erosion. Since that time numerous remedial actions have been undertaken by different interests, including private property owners, and agencies of the City and County of Honolulu, the State of Hawaiʻi, and the federal government. Unfortunately, the outcome of all of these years of construction and importation of sand has not been the creation of a beautiful, continuous white sand beach, but rather the alteration of the offshore bottom. The tons of foreign sand introduced inshore have for the most part escaped containment and have filled up depressions in the offshore reef and ocean bottom, causing a marked change in the breaking form of Waikīkī's famous surfing waves. Alternate solutions are still being sought in the hope of solving the problem of Waikīkī's drifting sands.

Outrigger Canoe Club Beach
2909 Kalākaua Avenue

F: showers; dressing rooms; concessions (food and beverage, beach equipment)
LG: private service provided by Outrigger Canoe Club
EP: Kūhiō Beach Park, Monsarrat at Kalākaua avenues
PP: Kaimana Beach Hotel, 2963 Kalākaua Avenue
FS: 381 Kapahulu Avenue, Waikīkī
H: Kaiser Medical Center, 1677 Ala Moana Boulevard; Queen's Medical Center, 1301 Punchbowl Street
SS: Monsarrat or Kapahulu avenues
WA: canoeing; diving; sailing; snorkeling; board surfing; swimming
WC: safe all year; inshore waters protected by offshore fringing reef

Soon after 1900, a major problem developed with
Waikīkī's invaluable shoreline. Private residences and a
few small hotels were beginning to take over the entire
beach frontage, to such an extent that local residents
were being shut off from the ocean. With this problem
in mind, the founders of the Outrigger Canoe Club
leased from the trustees of the Queen Emma Estate 1½
acres of beach land between the Seaside and the Moana
hotels. They guaranteed their landlords that the property would be used solely for the purpose of preserving
and promoting surfing on boards and in canoes, along
with other related sports and activities. It was here, for
example, that the first official life-saving course in the
United States was taught. Under the auspices of the
Royal Life-Saving Society of England, Mrs. Ellen
Fullard-Leo instructed the initial class in 1916. The
Outrigger Canoe Club remained at its original site from
1908 until the New Year's Eve of 1963. Four days later
the club opened its new facilities at its present home
across from Kapi'olani Park, at the far end of Waikīkī.
The old site is occupied now by the Outrigger Hotel.

   The beach in front of the present Outrigger Canoe
Club is about 150 yards long. Contrary to popular opin-
ion, this beach is not artificial, but actually is the former
beach somewhat restored. All of the sand there came
from the club's property, primarily from excavation for
one of the buildings, a part of which is constructed
below ground. The O.C.C. is the only private facility in
the entire area that has made an attempt to restore the
old beach, the sands of which extend inland to Kalākaua
Avenue.

Sans Souci

(part of Kapi'olani Regional Park, between Kaimana
Beach Hotel and the War Memorial Natatorium)

Sans Souci Beach is located in the land division formerly
known as Kapua. In 1884, a man named Allen Herbert
bought several acres of land there, which included this
particular beach. Herbert felt that Waikīkī needed a
"family resort," so he opened a lodging house that soon
became the showplace of Waikīkī. He named his resort
Sans Souci, the French phrase for "without a care,"
after the palace of Frederick the Great in Potsdam. In
1889, Robert Louis Stevenson and his family stayed in
Waikīkī following a trip through the South Pacific.
Stevenson and Herbert became acquainted, and the famous author spent many evenings at Sans Souci. Not
long after Stevenson's visit the resort was purchased by
Judge F. M. Hatch, who built a home for himself on the
property.

   In 1893, Sans Souci was leased by the property's best-
known landlord, George Lycurgus. Born in Sparta,
Greece, in 1865, Lycurgus came to the Hawaiian Islands
from California. He converted Sans Souci into one of
the notable hotels in Honolulu. When Robert Louis
Stevenson returned to Hawai'i in 1893, he stayed in a
bungalow on the premises of Lycurgus' hotel. "Uncle
George," as he was better known to island residents,
left Sans Souci in 1904 to become the famed manager of
the Volcano House on the Big Island.

   Sans Souci played a part in the establishment of the
first submarine communication cable to Hawai'i. In
1904 the Commerical Pacific Cable Company, Inc.,
placed an order with a factory in Silvertown, England,
for an underwater cable to extend from San Francisco
to Honolulu. The steamship *Silvertown,* freighted with
the first lengths of cable needed for traversing those
2,300 miles, arrived in San Francisco in December 1902.
The crossing to Hawai'i took twelve terrible days. The
Silvertown encountered tremendous winter storms, and
on several occasions serious debates arose on board as

Sans Souci Beach. A section of Waikīkī Beach popular among Honolulu residents for teaching children and other novice swimmers to swim and snorkel. The beach takes its name from a resort that once stood on the grounds now occupied by the Kaimana Beach Hotel.

to whether or not the cable should be cut. The steamship, however, successfully completed her mission and dropped anchor off Sans Souci, where the cable company had purchased a portion of the property. On the morning of December 28, 1902, the guideline for the submarine cable was brought ashore by a Hawaiian crew in a four-man canoe made of *koa,* named *Halekūlani.* The canoe was steered through Kapua Channel by one of the best watermen in Waikīkī, David Piʻikoi Kahanamoku, an uncle of Duke Kahanamoku. The final connection was made on January 1, 1903, and Hawaiʻi for the first time was linked telegraphically to the mainland. In addition to supplying a quick relay of information to Honolulu, this means of direct communication was of great importance to navigation in the Pacific. The longitude of a place is based upon that of Greenwich as a reference; and, of course, the difference in time between that of Greenwich and that of any particular point on Earth is a way of determining the actual longitude of that point. Now, ships crossing the Pacific could set their chronometers in Hawaiʻi instead of having to wait until they docked in San Francisco, thus making for more exact navigation. Remnants of the old submarine cable can still be found in Kapua Channel.

The cable hut was located in the park area just to the rear of the beach. The new cables connecting Oʻahu with California come ashore at Hanauma Bay.

Now the beach at Sans Souci extends from the Kaimana Hotel to the Natatorium wall. It is a very safe and shallow swimming area, providing a relatively calm place for little children. Kapua Channel, marking an ancient freshwater course, comes all the way into shore, where its sandy bottom attracts many recreational swimmers and snorkelers. The occasional accidents that do occur at Sans Souci usually happen when visitors jump or dive from the nearby pier or the Natatorium wall. The bottom in these shallow places is primarily coral, and ignorance of this danger can lead to some bad cuts and scrapes. The City and County lifeguards stationed in the Natatorium and at San Souci Beach are well aware of this danger and try to discourage diving.

War Memorial Natatorium
(part of Kapiʻolani Regional Park)
2815 Kalākaua Avenue

  F: 1 bathhouse; 1 100-meter saltwater swimming pool; 1 basketball court; 2 volleyball courts; 39 parking stalls
LG: daily service provided by City and County
EP: Kūhiō Beach Park, Monsarrat at Kalākaua avenues
PP: in park area rear of pool
FS: 381 Kapahulu Avenue, Waikīkī
  H: Kaiser Medical Center, 1677 Ala Moana Boulevard; Queen's Medical Center, 1301 Punchbowl Street
SS: Monsarrat or Kapahulu avenues
WA: pole fishing; swimming
WC: safe all year; no shallow end
PA: limited to hours posted on entrance gate (9:30 A.M. to 5:00 P.M.)
AI: headquarters of City and County lifeguard service

Soon after the end of the First World War, the people of Hawaiʻi decided to raise a memorial honoring the island men who had lost their lives while serving their country. Wishing to build a memorial that would be the beginning and not the end of honoring, the territory acquired the land of the former Irwin Estate next to San Souci at Waikīkī. In 1920, on Armistice Day, a newly established national holiday, dedicatory exercises were held and the property was turned over to the American Legion. Governor Charles J. McCarthy made the address of dedication and A. L. C. Atkinson the address of acceptance on behalf of the Legion. The monument itself was to be constructed at a later date in the new memorial park honoring Hawaiʻi's fallen sons.

During the late 1920s, plans for the memorial were finally completed. The planners had decided that a big swimming pool that could be used both for official competition and by the general public would be a fitting monument. Before the completion of the pool, all of Hawaiʻi's competitive swimming events were held off one of several piers in Honolulu Harbor. A temple of music, too, was supposed to be built on the memorial park grounds, but this part of the project was never realized.

Just before construction of the Natatorium was begun, an opening in the reef was dredged parallel to the beach in order to provide a swimming area for the "public baths," which had existed for many years in the section next to the memorial park. A portion of the channel was enlarged shoreward specifically to accommodate the proposed pool. The Natatorium building and its regulation pool were rushed to completion during the summer of 1927, just in time to accommodate the National Outdoor Swimming Meets held on August 23. The length of the pool was set at 100 meters (110 yards), because that was the size of an official Olympic Games pool at the time the plans were drawn. Governor Wallace R. Farrington made the dedicatory address, and Duke Kahanamoku, Hawaiʻi's Olympic champion, opened the pool with an exhibition swim.

The Natatorium was one of the first World War I memorials to be built in the United States and is still the largest saltwater swimming pool in the country. It is the only public swimming pool in Waikīkī, and the only public saltwater pool in the State. Since its completion in 1927 the "tank," as it is popularly known, has been a favorite place for swimmers of all ages.

Today the Natatorium is a part of Kapiʻolani Regional Park and is the headquarters for Honolulu's City and County lifeguards, who moved there in 1935 from their old central site on the beach before the Moana Hotel. In recent years there has been a great deal of talk about demolishing the Natatorium because it is sadly deteriorated and is in need of much repair. Proponents of the plan to destroy the tank wish to widen the shore between Queen's Surf Beach and Sans Souci, thereby making the area one complete and connected sand beach. Opposition to these plans has been very strong and vocal: to many island residents the Natatorium is still a living memorial and thus a very valuable part of Hawai'i.

The Natatorium's pool has no shallow end, so beginning swimmers should be restricted to nearby Sans Souci. The depth of water in the tank varies with the tide. It is deepest in the *makai* center portion, because of a high diving tower that once stood on this edge of the pool deck. The hours for swimming are posted on the entrance gate. A lifeguard is always on duty while the pool is open.

Kapi'olani Park Beach Center

(also Kapi'olani Beach Center)
(part of Kapi'olani Regional Park)
2745 Kalākaua Avenue

 F: 1 comfort station; 1 volleyball court; 24 parking stalls; 1 food concession
LG: service provided by lifeguard station at adjoining Queen's Surf Beach
EP: Kūhiō Beach Park, Monsarrat at Kalākaua avenues
PP: in comfort station
FS: 381 Kapahulu Avenue, Waikīkī
 H: Kaiser Medical Center, 1677 Ala Moana Boulevard; Queen's Medical Center, 1301 Punchbowl Street
SS: Monsarrat or Kapahulu avenues
WA: diving; pole fishing; board surfing; swimming
WC: safe all year; shoreline rocky in places; dangerous drop into channel from reef shelf
PA: unlimited

In December 1871, King Kamehameha V proclaimed June 11 of each year as a public holiday in memory of Kamehameha I, creator of the Kingdom of Hawai'i. In 1877, when Kalākaua had been king for more than three years, Kamehameha Day was marked by dedicating the island nation's first public park in honor of Queen Kapi'olani. It was opened formally with prayers, speeches, and horse races (the land having been acquired for that purpose as well as for the other uses to which a park can be put), and racing continued there until after the turn of the century. Nearly the entire extent of the park was Crown Land, but in 1877 the land was leased to the Ka-

pi'olani Park Association, among the members of which were Captain James Makee, Thomas Cummins, Sr., and A. S. Cleghorn. The park itself, controlled by the Board of Parks Commissioners, was a beautiful area with numerous trees, artificial ponds and winding streams, and an island where occasionally band concerts were held. Before Kapi'olani Park was created, Honolulu had only two other parks, Queen Emma Square and Thomas Square, both of which were looked after by Mr. Cleghorn.

During the early days of the Republic of Hawai'i nearly all of the shoreline parallel to Kapi'olani Park was disposed of to private individuals and many years passed before the government regained all rights to the sea frontage. This loss of Waikīkī's shoreline to private individuals created a serious problem, because people who did not actually live along the beach were left without rights-of-way to the beach and the sea beyond. In 1908, the same year that the Outrigger Canoe Club obtained some land to assure its members of a beach access, the City and County of Honolulu acquired the Kunst lot opposite the bandstand in Kapi'olani Park for a public recreational beach area. The "Public Baths," as everybody called it, provided facilities for showers, dressing rooms, a dance pavilion, and a lounging room. The sea bottom offshore was cleared and deepened by removing some of the coral. More than twenty years later, in January 1931, the then aging structures were torn down. On November 9, 1931, Mayor Fred Wright dedicated the newly built municipal public baths, hailed as one of the showcases of Waikīkī, with its complementary lighting and landscaping. The "new" public baths served O'ahu's beach-going populace for thirty more years until they, too, were replaced by the present bathhouse concession. The former public baths was renamed the Kapi'olani Park Beach Center. The only surviving reference to the former name is the popular surfing spot offshore, still known as "Public's."

Next to the public baths was a beautiful two-story, beachside mansion that was purchased in the 1930s by Christopher R. Holmes, heir to the Fleischmann yeast fortune. The mansion, sold to another owner, was converted into a restaurant in 1946. Named "the Queen's Surf" after the famous surfing break in Waikīkī, it soon became one of the most popular places in Honolulu. The City and County acquired the land in 1953, but

Christine A. Takata

Kapi'olani Beach Center. Pole fishermen wait patiently in the shallows between the Natatorium and the Waikīkī Aquarium for *'oama,* baby goat fish, to bite. This beach park is the only place along the Waikīkī shoreline that has public cooking and picnicking facilities.

allowed the restaurant to remain open on a short-term lease. In 1961 the SpenceCliff Corporation bid for and won the new lease. Their nightclub-restaurant venture made the Queen's Surf one of the largest gathering places in Waikīkī not only for visitors but also for residents. The SpenceCliff Corporation's lease ended in 1970. The only evidence of the former mansion left today is the floor of the main dining room and show room that was retained for use as a public stage and pavilion. The rest of the building was completely demolished by June 1971 in order to expand the beach park area. This stretch of beach, however, is still widely known as Queen's Surf.

The last bit of private property acquired to make up the present Kapi'olani Park shoreline was the Cunha estate. Today it is completely an open area, with no structures at all on it. The only remaining reference to the former owners is a deep-water surfing break offshore from the Kapahulu groin, called "Cunha's."

The best section of Kapi'olani Park's beach is the Queen's Surf area. It has the widest beach in the park, and the waters offshore have a rock-free sandy bottom. The section of the shoreline between the Kapahulu groin and Queen's Surf is narrow, with coarse sand and a shallow, uninviting coral bottom. There are no good places to swim in this area.

The only real hazards throughout the entire length of the Kapi'olani Park Beach are found at either end. In front of the Aquarium the reef shelf drops off abruptly into the old boat channel and presents a danger to nonswimmers or wading children. At the other end of the beach there is small but ridable surf around "the Wall," as the Kapahulu groin is called, so swimmers must beware of runaway boards and novice riders. The Wall has long been a popular bodysurfing area so, by regulation of the State Board of Transportation, the waters within a radius of 150 yards from it are off limits to board surfers. The enforcement of this regulation, however, is very difficult at times, and is a constant problem for lifeguards stationed nearby as well as for bodysurfers.

Queen's Surf Beach Park

(part of Kapi'olani Regional Park)
western side of Kapi'olani Park Beach Center

 F: 1 comfort station; 1 lifeguard tower; 1 open-side picnic pavilion; 87 parking stalls
LG: daily service provided by City and County
EP: Kūhiō Beach Park, Monsarrat at Kalākaua avenues
PP: in comfort station
FS: 381 Kapahulu Avenue, Waikīkī
 H: Kaiser Medical Center, 1677 Ala Moana Boulevard; Queen's Medical Center, 1301 Punchbowl Street
SS: Monsarrat or Kapahulu avenues
WA: diving; snorkeling; board surfing; swimming
WC: safe all year; wide, shallow, sand-bottom swimming area bordered by coral reef
PA: unlimited
 AI: see text for Kapi'olani Park Beach Center

Kūhiō Beach Park

2453 Kalākaua Avenue

 F: 1 volleyball court; 1 food concession; 2 lifeguard towers
LG: daily service provided by City and County
EP: in park area
PP: in park area
FS: 381 Kapahulu Avenue, Waikīkī
 H: Kaiser Medical Center, 1677 Ala Moana Boulevard; Queen's Medical Center, 1301 Punchbowl Street

SS: Kapahulu Avenue
WA: diving; snorkeling; board surfing; bodysurfing; paipo board surfing; swimming
WC: safe all year; western end of beach (Queen's Surf Beach to Kapahulu groin) has poor swimming, shallow ocean bottom made up of coral reef; eastern end (Kapahulu groin to Waikīkī Beach Center) allows good swimming, primarily sand bottom throughout area; specific hazards: jumping off Kapahulu groin is dangerous because of shallow reef surrounding; easy to lose footing on "Slippery Wall"; occasional rip current in small channel seaward of "Slippery Wall"
PA: unlimited

Jonah Kūhiō Kalaniana'ole, the youngest son of Kekaulike Kinoiki II and High Chief David Kahalepouli Pi'ikoi, was born on March 26, 1871, at Hoai, Kualu, in the Kōloa district of Kaua'i. His mother died soon after his birth, so he and his two older brothers were adopted by his mother's sister, Kapi'olani. Because Kapi'olani and her husband Kalākaua had no children, when he ascended the throne in 1874 the king officially gave each of the boys the title of prince. When the revolution that deposed Queen Lili'uokalani, Kalākaua's sister and successor, put an end to the possible ascendancy of any of the boys, they retired to their mother's home, "Pualeilani," in Waikīkī.

In 1895 Prince Kūhiō, like many other Royalists, was involved in Robert Wilcox's unsuccessful attempt to overthrow the Republic of Hawai'i and to restore the queen to her throne. He served one year in jail as a political prisoner and was released on October 8, 1896, the same day on which the former queen was granted her freedom.

In the ensuing years, Prince Kūhiō was elected as Hawai'i's second delegate to the American Congress, defeating Robert Wilcox for the position. He served from November 1902 until his death in January 1922. His greatest ambition in Congress was to promote the rehabilitation of the Hawaiian people. In 1910 he obtained an amendment to the Organic Act, which opened public lands in Hawai'i to homesteading. The amendment, however, still did not protect the Hawaiians, so Kūhiō sought to establish homesteading lands for Hawaiians only. In arguing his case, the prince told congressmen of his anxiety over the dying Hawaiian people. He explained that the Hawaiians had lost their lands to people of more aggressive races who had settled in the islands.

Kūhiō Beach Park. Youngsters line "Slippery Wall," a major sand-retaining wall in Kūhiō Beach Park, waiting for waves to wash over. Injuries from slips and falls on this wall are frequent and occasionally very serious.

At home he was just as outspoken in telling the Hawaiian people that in work lay their only salvation, that hard work and education would enable them to compete with the aggressive races from Europe, America, and Asia. The original rehabilitation act was enacted in 1921 and the way was opened for setting aside homesteads for Hawaiians.

In the heart of Waikīkī, Queen Lili'uokalani had owned an extensive tract of land called Hamohamo, that ran inland from the beach, through swamps, to what eventually became the Ala Wai Canal. Prince Kūhiō and his wife Princess Elizabeth Kahanu had their home at Pualeilani, on the seashore of Hamohamo. On July 22, 1918, the prince removed the high board fence around his property and opened this section of beach to the public. Although it had already been named Kūhiō Park in his honor, when the beloved prince died of heart disease at his Waikīkī home on January 7, 1922, Pualeilani was given to the city. The park was not officially dedicated until 1940, when a plaque was set into one of the retaining walls along the shore. The inconspicuous memorial is still in place.

Kūhiō Beach Park is situated between the Kapahulu groin and the Waikīkī Beach Center. In the early days of modern Waikīkī, the Diamond Head end of Kūhiō Beach had no sand at all and was called "Stonewall" because of the high retaining dike constructed there to support Kalākaua Avenue. The former Kuekaunahe Stream emptied into the ocean in the Stonewall area. In recent years this region has been rebuilt and improved. The first major restoration, called the Waikīkī Beach Improvement Project, was completed in July 1951 by James W. Glover, Ltd. This project included construction of the Kapahulu groin, which is an extension of the storm drain running under Kapahulu Avenue; construction of the retaining wall on the Diamond Head side of the groin; and the importation of sand for the shore on both sides of the groin. Today the Stonewall section is the widest part of Kūhiō Beach Park and the most heavily used.

There are several hazards in this area of which swimmers should be aware. A low retaining wall was constructed some years ago perpendicular to the Kapahulu groin to keep the sand from eroding away. "Slippery Wall," as it is known locally, is covered with a growth of fine seaweed that creates a very slick surface when wet. Younger people who frequent the area often can be seen sliding on their feet across the wet, slippery sections of the wall with no apparent effort, or ill effect. Visitors who attempt to join in this sport, however, often take some bad spills which occasionally have resulted in serious injuries. Even people simply trying to walk across Slippery Wall can lose their footing. It is a good place to avoid. Another hazard is the short stretch of water between the beach and Slippery Wall. The currents swirling through a break in the low wall often dig up and shift the sand bottom. The expected shallowness of the area is not always present, as the depth varies with surf conditions. Little children should be especially watched. Another danger awaits children playing on "The Wall," the Kapahulu groin: the water on both sides is extremely shallow, with a rough coral bottom, into which youngsters still persist in jumping and diving. There have been many instances of serious lacerations from these foolhardy activities. The last danger at this end of Kūhiō Beach Park is the narrow channel cutting through the reef outside Slippery Wall. This channel, cut long ago by Kuekaunahe Stream, occasionally has a strong rip current that catches unwary swimmers.

The 'Ewa end of this park, formerly known to Hawaiians as Kapuni, has very little sand on its beach. The sand bottom slopes gently into deeper areas, and in general there are no significant hazards.

Waikīkī Beach Center
(formerly known as Tavern's or Kapuni)
2435 Kalākaua Avenue

 F: 1 comfort station; 1 lifeguard tower; 1 surfboard/canoe rental concession; surfboard lockers
LG: daily service provided by City and County
EP: in park area
PP: in park area
FS: 381 Kapahulu Avenue, Waikīkī
 H: Kaiser Medical Center, 1677 Ala Moana Boulevard; Queen's Medical Center, 1301 Punchbowl Street
SS: Kapahulu Avenue
WA: canoeing; snorkeling; board surfing; swimming
WC: safe all year; inshore ocean bottom primarily sandy and coral-free (excellent swimming); major danger is mixing of commercial canoeing, expert and novice board surfing
PA: unlimited
AI: 4 large boulders at rear of Waikīkī Beach Center known as the "Wizard Stones" of Kapaemahu

In ancient times four learned men, Kapaemahu, Kahaloa, Kapuni, and Kinohi, came to Hawai'i from a distant land. They were well received by the Hawaiians and became very famous throughout the islands for their wonderful powers of healing and curing and for their great wisdom. When the time for their departure drew near, they decided to leave some tangible evidence of their stay on O'ahu. The *kahunas* agreed that the people should erect four stone monuments as permanent reminders, two to be placed on the ground of their habitation and two at their usual swimming places in the ocean. Four large boulders were brought from Kaimukī and taken to the beach at Ulukou in Waikīkī, the area now occupied by the Moana Hotel and the Waikīkī Beach Center. The stone of Kapuni was placed where the surf rolled into the beach, the shallows that surfers now know as "Baby Queens." The stone of Kahaloa was taken to the 'Ewa side of Apuakehau Stream, to the waters fronting the present Royal Hawaiian Hotel. Eventually the shorelines in both of these places took the names of the stone monuments. The stones of Kapaemahu and Kinohi were set above the waterline on the beach at Ulukou, where the four *kahunas* had dwelt. After the four stones had been put in place, a ceremony was held transferring the powers of the *kahunas* to their monuments. Then the four men departed.

During the early 1900s, the four boulders were unearthed in the beach lands of the late Princess Ka'iulani, the daughter of former Governor Archibald Cleghorn. He ordered them returned to their shoreline locality, where they still sit inconspicuously near the sidewalk passing by the Waikīkī Beach Center.

For many years one of the best-known places in Waikīkī was the tavern that once stood on the premises now housing the beach center. The first building was constructed on the site in 1884. In the ensuing years it underwent numerous alterations and was known by a variety of names, such as Waikīkī Inn, Heinie's Tavern, and finally Waikīkī Tavern. These restaurant ventures, however, came to an end in 1960, when the Waikīkī Tavern was demolished to make way for the Waikīkī Beach Center. The City and County paid $26.65 per square foot for the premises, the entire parcel costing more than $1,500,000. Among old-timers the Waikīkī Beach Center is still known as "Tavern's."

The inshore waters in front of the beach center are as safe as can be desired by any recreational swimmer. The shallow offshore bottom is primarily sand, with scattered patches of coral.

Royal-Moana Beach

(Royal area formerly called Kahaloa;
Moana area formerly called Ulukou) shoreline from the Moana-Surfrider Hotel to the Royal Hawaiian Hotel

  F: 1 lifeguard tower; concessions (food, surfboard, canoe, catamaran, and beach equipment)
 LG: daily service provided by City and County
 EP: Waikīkī Beach Center

 PP: Banyan Court, Moana Hotel, 2365 Kalākaua Avenue
 FS: 381 Kapahulu Avenue, Waikīkī
  H: Kaiser Medical Center, 1677 Ala Moana Boulevard; Queen's Medical Center, 1301 Punchbowl Street
 SS: Kapahulu Avenue
 WA: canoeing; sailing; snorkeling; board surfing; swimming
 WC: safe all year; ocean bottom primarily sandy and coral-free; major hazard is small offshore channel which is deeper than surrounding areas and sometimes has a strong rip current
 PA: unlimited
 AI: Royal-Moana area is the traditional "Heart of Waikīkī" beach

The sandy shoreline fronting the Moana Hotel and extending down to the Royal Hawaiian Hotel is the heart of Waikīkī Beach. Here the first large hotels were built, and to this day the area remains the focal point for other hotels, shops, nightclubs, travel offices, and similar visitor-oriented businesses. The beach between the Royal and the Moana was divided by 'Āpuakēhau Stream, which emptied into the sea on the Diamond Head side of the present Outrigger Hotel. The Moana side of the stream was called Ulukou, "the *kou* tree grove"; and the Royal Hawaiian side was known as Kahaloa, "the long place," noted for its fragrant *limu lipoa*. Remembrance of these Hawaiian names has waned during the years through lack of use: for most people it is much easier to refer to a place on the beach simply by mentioning the nearest hotel.

Before the completion of the Waikīkī Reformation Project in 1926, 'Āpuakēhau Stream was one of two branches of the united Mānoa-Pālolo Stream that flowed through the rice paddies, ponds, and swamps that made up the backlands of Waikīkī. 'Āpuakēhau carved a small channel in the sea bottom at the place where its freshwater coursed and dispersed. For a while the surf near this channel was called "Cornucopia," for the traditional horn of plenty, because the first *haole* surfers in Waikīkī thought that the pattern of the dying waves converging upon the channel from the outside breaks resembled a cornucopia. The small surf and crosswaves that come in at Cornucopia are primarily a beginners' break. By 1926 the waters in 'Āpuakēhau Stream were cut off by the completion of the Ala Wai Canal, but the old channel it had cleared in the ocean bottom remains, although it has filled considerably with sand from erod-

Royal-Moana Beach. The traditional heart of Waikīkī Beach. Two of the oldest and most famous hotels in Waikīkī can still be seen nestled among the towering high rises. The Moana Hotel is the white building on the right and the Royal Hawaiian Hotel is the low rise just to the right of the catamaran. Still the most popular section of Waikīkī Beach, this area has the highest concentration of sunbathers, swimmers, surfers, and rental concessions.

ing beaches. The channel still presents a danger because occasionally strong currents run through it. City and County lifeguards make a number of rescues in this area every year. The inshore waters of the Royal-Moana Beach, however, provide a safe, calm, and relatively coral-free swimming spot. The sand bottom is shallow and slopes gently toward the deeper areas. Offshore from the Royal-Moana Beach are Waikīkī's two most famous surfing breaks, "Queen's Surf" (not to be con-

fused with the beach of the same name) and "Canoes' Surf." Queen's was named for Queen Lili'uokalani, who had a beach home called Pualeilani on the land that now comprises Kūhiō Beach Park. Between 1900 and 1905, two young boys, Larry Kerr and Dude Miller, began board surfing in the break directly offshore from the Queen's house, and they called this favorite place "Queen's Surf." The name has been retained ever since that time. The waves at "Queen's" are steeper and break faster than do those at Canoes. The heavy, old-style *koa*-wood canoes could not successfully ride these waves, so their paddlers stayed in the slower-breaking, more rolling surf at the 'Ewa side of Queen's. For this reason this slower break was named "Canoes."

Besides being the place for canoe-surfing, Canoes is the major board-surfing break in Waikīkī for beginners. On days when the surf is good, the combination of canoe riding and beginning board surfing creates a dangerous mixture. During the summer months, when the situation is especially chaotic, the lifeguards usually keep one man in the water on a roving surf patrol.

Gray's Beach
(also Halekūlani Beach)
fronting Halekūlani Hotel

F: public parking facilities in Kālia Road area; concessions (surfboard, canoe, sailing craft, beach equipment, food, and catamaran rides)
LG: service provided by beach concessions personnel
EP: Waikīkī Beach Center
PP: Kālia Road
FS: 381 Kapahulu Avenue, Waikīkī
H: Kaiser Medical Center, 1677 Ala Moana Boulevard; Queen's Medical Center, 1301 Punchbowl Street
SS: Kalākaua at 'Ena Road; McCully Street; Maluhia Road
WA: canoeing; sailing; snorkeling; board surfing; swimming
WC: safe all year; best swimming in Gray's channel; large, sand-bottom channel running out through reef; rocky ocean bottom surrounding channel
PA: 1 public right-of-way from Kālia Road between Halekūlani and Reef hotels

In the late 1800s, Mrs. Cordelia Brown purchased from a man named Hall a large section of beachfront property located in the Kālia area of Waikīkī. In the deed from Mr. Hall to Mrs. Brown, the estate was referred to as "Oneonta." There was also a sign bearing this name at the entrance to the property from Kālia Road. Oneonta is of interest because it is not a Hawaiian word. It is an Indian name, meaning "place of peace," and was first used as a place name in the state of New York: the town of Oneonta lies just south of Cooperstown. The name apparently traveled with the pioneers across the con-

tinental United States. In 1883 a Mississippi River side-wheel steamboat was built at Cascades, Oregon, and named the *Oneonta*. She was operated on the Columbia River by the Oregon Steam Navigation Company until 1877. Oneonta Gorge in Multnomah County, Oregon, is thought to have been named for some incident connected with the boat. How the name happened to be given to the property in Waikīkī that Mrs. Brown purchased is not known. In Hawai'i Oneonta also is remembered as the name of a racehorse during that time, but the connection, if any, between the horse and the Waikīkī property has never been established.

Hawaiians called this area Kawehewehe, "the removal." They believed that the beach of Kawehewehe was a place of healing where the sick were brought to be bathed in the waters of the ocean.

The Oneonta estate eventually was divided among Mrs. Brown's sons, Jacob and Arthur, and her daughter, Mrs. J. A. Gilman. In 1903 the Gilman family constructed a two-story home on their portion of the estate, but later moved out of the large house into a smaller one nearby. In 1912 the two-story house was rented to La Vancha Maria Chapin Gray, who converted it into a boardinghouse that was officially known as "Grays-by-the-Sea." Because of that the area was soon known as "Gray's Beach," and the natural sand-filled channel that ran westward through the reef was called "Gray's Channel." Gray's Beach was the only good sandy place in the immediate area, and its fame spread throughout Waikīkī. Often tourists would walk from the old Seaside Hotel (on the grounds of the present Royal Hawaiian), and occasionally even from the Moana Hotel, to swim there. In 1929 the boardinghouse closed its doors when Mrs. Gilman sold her portion of the estate to Clifford Kimball.

Arthur Brown had built a beautiful home on his parcel of the estate, which Kimball also acquired. Kimball named the mansion Halekūlani, "house befitting heaven," and converted the combined premises into one of Waikīkī's most prominent and well-loved hotels, a reputation the hotel still enjoys. Author Earl Derr Biggers stayed at the Halekūlani while he visited Honolulu. Later, he wrote a murder mystery called "The House without a Key," basing his title upon the fact that in those days people in Honolulu never locked their doors.

Gray's Beach. Named for Gray's-by-the-Sea, a lodging house that was located just to the rear of the beach prior to the development of the Halekulani Hotel. The Sheraton Waikīkī looms in the background in marked contrast to the low-rise graciousness of the Halekulani.

The principal character in the story was the celebrated Chinese detective, Charlie Chan, patterned after Honolulu's detective Chang ("Chan") Apana. In memory of the author and his novel, the Halekūlani named its famed bar and *lanai* under the *kiawe* tree "The House without a Key." The *lanai* and the house remain much the same as they were originally, except for the glass partitions and some other minor additions.

In spite of the prominence of the Halekūlani Hotel, the strand in front of it kept the name Gray's Beach, and is still known as such to most *kama'āina* on O'ahu. Gray's Beach is an ideal place for recreational swimmers. The inshore waters are calm, shallow, and relatively sandy, with only scattered patches of coral. The most frequently used swimming place is Gray's Channel, the wide, sand bottom that crosses the reef between the surfing spots called "Paradise" and "Number Threes." There is a public right-of-way to the beach from Kālia Road, on the 'Ewa side of the Halekūlani Hotel.

Fort DeRussy Beach
Kālia Road

   F: volleyball courts; cooking stands and tables; dressing rooms and showers; concessions (food and beverage)
  LG: service provided by military personnel
  EP: Waikīkī Beach Center
  PP: on Kālia Road
  FS: 1610 Makaloa Street, Pāwaʻa
   H: Kaiser Medical Center, 1677 Ala Moana Boulevard; Queen's Medical Center, 1301 Punchbowl Street
  SS: Kalākaua Avenue at ʻEna Road; at McCully Street; at Maluhia Road
  WA: snorkeling; board surfing; swimming
  WC: safe all year; wide, sandy beach; ocean bottom is mixture of coral patches and sand pockets
  PA: limited to beach areas; facilities in Fort DeRussy are for military personnel only; public rights-of-way on Kālia Road and DeRussy Place

The first steps to acquire the lands that make up Fort DeRussy were taken in 1904. The major portion of the reservation, originally privately owned, was obtained by the federal government by purchase and condemnation proceedings. Only a narrow strip just inland of the present seawall was taken for the government by presidential executive order. The newly acquired acreage was known initially as the Kālia Military Reservation, after the Hawaiian name for those lands. The entire region consisted of duck ponds and swamps, and a great deal of filling was required to make a foundation for the fort. In January 1909, War Department Orders 15 officially established the area as a military reservation, and during the following month it was formally named Fort DeRussy. Brigadier-General René Edward DeRussy served with distinction as a member of the Engineer Corps in both the War of 1812 and the Civil War. In keeping with the development of neighboring Waikīkī as a vacation resort area, Fort DeRussy eventually became a focal point for Army recreational activities. Today the post is used as an armed forces recreation center and as an "R & R" (rest and recreation) site for armed forces personnel. Some of its facilities are used by the local army reserves also.

For many years there has been a great deal of controversy concerning the lands of Fort DeRussy, because it represents so large a part of the invaluable Waikīkī shoreline. Many individuals who do not agree that the military should hold such an area contend that the reservation be returned to the State. These people, however, overlook the fact that the federal government acquired almost the entire acreage by purchasing it outright and not by presidential executive order. In addition, the area was originally a relatively unwanted wasteland that the government developed at its own expense. The destiny of the reservation was sealed, however, in 1967 by the Ninetieth Congress: Public Law 90–110 states that "none of the lands constituting Fort DeRussy may be sold, leased, transferred, or otherwise disposed of by the Department of Defense unless authorized by law" (in other words, by Congress).

According to state law, all beaches in Hawaiʻi are public property and the beachfront at Fort DeRussy is no exception. The beach was closed to the public only during World War II; it was reopened in August 1946. The rest of the reservation's facilities are available only to active and retired military personnel and their dependents and guests, except for Battery Randolph which is maintained as a World War II museum, and is open to the public. These facilities, the majority of which are low, single-story buildings, give Fort DeRussy an enviable distinction: it is the last big section in Waikīkī that is still green and undeveloped.

The entire shorefront has been improved in recent years and is definitely the widest single stretch of beach in Waikīkī. The inshore waters are calm and safe for swimming, but the sea bottom is primarily rough coral with scattered sand pockets. Most nonmilitary personnel prefer the sandier beaches at either side of DeRussy.

Fort DeRussy Beach Park
end of Paoa Place

   F: none; half-acre landscaped minipark; concessions and facilities in Hale Koa Hotel for military personnel only (not part of public park)
  LG: service provided by military personnel
  EP: none
  PP: next to concession in rear of the Hale Koa Hotel
  FS: 1610 Makaloa Street, Pāwaʻa
   H: Kaiser Medical Center, 1677 Ala Moana Boulevard; Queen's Medical Center, 1301 Punchbowl Street

SS: Kalākaua Avenue
WA: snorkeling; surfing; swimming
WC: safe all year; sandy beach
PA: unlimited

Kahanamoku Beach and Lagoon
2005 Kālia Road
(fronting Hilton Hawaiian Village)

 F: concessions (surfboard, beach equipment, food and beverage); catamaran cruises; showers; 1 volleyball court (sand); public parking in Ala Wai Yacht Harbor area
LG: service provided by beach concession personnel
EP: Ala Moana Park, Waikīkī (east) concession, 1201 Ala Moana Boulevard
PP: hotel to rear of beach
FS: 1610 Makaloa Street, Pāwaʻa
 H: Kaiser Medical Center, 1677 Ala Moana Boulevard; Queen's Medical Center, 1301 Punchbowl Street
SS: Kalākaua Avenue at ʻEna Road; McCully Street; Maluhia Road
WA: diving; snorkeling; board surfing; swimming
WC: both beach and lagoon are safe all year; sandy ocean bottom in both areas
PA: unlimited
 AI: beach and lagoon are man-made; completed in 1956, through a joint dredging/sand-filling venture between Henry J. Kaiser and the Board of Harbor Commissioners

When Henry J. Kaiser constructed his Hawaiian Village in the Kālia area, both he and the Board of Harbor Commissioners cooperated in a joint dredging and sand-filling venture to create a new beach. The beach and the adjoining lagoon were completed in 1955 (when the Village opened), and both were filled with sand by the following year. In May 1958 the City Planning Commission voted to name the newly constructed sand crescent Kahanamoku Beach in honor of Duke Paoa Kahanamoku, one of Hawaiʻi's most beloved sons.

In 1869, Alfred Ernest Albert, Great Britian's Duke of Edinburgh, visited Honolulu. Halapu Kahanamoku was born in that same year, and at the suggestion of Princess Bernice Pauahi Bishop he was named "Duke," to commemorate the visit of the English nobleman. "Duke" Halapu Kahanamoku married Julia Paʻakonia

Lonokahikini, and when their first child was born, on August 24, 1890, they named him Duke Paoa. The young Duke was followed by eight brothers and sisters. They spent much of their childhood between their parents' home at "Haleakalā," Mrs. Bishop's residence in central Honolulu, and their grandfather's home in Kālia, Waikīkī. Duke learned to swim in the waters of Kālia.

In 1910, when Duke was twenty years old, he swam a fifty-yard sprint and was clocked at the unbelievable time of twenty-three seconds, thereby establishing a new world record. Even today, with our more sophisticated and intensive training methods, twenty-three seconds still remains a very respectable time for swimming fifty yards freestyle. Furthermore, it must be remembered, Duke swam this sprint over a straight, open, saltwater course. In 1912 Duke was named a member of the United States Olympic swimming squad and won the gold medal in the 100-meter freestyle. He also participated in the 1920, 1924, and 1932 Olympic Games. He remained an active supporter of all water sports until his death in 1968. Kahanamoku Beach was named most appropriately for this son of Hawaiʻi who learned to swim in the waters offshore.

Kahanamoku Beach is a safe and protected swimming area. The inshore waters are completely enclosed by the hotel's catamaran pier on the Diamond Head side, a heavy breakwater on the ʻEwa side, and by a strip of shallow reef offshore that runs between the two. The strip was left deliberately when the area was dredged, in order to provide a secure, protected swimming beach. The ocean is deep on the outer side of the reef, for the sake of catamarans, and deep on the inner side for comfortable swimming. From the beach itself the sand bottom slopes gently toward the deeper places. Kahanamoku Lagoon is adjacent to Kahanamoku Beach. Fresh ocean water flows into the sandy lagoon through two 36-inch pipes. A small concrete structure located on the west side of the lagoon contains a pump which constantly releases water from the lagoon into the nearby yacht basin. This circulation system insures the freshness and purity of the water in the lagoon. The enclosing beach is sandy, and the bottom slopes gently to the deeper regions of the lagoon, which attains a depth of fourteen feet at the center.

Christine A. Takata

Kahanamoku Lagoon. Looking *mauka* across the man-made lagoon. The lagoon and the adjoining beach that fronts the Hilton Hawaiian Village were named in honor of Duke Kahanamoku, a former Olympic swimming champion from Hawaii. The Duke spent much of his youth swimming in the ocean in this area, which was known as Kālia to the Hawaiians.

Magic Island Beach

(officially named 'Āina Moana in 1972)
eastern end of Ala Moana Beach Park

   F: 1 comfort station; 1 lifeguard tower; concessions (food and beverage in Ala Moana Park); landscaped park; 100 parking stalls
 LG: none; summon from Ala Moana Beach
 EP: Ala Moana Park, Waikīkī (east) concession
 PP: Ala Moana Park, Waikīkī (east) concession
 FS: 1610 Makaloa Street, Pāwa'a
   H: Kaiser Medical Center, 1677 Ala Moana Boulevard; Queen's Medical Center, 1301 Punchbowl Street

  SS: Ala Moana Boulevard; Ward Avenue
 WA: diving; pole fishing; snorkeling; board surfing; swimming; throw-netting
 WC: safe all year; sandy bottom in lagoon; deep channels in open ocean on either side of lagoon and park area; dangerous waves come directly to rocks
 PA: unlimited
  AI: owned and maintained by the State of Hawai'i

The man-made peninsula bordering the Ala Wai Channel was completed in 1964 through the reclamation of about thirty acres of shallow reef. Called "Magic Island" by its developers, the peninsula was the first

60

Christine A. Takata

Magic Island Lagoon. Looking across the beach and a portion of the lagoon at the *makai* end of this man-made peninsula. Created largely from the deposition of dredged material, Magic Island's official state park name is 'Āina Moana, "land from the ocean."

phase of an intended resort hotel complex. The promoters of the venture ran into financial difficulties, however, so the undertaking never moved farther than the completion of Magic Island. The original plans called for two more such islands to be constructed opposite the front of Ala Moana Beach Park. The project presented the State with an artificial peninsula, which it has converted into a public park. In 1972 Magic Island was officially renamed 'Āina Moana, "land from the sea," referring to the fact that the entire park is primarily coral fill.

With the installation of walkways, benches, and other improvements, a very beautiful park was created. The man-made beach in the park is located at the seaward end of 'Āina Moana, where it is protected by thick sec-

tions of seawall made from heavy rocks. The peninsula was built right into two well-used surfing breaks, so the retaining wall was necessary to protect the sand from being eroded by the strong summer surf and by swells caused by the prevailing trade winds. These sections of the wall form a small, safe lagoon. The bottom is sandy and slopes gently toward the deeper areas. The hazards here are not in the swimming beach itself, but rather in the area surrounding it. The seawall enclosing the beach is made of boulders that are positioned to allow the seawater to flow into and out of the lagoon. On several occasions someone climbing over the rocks has slipped and wedged a foot or a leg in the cracks. Outside the seawall is a surfing spot whose waves wash directly upon the huge boulders. Besides taking its toll of runaway surfboards, the wall occasionally cuts up a careless surfer who takes a chance with the dangers of this once-open break. The other major hazards of Magic Island are the deep boat channels on either side of the peninsula. Children like to climb up and down the retaining walls, especially on the boat harbor side, where all sorts of driftwood and marine flotsam lodges on the rocks. Enthusiastic youngsters should be watched very carefully because the channels are deep and the drops into both are very abrupt.

Magic Island, or 'Āina Moana, is a State beach park at present, although eventually it is to be turned over to the City and County to become an additional section of Ala Moana Beach Park.

Ala Moana Beach Park
1201 Ala Moana Boulevard

F: 2 comfort stations; 2 food and beverage concessions; 1 recreation building with banyan court; 10 tennis courts; 1 bowling green; 6 softball fields; 5 lifeguard towers; 582 parking stalls
LG: daily service provided by City and County
EP: 2 in park area (1 located next to each concession)
PP: 2 in park area (1 located next to each concession)
FS: 1610 Makaloa Street, Pāwa'a
H: Kaiser Medical Center, 1677 Ala Moana Boulevard; Queen's Medical Center, 1301 Punchbowl Street
SS: Ala Moana Boulevard; Ward Avenue
WA: diving; pole fishing; board surfing; swimming
WC: safe all year; deep swimming channel runs length of entire beach; often gusty trade winds are potentially hazardous to children playing with inflatable toys or supported by flotation gear
PA: unlimited
AI: the most popular beach park in urban Honolulu

Ala Moana is the finest and most popular beach park in all of urban Honolulu. On weekends, holidays, and during the summer months, the entire seventy-six-acre park is completely filled with tennis players, joggers, huge groups of picnickers, fishermen, model airplane enthusiasts, model boat sailors, sunbathers, surfers, and swimmers. For Honolulu's residents, Ala Moana provides the combined pleasures of numerous park activities and

of the beach without the crowds and traffic of Waikīkī. The beach is not frequented by many out-of-state visitors, who generally prefer the sands of Waikīkī, with its rentable canoes and surfboards and its famous (if crowded) swimming beach.

Before it was developed, the area now called Ala Moana Park was a vast swamp, a mixture of bullrushes and duck ponds, with scattered patches of land bearing *kiawe* trees and coconut palms. The entire shoreline was a coral wasteland bordered by mud flats. In time this stretch of coast between Kewalo Basin and Waikīkī became the site of the Honolulu garbage dump, which burned almost continually. In 1931 the entire area was officially designated as Moana Park by the City and County Parks Board, but the actual beach and park complex was not finished until 1934. In the summer of that year the dedication was made by President Franklin D. Roosevelt, who participated in the opening ceremonies during a visit to Honolulu.

After World War II, many other uses were suggested for the land, including a housing development, a rest camp for military personnel, and a quarantine station, but fortunately none of these plans was ever realized, and the area remained a park. In 1947 its name was changed officially to Ala Moana, "the path to the sea."

The entire swimming area along the front of the park is an old boat channel that was cut through the coral reef to join Kewalo Basin with the Ala Wai Canal. When the Ala Wai channel was dredged, the long channel parallel with the park became unnecessary for commercial boat traffic, but it continued to attract sailors of pleasure craft. With the development of the park, conflicts arose between swimmers and boating enthusiasts. Finally in 1955 Hawaiian Dredging Company completed a contract to grade and close off the old channel at the 'Ewa end. Sand was brought in from Yokohama Bay in Keawa'ula of Wai'anae to cover the coral fill. Still later, the construction of "Magic Island" closed off the Waikīkī end of the channel.

Even though the Ala Moana Beach Park channel is calm and free of strong currents, it still poses some serious hazards. Because initially it was planned for boat traffic, it is deep, reaching depths of twenty to thirty feet offshore from the center of the beach. The slope into the channel is fairly gradual along the entire shore-

Ala Moana Beach Park. The most popular beach park among Honolulu residents. The deep boat channel just offshore from these swimmers poses a threat to unsupervised children and all weak or non-swimmers. Lifeguards are stationed here and elsewhere along the beach every day of the year.

line, but low tides present a problem. The lower the tide, the closer is the water's edge to the channel's drop-off. This situation often is deceiving and dangerous to younger children, who are not aware of tidal variations. The channel itself presents another problem. Many swimmers accept the visual challenge to swim across its width to gain the shallow coral flats on its seaward border. Children and poor swimmers often misjudge the distance and, lacking the strength, run into serious trouble in water far too deep for them.

Another common difficulty happens to children playing with flotation gear or light, inflatable toys. The trade winds blowing across the shallow areas often catch floating balls and other such playthings and carry them out into the deeper waters. And, all too often, children caught up in the excitement of their games will chase after their wind-stolen toys. Before the children realize the danger, they exceed their limits. Children using flotation gear, such as air mattresses and inner tubes, also invite trouble: the gusty trades can so easily overcome a child's paddling abilities and send him drifting helplessly away from shore. All these situations have caused perilous incidents, and sometimes drownings, at Ala Moana Beach Park.

Point Panic Beach Park

(Formerly Kaʻākaukukui)
41 Ahui Street

F: 21 parking stalls; 1 shower; 1 asphalt path to point area; landscaped grounds
LG: none
EP: Ala Moana Beach Park, 1201 Ala Moana Boulevard
PP: Fisherman's Wharf, 1009 Ala Moana Boulevard
FS: 555 Queen Street, Kakaʻako
H: Queen's Medical Center, 1301 Punchbowl Street
WA: board surfing; bodysurfing; pole fishing
WC: no sand area; park shoreline bordered entirely by retaining wall; abrupt drop from shallow reef shelf at bottom of wall into Kewalo Channel; bodysurfing potentially dangerous—all waves wash into retaining wall; sharks common in area
PA: limited to specific area provided
AI: entire park and its facilities are owned and maintained by the University of Hawaii; park was created on the grounds of the Pacific Biomedical Research Center to accommodate the numerous surfers and bodysurfers who frequent the area; is considered to be one of the finest bodysurfing areas in Hawaiʻi; its waves break best on a big south swell

Kewalo Basin was developed as a small boat harbor to prevent overcrowding Honolulu Harbor by the tuna fishing fleet. During the 1920s, the sampan fleet that congregated in the harbor near the River Street fish-markets numbered about fifty vessels. The Kewalo Basin wharf and channel were completed in 1925 by the Hawaiian Dredging Company, and all ships of the fishing fleet were relocated to their new home by 1930.

During this period of development a settlement of relatively poor people grew up around Kewalo Basin. On the Waikīkī side of Kewalo there was a small camp called "Blue Pond," after a large and deep pool near shore that remained full of saltwater even when the tides receded beyond the shallow coral flats. The much-larger settlement on the ʻEwa side of Kewalo was called "Squattersville" because the residents were living without authorization on government land. The shoreline land that Squattersville occupied was known as Kaʻā-kaukukui, commonly shortened to ʻĀkaukukui. The majority of the homes were comfortable and sturdily built. The dwellings that lined the seashore, where the present Olomehani Street now runs, were protected from the ocean by a low sea wall about three feet high. Relatives and friends of the residents often went there to spend weekends and summers. By the mid-1920s, the community numbered about 700 Hawaiians and part-Hawaiians, but because of the illegality of their settlement all of the families were evicted by May 1926 and all of the dwellings were razed.

During the 1930s and 1940s, the Kaʻākaukukui area continued to be heavily utilized as a fishing and swimming area, especially by children from the nearby community of Kakaʻako. The children surfed on redwood planks in the break they called "Stonewall." Many varieties of fish were abundant. Younger divers were warned by the old-time residents to stay away from the large shark hole on the Waikīkī side of Kewalo Channel. Many people came to this area to pick *limu* and *wana,* and also to catch squid on the shallow reef.

In August 1948 a severe change took place. The City and County began work on a project to provide a dump for the noncombustible material from the nearby incinerator. A huge seawall was constructed, 10 feet high, 10 feet wide on top, 30 feet wide at the base, and it extended 500 feet seaward from the old shoreline. From its outer extremity, along the edge of Kewalo Channel, the wall was continued parallel to the coast all the way to Fort Armstrong. The large boulders laid in the part of the wall lining Kewalo Channel and around the point for about 150 feet toward Fort Armstrong were obtained from a construction project in ʻĀina Haina. A substantial amount of the boulders that completed the seawall came from Punchbowl Crater. At that time James W. Glover, Ltd., was cutting the access road into Punchbowl's Crater and excavating the crater floor in the initial development of the National Memorial Cemetary of the Pacific. With the completion of the seawall in 1949, filling operations began and by the mid-1950s the shallow reef of Kaʻākaukukui was completely covered over. Twenty-nine acres of new land had been added to the old shoreline.

During the 1960s the almost explosive growth of board surfing pushed many surfers out of Waikīkī's waters. In search of other uncrowded places, surfers found their way to the numerous breaks in front of Ala Moana Beach Park and Kewalo. The break on the

Waikīkī end of Kewalo Channel they called "Shark Hole." The break on the 'Ewa side now fronting the marine laboratories of the University of Hawaii's Pacific Biomedical Research Center they called "Point Panic." The surf at Point Panic rolls almost directly into the sea wall, and thereby often causes a troublesome situation for any surfer or his board.

During the 1960s, bodysurfers also discovered the excellent waves at Point Panic. Since then this break has become one of the most popular bodysurfing areas on O'ahu. Because of the extensive use of the Point Panic area by both board surfers and bodysurfers, the University of Hawaii set aside a portion of its research facility's grounds for a parking lot and installed a freshwater shower, thus creating a small if unofficial beach park. It is located adjacent to the facility at the end of 'Āhui Street in Kaka'ako.

Sand Island State Beach Park

(on Sand Island near entrance to Honolulu Harbor)

 F: 1 comfort station; picnic facilities; bikeways; walkways; 2 parking lots
LG: none
EP: none
PP: Ke'ehi Marina, Sand Island Access Road (near drawbridge)
FS: 1334 Nimitz Highway, Kalihi Kai
 H: Queen's Medical Center, 1301 Punchbowl Street
SS: Nimitz Highway
WA: pole fishing; board surfing; swimming
WC: narrow, coarse sand beach; rocky and uneven ocean bottom
PA: unlimited; boats can be easily launched in various areas of Sand Island shoreline; paved boat ramp located in Ke'ehi Marina on Sand Island Access Road near the drawbridge

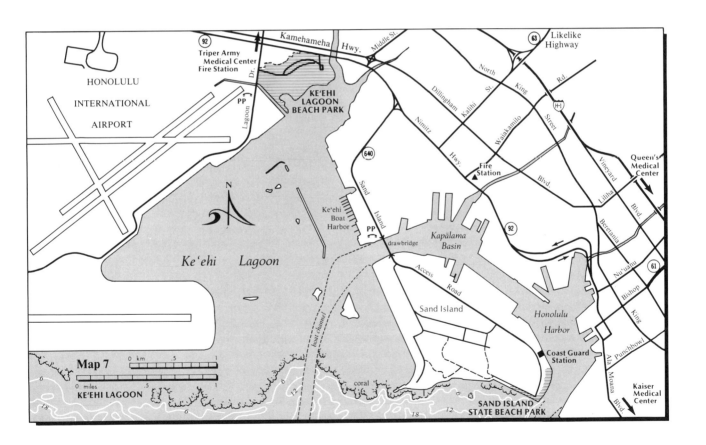

AI: take Sand Island Access Road from Nimitz Highway; developed section of park borders the main entrance to Honolulu Harbor

The original Sand Island was a low, man-made fill built along the western side of the channel into Honolulu Harbor in order to protect the harbor from the sea. It was named Sand Island because it was created on the shallow offshore reef by deposition of spoil material from successive dredging operations in the area. Near Sand Island was another shoal called Mauliola, "breath of life," after a god of good health. This neighboring islet was known also as Quarantine Island. The word Quarantine refers to the period of forty days during which vessels arriving from suspected plague areas were detained before being allowed to discharge their cargoes or passengers. This form of plague prevention was first established in Venice in 1348. Because Hawai'i was always threatened with entry of foreign pestilences, and some actually were introduced, despite efforts to inspect incoming ships and passengers, a quarantine station was set up on Mauliola in 1869, and passengers of all suspect ships were detained at the station.

In 1940, the original Sand Island and Mauliola were joined and enlarged. Today Sand Island is 500 acres in extent. The shoreline is primarily rocky, but there is one small sand beach on the seaward side of the island near the entrance to Honolulu Harbor. It is a short, steep beach made up of coarse sand and pebbles. It offers no place favorable for swimming, because of the rough coral reef immediately offshore. Another drawback to any water sports there was registered when the 1970/71 O'ahu Sewage Study by the City and County showed that the entire area is so polluted as to be unfit for swimming. Ships in the adjacent harbor and the Honolulu sewer system's outfall offshore are the primary sources of that pollution. Consequently the beach is frequented mainly by fishermen and surfers. The surfing break, known in the old days as Ke Kai o Māmala, the Sea of Māmala, was said to have provided the finest surfing waves west of Waikīkī. The Sand Island surf today, although consistent, is only average in comparison with that of the many other spots around O'ahu. The entire beach area is part of a 140 acre state park. A 14-acre portion of the park fronting the main channel of Honolulu Harbor has been landscaped.

Ke'ehi Lagoon Beach Park
465 Lagoon Drive

F: 2 comfort station/pavilion; 4 tennis courts; 1 basketball court; 2 softball fields; 1 rugby field; 1 maintenance shed; 472 parking stalls
LG: none
EP: none
PP: on Lagoon Drive
FS: 2835 Ala 'Ilima Street, Moanalua
H: Queen's Medical Center, 1301 Punchbowl Street
SS: Lagoon Drive
WA: crabbing; pole fishing; swimming
WC: safe all year; lagoon water is dirty and polluted; shoreline of park is rubble and mud flats
PA: unlimited

The Beaches of 'Ewa District

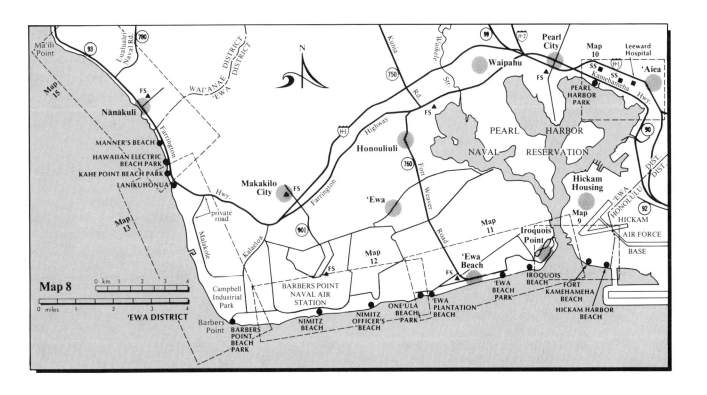

Map 8

'EWA DISTRICT

Mā'ili Point

Lualualei Naval Rd.

93

780

WAI'ANAE DISTRICT
'EWA DISTRICT

N

99

H-2

Pearl City

Map 10

Leeward Hospital

Waipahu

SS

H-1

'Aiea

FS

Map 15

Nānākuli

Farrington

MANNER'S BEACH

HAWAIIAN ELECTRIC BEACH PARK

KAHE POINT BEACH PARK

LANIKUHONUA

Map 13

Malakole

Kunia Rd.

Waikele Str.

750

FS

Kamehameha

PEARL HARBOR PARK

90

FS

H-1

Highway

Honouliuli

760

PEARL HARBOR

NAVAL RESERVATION

Hickam Housing

'EWA
HONOLULU DIST. DIST.

Hwy.

private road

Makakilo City

FS

Farrington

'Ewa

Fort Weaver Road

Map 11

Iroquois Point

Map 9

HICKAM AIR FORCE BASE

92

HICKAM

Kalaeloa

901

Map 12

FS

'Ewa Beach

FS

'EWA BEACH PARK

IROQUOIS BEACH

FORT KAMEHAMEHA BEACH

Campbell Industrial Park

BARBERS POINT NAVAL AIR STATION

HICKAM HARBOR BEACH

Barbers Point

BARBERS POINT BEACH PARK

NIMITZ BEACH

NIMITZ OFFICER'S BEACH

ONE'ULA BEACH PARK

'EWA PLANTATION BEACH

0 km 1 2 3 4

0 miles 1 2 3 4

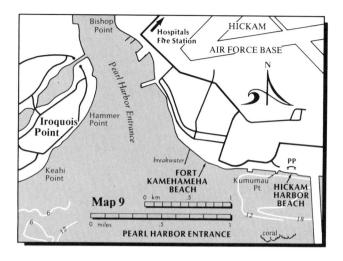

Map 9

PEARL HARBOR ENTRANCE

where the *'anae-holo,* the sea-going mullet, passed through on their yearly journey from Pearl Harbor to Lā'ie.

During the 1960s the Air Force obtained a permit from the Army to build a shoreline recreational facility in the Kumumau section of Fort Kamehameha. Known officially as Hickam Harbor, the project was completed and formally opened in 1965. The beach at Hickam Harbor was cut out of the surrounding coral flats. Sand was brought in from other military installations on O'ahu, primarily from Bellows' Field at Waimānalo and Dillingham Air Force Base near Mokulē'ia. The entire project was constructed through a self-help program with the assistance of Hickam's civil engineers and Kāne'ohe marines.

The man-made beach in the complex is short and narrow and composed primarily of coarse sand and coral fill. It drops off rather abruptly into the deeper offshore waters. Use of the area is restricted to active and retired military personnel, their dependents, and guests.

Hickam Harbor Beach

(Kumumau area of Fort Kamehameha)

  F: 1 lifeguard tower; 1 restaurant; 1 snack bar; 1 comfort station; picnic grounds; boating area
LG: service provided by military personnel
EP: none
PP: in beach area
FS: Military: Hanger Avenue and D Street, Hickam; Civilian: 2835 Ala 'Ilima Street, Moanalua
  H: Military: Tripler Army Medical Center, Jarrett White Road (off Moanalua Road); Civilian: Queen's Medical Center, 1301 Punchbowl Street
SS: Military: Hickam; Civilian: Lagoon Drive
WA: boating; swimming
WC: safe all year; ocean bottom a combination of coral reef and sand pockets; bottom slopes sharply into deeper waters; line of permanent, floating buoys offshore marks outer limits of swimming area
PA: limited to military personnel
  AI: man-made beach blasted out of coral in joint effort of Hickam civil engineers and Kāne'ohe Marines; completed in 1965; land part of Fort Kamehameha, but used by Air Force on permit from Army

When the lands that make up Fort Kamehameha were acquired by the United States government in 1901, a section of the site included a large fishpond called Lelepaua. A small waterway ran seaward from the pond. The shoreline where the ditch emptied into the ocean was known as Kumumau. It was noted as one of the places

Fort Kamehameha Beach

(along shoreline of Fort Kamehameha Housing area, adjoining entrance to Pearl Harbor)

  F: none
LG: none
EP: none
PP: Hickam Harbor Beach
FS: Military: Hanger Avenue and D Street, Hickam; Civilian: 2835 Ala 'Ilima Street, Moanalua
  H: Military: Tripler Army Medical Center, Jarrett White Road (off Moanalua Road); Civilian: Queen's Medical Center, 1301 Punchbowl Street
SS: Military: Hickam; Civilian: Lagoon Drive or Nimitz Highway
WA: crabbing; pole fishing; swimming; throw-netting
WC: safe all year; very narrow beach composed of sand, dirt, gravel; bottom primarily coral and mud flats, very similar to beaches in Paikō, Niu, and 'Āina Haina areas
PA: limited to military personnel

Soon after Hawai'i was annexed by the United States in 1898, the dredging of the narrow channel entrance to Pearl Harbor commenced. Before the full value of the huge, protected harbor could be realized, the channel through the reef had to be deepened and widened and a drydock built to accommodate the large American battleships. In 1901, in anticipation of Pearl Harbor's importance as a naval base, the federal government acquired a tract of land on the Waikīkī side of the harbor entrance and built there a coastal defense unit to guard the entrance to Pearl Harbor. The installation was named Fort Upton, for Brevet-Major General Emery Upton, but in January 1909 it was renamed Fort Kamehameha, in honor of the first king of Hawai'i.

The very narrow beach fronting Fort Kamehameha is composed of a mixture of sand, mud, and gravel. The offshore bottom is primarily shallow mud over coral flats, very much like those in the Paikō, Niu, and 'Āina Haina areas near Koko Head. At high tide, nearly the entire beach disappears underwater. The beach is attractive primarily to fishermen. The public has no access to the area.

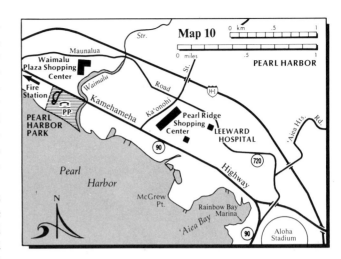

Pearl Harbor Park

98–319 Kamehameha Highway

 F: 1 comfort station/pavilion; picnic facilities; 68 parking stalls
LG: none
EP: none
PP: in park
FS: 885 1st Street, Pearl City
 H: Leeward Hospital, 98–1010 Haukapila Road
SS: Kamehameha Highway, Waiau or Waimalu
WA: pole fishing and crabbing
WC: shallow mud flats on *makai* edge of park; water too polluted for swimming; Waimalu Stream bordering the eastern boundary of the park is potentially dangerous to wandering children
PA: unlimited

British sailors were the first foreigners to discover Pearl Harbor, as Captain Nathaniel Portlock's journal of 1789 indicates.

The full value of Pearl Harbor was first made known to the United States in 1840, through the efforts of Navy Lieutenant Charles Wilkes, commander of the U.S. Exploring Expedition to the Pacific, and of the first geodetic survey made in the Hawaiian Islands. Wilkes' surveyors found only fifteen feet of water over the reef barring the entrance to the huge inner lochs. He reported that the coral bar could be easily dredged, thereby providing passage into the harbor for the world's largest ships.

In 1884 King Kalākaua and the Hawaiian government granted the United States exclusive rights to establish a coaling and naval station in Pearl Harbor. Although surveys with that end in mind were made in 1887 and 1897, no action was taken until after annexation of the islands in 1898.

After annexation, work was initiated to deepen the crooked and shallow natural channel. In 1908 construction was begun upon a drydock and a coaling station. By 1912 the channel work was finished and the drydock was nearing completion. During the following year, progress was halted abruptly when, within a few violent moments, the drydock collapsed into ruins. The collapse, according to Hawaiians, was the consequence of the breaking of a *kapu* by the Americans. The Hawaiians knew Pearl Harbor as Pu'uloa, and they believed that there, dwelling in a large cavern on the Honouliuli side of the harbor, Ka'ahupāhau, the queen of all sharks on O'ahu, made her home. Her chief guard was a brother shark, who lived in a pit at the entrance to the lochs. The Hawaiian people said that the drydock was built over the cavern of Ka'ahupāhau's son, who also lived in Pu'uloa. Angered by the violation of his home, the shark prince destroyed the imposing structure. The engineers in charge of the project attributed the collapse of the foundation to hydrostatic pressure. Whatever the cause, several years' work was wrecked within minutes. The engineers changed their method of construction, but this time, before starting to rebuild, they asked the Hawaiians to bless the site. After that the work continued without further trouble. On August 21, 1919, the Pearl Harbor drydock was dedicated by Governor C. J. McCarthy and Josephus Daniels, the Secretary of the Navy.

The Hawaiian name of the land west of the harbor was Pu'uloa. The harbor itself took its English name from Waimomi, "water of the pearl," a river that ran into the lochs. In the 1830s, pearl oysters were reported there in abundance, and small pearls were found frequently when the oysters were harvested for food and for mother-of-pearl. A species of speckled clam also grew in the harbor that, in addition to being good eating, contained milk-white pearls of an exquisite luster.

The original beds of mollusks were destroyed by pollution of the waters in the harbor. With the introduction of cattle to the uplands, the watersheds were denuded of vegetation and vast quantities of earth were washed into the lagoons. Later, sewage and oil spills from Navy ships added to the spoiling. Only recently have attempts been made to reduce pollution. Today an edible, non-pearl-bearing oyster introduced from the East Coast of the United States is being grown successfully in the harbor's mud flats.

Most of the shoreline of Pearl Harbor, which once accommodated more fishponds than any other single district in the islands, has been altered completely to provide berthing and shipyard facilities. The other shore areas within the harbor are either mud flats or gravel beaches. They are not used at all for recreational swimming because the water is too polluted. The only acquatic recreational area within the harbor is located at 'Aiea Bay, to accommodate the Pearl Harbor Yacht Club, a group of boat owners based at the Rainbow Bay Marina, a military facility. A joint venture between the Navy and the State of Hawai'i has been considered for the development of a public park and marina in the bay, but at present the "Rainbow Bay project," as it is called, is in limbo.

There is one public park on the shores of Pearl Harbor, Pearl Harbor Park located on Kamehameha Highway at the intersection of Ka'ahumanu Street. It is frequented primarily by fishermen, picnickers, and sports leagues.

Iroquois Beach

(also Capehart or Annex beaches; formerly
Keahi Beach)
(undeveloped beach along Iroquois Drive and Edgewater Drive, Capehart Housing; Iroquois Beach recreational area located between housing area and U.S.M.C.
rifle range)

F: 1 comfort station; 1 food and beverage concession and pavilion; picnic facilities; 1 lifeguard tower; 1 unmarked parking lot
LG: service provided by military personnel
EP: none
PP: in beach area
FS: 91–832 Pōhakupuna Road, 'Ewa Beach
H: Military: Tripler Army Medical Center, Jarrett White Road (off Moanalua Road); Civilian: Leeward Hospital, 98–1010 Haukapila Road
SS: Military: Cormorant Road; Civilian: 'Ewa Beach
WA: diving; snorkeling; board surfing; swimming
WC: safe all year; small shorebreak forms when surf is big
PA: limited to military personnel

Once upon a time Keahi Point was noted as one of the finest places on O'ahu for catching 'ō'io. Prized as one of the most delicious fish to eat raw, 'ō'io sold very readily in the markets of Honolulu. The 'ō'io from Keahi had a unique fragrance, somewhat like that of *limu lipoa,* and this made it particularly desirable. Before the channel into Pearl Harbor was widened and dredged, Keahi was also well known for the formation of its surfing waves.

Today Keahi is part of a U.S. naval housing area commonly called "Capehart Housing." Iroquois Drive is the main road along the shoreline in the subdivision, so the Keahi area is now known as Iroquois Beach. The beach itself is narrow and made of coarse sand and pebbles. It is well protected by a shallow offshore reef shelf and has occasional sand pockets that can easily ac-

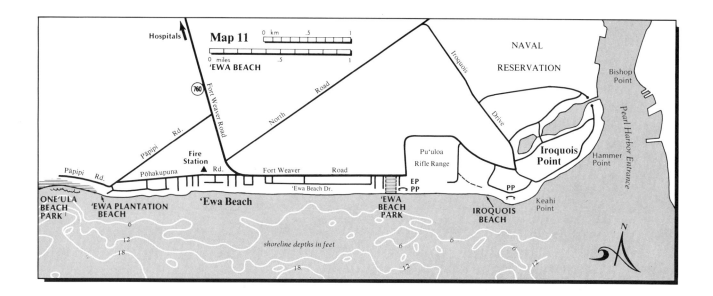

commodate recreational swimmers. Low shrubs and other shoreline vegetation cover much of the beach to the high-water mark.

At the end of Iroquois Beach, between the housing area and the Puʻuloa Rifle Range, the Navy has developed a permanent beach recreation center with a snack-bar/pavilion, comfort station, and picnic grounds. The beach in front of the complex has been improved and provides a small but attractive swimming and sunbathing area. Iroquois Beach is also known as "Capehart Beach" or "Annex Beach." There are no particular water hazards in the area. Access to the beach is limited to military personnel.

ʻEwa Beach Park

(formerly Puʻuloa Beach Park or Kūpaka)
91-027 Fort Weaver Road

F: 1 comfort station/pavilion; 1 basketball court; 2 volleyball courts; 1 softball field; children's play apparatus; camping and picnic equipment; 74 parking stalls
LG: none
EP: in park area
PP: in park area
FS: 91-832 Pōhakupuna Road, ʻEwa Beach

H: Leeward Hospital, 98-1010 Haukapila Road
SS: ʻEwa Beach
WA: diving; pole fishing; snorkeling; board surfing; swimming; throw-netting
WC: safe all year; bottom slopes sharply to deeper water; water often murky
PA: unlimited
AI: park is known island-wide as good seaweed grounds

In ancient times, the two great gods Kāne and Kanaloa once traveled around Oʻahu to inspect the island. They decided to mark off the different land divisions by the throwing of stones—where a stone fell determined a division's boundary line. In this part of Oʻahu, however, they could not find the stone they had thrown, so they named the district ʻEwa, "strayed," for the stone that strayed.

When a sugar factory was built at Honouliuli in 1891, it was given the district's name, as was the plantation town that eventually grew up around the mill. The shoreline closest to the inland mill was several miles away, along the lands once called Puʻuloa. With the ever-increasing use of the beaches in the Puʻuloa area by ʻEwa plantation employees, people began to call the region "ʻEwa Beach." Today ʻEwa Beach is a thriving community.

ʻEwa Beach Park is located on Fort Weaver Road, next to the Puʻuloa Rifle Range. Hawaiians called this

71

'Ewa Beach Park. Probably the best-known seaweed foraging area on O'ahu. People come here from all over the island to look for their favorite seaweeds among the varieties that wash ashore in front of the beach park. The most highly prized is the *limu manauea,* or *ogo,* which is often eaten mixed with raw fish or octopus, or simply eaten alone, either fresh or pickled, as a relish.

section of the shoreline Kūpaka. The very popular five-acre park there provides a bathhouse/pavilion, camping and picnic facilities, and a good swimming beach. The beach itself is narrow and often fairly steep, but a wide, irregular reef protects the inner waters from waves and strong currents. The only danger is the rather abrupt drop to overhead depths not far offshore, which is hazardous for little children. The bottom is made up of sand pockets and low coral heads, but it easily accommodates recreational swimmers. 'Ewa Beach is well known for its abundance of edible *limu* and attracts gatherers from all over O'ahu. The often murky waters are frequented also by net fishermen looking for *'ō'io* and *moi.*

'Ewa Plantation Beach
(also Hau Bush Beach)
Pāpipi Road, 'Ewa Beach

  F: 1 comfort station; camping and picnic equipment; un-marked parking areas
LG: none
 EP: One'ula Beach Park
 PP: none
 FS: 91–832 Pōhakupuna Road, 'Ewa Beach
  H: Leeward Hospital, 98–1010 Haukapila Road
 SS: 'Ewa Beach
WA: diving; snorkeling; board surfing; swimming
WC: safe all year; rocky ocean bottom; many outcroppings of coral and beachrock along shoreline
 PA: limited to members of 'Ewa Recreational Association and 'Ewa Sugar Company employees

72

The 'Ewa Plantation Beach is a recreational area maintained by the 'Ewa Recreational Association and the 'Ewa Sugar Company. It is primarily for plantation employees and their guests, so the facilities are not available to the general public. This beach is more commonly known as "Hau Bush" because of the prevalence of *hau* trees on the property. Surfers, as well as fishermen, frequent the area; the surfers probably are the ones who gave the name Hau Bush to this beach.

One'ula Beach Park

(formerly 'Ewa Beach Hau Bush Beach Park)
91–101 Pāpipi Road, 'Ewa Beach

  F: 30 acres; 1 comfort station; 44 parking stalls
LG: none
EP: in park area
PP: none
 FS: 91–832 Pōhakupuna Road, 'Ewa Beach
  H: Leeward Hospital, 98–1010 Haukapila Road
 SS: 'Ewa Beach
WA: diving; board surfing; swimming
WC: safe all year; rocky ocean bottom; almost entire shoreline fronted by outcroppings of coral reef and beachrock; water often murky
 PA: unlimited

One'ula means "red sand." The name probably was given to this shoreline because of a large drainage ditch from the mountains that once emptied quantities of red dirt upon the beach and into the surrounding ocean. Parts of the ditch can still be located in the area.

An alternate version of the naming of One'ula has been suggested. During the early 1900s, a fisherman named Kapu lived on the beach near the One'ula area. He was known both by the English name "Red" and by the Hawaiian name 'Ula'ula, which means red. Kapu had several canoes and many feet of fish net, and he fished extensively in the waters nearby. Transient fishermen often referred to the beach that Kapu frequented as "'Ula'ula." The name One'ula may have been another way of saying "Red's Beach."

Japanese fishermen from 'Ewa called this region Kanaka-umi. *Kanaka* is Hawaiian for "man," and *umi* is Japanese for "ocean" or "sea." The combined words,

Kanaka-umi, were intended to mean the ocean where Hawaiians fished.

One'ula Beach Park extends from the raised coral shoreline at the Pāpipi Road end of 'Ewa Beach for approximately 3,000 feet westward to a broad, low, rocky point. This point formerly was called Keku Point, for an old Hawaiian man of that name who lived alone there for many years. The beach has a rather steep foreshore with the offshore bottom being comprised primarily of coral and sand pockets. The thirty-acre park is partially improved and provides only fair swimming. It is reached by means of a secondary dirt road.

The best swimming area at One'ula is an open, rock-free section of shoreline, located directly in front of the adjacent 'Ewa Plantation Beach recreational site. The rest of the beach is made up of patches of coral outcropping along the water's edge. When the public section of One'ula was first designated as a park, it was called 'Ewa Hau Bush Beach Park after Hau Bush Beach, the common name for the area.

Nimitz Beach

(formerly Kualaka'i Beach)
Coral Sea Road, Barber's Point Naval Air Station

  F: separate beaches for officers and enlisted personnel; each area includes a comfort station, food and beverage concession, lifeguard towers, picnic area, and parking area
LG: service provided by military personnel
EP: none
PP: in concession areas
 FS: Military: 1701 Midway Street off Enterprise, Barber's Point; Civilian: 91–832 Pōhakupuna Road, 'Ewa Beach
  H: Military: Tripler Army Medical Center, Jarrett White Road (off Moanalua Road); Civilian: Leeward Hospital, 98–1010 Haukapila Road
 SS: Military: Barber's Point; Civilian: 'Ewa Beach
WA: diving; snorkeling; board surfing; swimming
WC: safe all year; shallow ocean bottom; combination of patches of reef and pockets of sand
 PA: limited to military personnel
 AI: surfing area fronting officer's section is excellent for novice surfers

The *kapu* system of ancient Hawai'i was complicated in the extreme. At its height of power the system covered

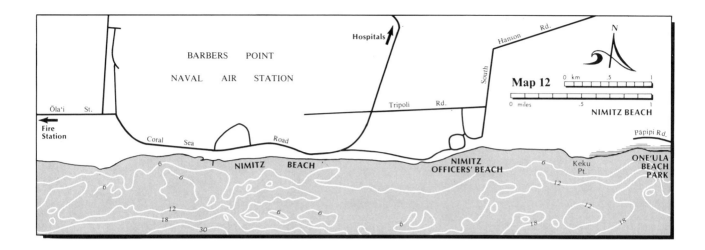

practically every phase of the lives of the people, enmeshing them in a code that punished severely every breaking of the *kapu,* sometimes with the penalty of death. The entire framework of rules and officials supporting the *kapu* system was much weakened when Kamehameha the Great died in 1819.

Among those who had ceased to believe in the powers of the old gods were many high chiefs and priests and the two principal wives of Kamehameha I, Ka'ahumanu and Keopuolani.

When Liholiho inherited the kingdom as Kamehameha II, Ka'ahumanu proposed that the *kapu* system be ended, but Liholiho, not yet having ascertained the attitude of his subjects, withheld consent. Upon learning of Liholiho's hesitation, Keopuolani, his mother and the highest *kapu* chiefess in the islands, requested that he send her his younger brother Kau'ikeaouli, a boy six or seven years of age, so that they might eat together. Liholiho consented to that serious violation of the *kapu,* although he himself was very careful not to follow their example. The queen mother and the boy ate their evening meal together, and thus Keopuolani, the highest *kapu* chiefess in Hawaii, set a shocking precedent by openly violating the *kapu* that forbade men and women to eat together.

This incident is anticipated in a legend about two children of 'Ewa, the story of Ka 'ai malu, "the secret eating place." A young brother and sister always fished at Kualaka'i. They were excellent fishermen and never went home empty-handed. One day they laid their nets in all their favorite places, but they caught nothing except one *palani,* a fish that only women could eat. On their way home the little girl talked her brother into sharing the fish with her. They stopped at a secluded place near a stream and ate it. Their breaking of the *kapu* was discovered. Their daring to do so was a kind of prediction, in legend, of the time when the *kapu* system would be overthrown.

Kualaka'i, the place where those legendary children went fishing, is located within the military reservation at Barber's Point. *Kualaka'i* is the name of a sea cucumber that squirts a purple fluid when squeezed. *Kualaka'i* are also known as *kumia, mia* being a variant form of the verb *mimi,* to urinate.

When the naval air station was commissioned on April 15, 1945, the Kualaka'i shoreline was called Nimitz Beach, after Fleet Admiral Chester W. Nimitz (1885–1966), commander-in-chief of the Pacific Forces during most of World War II. The entire beach park is man-made. Both the officers' and the enlisted men's beaches were cut out of the rocky shoreline that forms the entire coast of Barber's Point. Sand was imported to complete both areas.

When the naval station first opened, the original beach adjoining the Nimitz Recreational Field was nicknamed "Horseshoe Beach" because of its shape. This beach, reserved now for officers, is presently straight and sandy. Enlisted personnel use another area at the western end of Nimitz Beach.

The surfing break offshore from the officers' beach provides an excellent place for novices to learn to surf. It is used primarily by military dependents and occasionally by civilians who paddle or walk over from One'ula. As with the rest of Barber's Point, the waters off Nimitz Beach are only fair for swimming because shallow coral reefs extend throughout the area.

Barber's Point Beach Park

(formerly Kalaeloa Beach)
91–121 Ōla'i Street, Campbell Industrial Park

  F: 1 comfort station; picnic area and equipment; 52 parking stalls
LG: none
EP: in park area
PP: Kahe Point Beach Park
FS: 92–885 Makakilo Drive, Makakilo
  H: Leeward Hospital, 98–1010 Haukapila Road
SS: Farrington Highway, Nānākuli
WA: diving; pole fishing; swimming; throw-netting
WC: potentially dangerous currents and surf from October through March; generally safe during summer; poor beach; rocky shoreline; sharp limestone shelf fronting park; small sand beach at western end of park
PA: unlimited

Captain Henry Barber first arrived in Hawai'i in his trading brig, the *Arthur,* in October 1795, on his way to China. Needing supplies and provisions, he bought them at Waikīkī and then sailed for Kaua'i. Soon after the *Arthur* had passed the entrance to Pearl Harbor she was wrecked on a shoal westward of the harbor's entrance. Captain Barber and his crew of twenty-two took to their small boats. Six men drowned, but the rest succeeded in reaching shore at Kalaeloa. The cargo of sea-otter skins was salvaged, although the *Arthur* was completely destroyed. The survivors and the cargo went to Kealakekua on the Big Island. Eventually all reached China aboard a ship whose name is not known. Kalae-

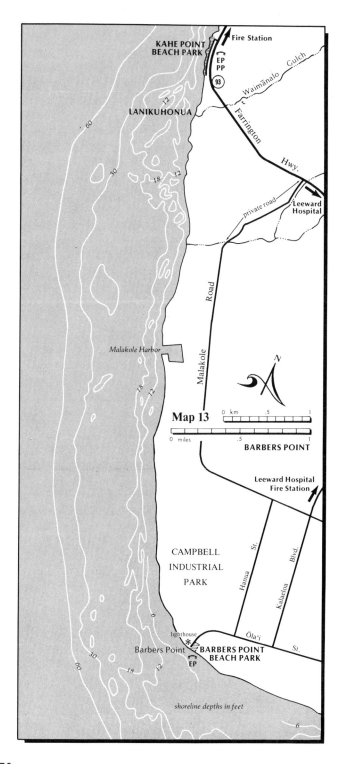

loa, "the long point," was renamed Barber's Point in memory of the incident.

In 1802 Captain Barber again passed through Hawai'i on his way to China. While resupplying his ship, he learned that King Kamehameha had a battery of cannons for the defense of a newly built fort in Lahaina and that the guns had come from Barber's wrecked brig *Arthur.* Barber sought out Kamehameha and demanded the return of his cannons. The guns, however, had been salvaged with a great deal of effort and risk by the Hawaiians. Without the benefit of any modern underwater gear, the divers had located and dislodged the cannons from the submerged wreck. The prowess of Hawaiian divers in the water was incredible. John Turnbull's book, *Voyage Around the World* (1800–1804), gives eye witness accounts of Hawaiians free-diving to incredible depths and remaining underwater for amazing lengths of time. He tells of men hired to dive beneath large vessels in order to nail copper sheeting to the ships' bottoms. The divers remained submerged for three to four minutes at a time, and made numerous dives to accomplish the job. Naturally, then, after considering the tremendous effort that went into salvaging the *Arthur*'s cannons (not to mention their defensive worth to the fort in Lahaina), Kamehameha flatly refused Barber's demand to return the guns. Furthermore, the king demanded that Barber pay for his supplies not in gold but in gunpowder. From all accounts Barber was a tyrannical, unscrupulous, and extremely determined trader. Kamehameha was one of the few people who held his own against Barber and bested him. Kamehameha kept the guns and was given the powder.

Barber's Point Beach Park's seven acres are situated at the Wai'anae end of Campbell Industrial Park. Located at 91–121 Ōla'i Street, the beach park is relatively unknown to most of O'ahu's residents. Besides having no housing areas nearby, it is fairly well off the beaten track of Farrington Highway. Furthermore, the beach is very poor, nothing more than a rough limestone shelf at the shoreline, with a narrow strip of rough, coarse sand and gravel behind it. The only feasible swimming place is a tiny sand beach located in front of a private residence between the park and the lighthouse. The area is frequented primarily by picnickers and fishermen.

Lanikuhonua Beach

Alice Kamokila Campbell was one of four daughters of the wealthy landowner James Campbell, whose estate was estimated to be worth $100 million in 1945. During her life of eighty-seven years, she became one of the most colorful figures in the islands, and interesting stories about her abound among Hawai'i's *kama'āina* families.

In 1940 or 1941 Kamokila leased from the Campbell Estate about thirty-seven acres of beachfront property in the Waimānalo area of Honouliuli. This beach place, which she named "Lanikuaka'a," included a thatched Hawaiian house and three "sacred pools" where Ka'ahumanu, a favorite wife of Kamehameha I, was supposed to have bathed and performed certain religious rites. During the Second World War, this one of Kamokila's several homes was used as a recreation center by Army and Navy servicemen, who nicknamed it "Camp Bell." In later years Kamokila renamed her beachfront estate "Lanikuhonua."

Probably it is Kamokila's "Lanikuhonua" with its sacred pools that is referred to in Hawaiian history as Ko'olina, a lovely place in Waimānalo near the boundary of 'Ewa and Wai'anae. The caretaker of Ko'olina was Napua'ikamao, and the area was a favorite vacationing spot of the high chief Kakuhihewa.

Before Kamokila leased Ko'olina, the pools were frequented by many teen-aged children from the neighboring camps of 'Ewa Plantation. In those days, convenient public transportation to 'Ewa Beach was not available, so the children caught the train to the pools. The former railway line passed just inland of the area. The westernmost pool was their favorite, and the kids called it "D.P.D."; the meaning of this name is now forgotten.

The shoreline fronting Lanikuhonua is a shelf composed primarily of lava rock and raised coral reef. There is a small sand beach. The large saltwater pools are situated at the shore's edge, and each has a small sandy area in front of it. They are separated from the ocean by natural walls of reef over which the waves flow to fill the pools. The rocky shoreline is noted among fishermen as good *moi* grounds. There is no public access to the estate, which is now owned by a local real estate developer. He has renamed the area "West Beach."

Kahe Beach

Kahe is the last shoreline section at the western end of the district of 'Ewa: the edge of Kahe Beach marks the *makai* boundary that separates 'Ewa and Wai'anae. Formerly there were two drainage ditches in the area that ran down to the ocean, Keone'ō'io and Limaloa. The name Keone'ō'io, "the '*ō'io* sands," refers to the fact that the beach once attracted large schools of '*ō'io,* a fish that frequents such sand-bottom areas. The Kahe

area was acquired by the Campbell Estate in the late 1800s, but was relinquished to the State in 1960, when the land was condemned as an electric power plant site.

The shoreline here is made up of three distinct sections, Kahe Point Beach Park, the Hawaiian Electric Beach Park, and Manner's Beach.

Kahe Point Beach Park
92–301 Farrington Highway

F: 2 comfort stations; 1 pavilion; camping and picnic equipment; 14 marked camping sites with parking; 44 parking stalls

Christine A. Takata

Kahe Point Beach Park. Low sea cliffs make up the majority of the park's shoreline. The pier was intended to be a temporary structure, built to facilitate a construction project in this popular fishing and camping area.

77

LG: none
EP: in park area
PP: in park area
FS: 89–334 Nānākuli Avenue, Nānākuli
 H: Leeward Hospital, 98–1010 Haukapila Road
SS: Farrington Highway, Nānākuli
WA: diving; pole fishing; snorkeling; board surfing; swimming
WC: potentially dangerous currents and surf from October through April; generally calm during summer; entire park situated above ocean on low sea cliff; no access to ocean; small cove about 150 yards east of improved park area where swimming is possible on calm days
PA: unlimited

Kahe Point Beach Park, maintained by the City and County, is situated directly on the cliffs of Kahe Point. Except for a small rocky cove at the eastern end of the park, there is no easy access to the ocean for recreational swimming. The park is used primarily by picnickers, shore casters, and occasionally by divers who climb down the rocks above the cove to fish in the offshore waters. The area was formerly known as Brown's Camp.

Hawaiian Electric Beach Park

(includes former Waipahu Beach; known to surfers as "Tracks")
92–200 Farrington Highway, Kahe (across from Hawaiian Electric Power Plant)

 F: landscaped picnic area; cooking stands and picnic tables; 1 comfort station; showers; roadside parking along Farrington Highway
LG: none
EP: Kahe Point Beach Park
PP: Kahe Point Beach Park
FS: 89–334 Nānākuli Avenue, Nānākuli
 H: Leeward Hospital, 98–1010 Haukapila Road
SS: Farrington Highway, Nānākuli
WA: diving; shore casting; board surfing; bodysurfing; swimming
WC: generally safe all year; occasional strong currents when surf is big offshore
PA: beach park owned and maintained by the Hawaiian Electric Company; use of facilities extended to general public

Keoneʻōʻio, the Hawaiian Electric Beach Park, located in the center of the beach, is private property. Although it is owned and maintained by the Hawaiian Electric Company, use of the facilities is extended the year around to the general public. Since its development the park has proved to be one of the most popular places in the area. The wide sand beach generally is safe for swimming, the ocean bottom being sandy for the most part, with a gentle slope to deeper waters. The only strong currents in the inshore areas are generated by large waves that usually roll in during the winter months. The relatively gentle surf here has long attracted children from Waiʻanae to Honolulu. In the old days youngsters from Honolulu or other distant places would ride the train to Kahe to bodysurf.

While the railroad was still in operation, Keoneʻōʻio was best known as "Waipahu Beach," so called because of the recreational area that was built there specifically for employees of the Oʻahu Sugar Company, most of whom lived at Waipahu.

During the late 1950s and early 1960s, the break became a popular board-surfing spot. It was called "Tracks," of course, because of the railroad tracks that still parallel the highway. Even now the beach is commonly known as "Tracks."

Manner's Beach

92–200 Farrington Highway, Kahe

 F: none; roadside parking along Farrington Highway
LG: none
EP: Kahe Point Beach Park
PP: Kahe Point Beach Park
FS: 89–334 Nānākuli Avenue, Nānākuli
 H: Leeward Hospital, 98–1010 Haukapila Road
SS: Farrington Highway, Nānākuli
WA: diving; shorecasting; swimming
WC: generally safe all year; strong currents when surf is big
PA: follow shoreline from Hawaiian Electric Beach Park

During World War II, the Navy constructed several buildings on the western end of Kahe Beach to establish a small recreational complex. In 1946 Francis J. Manner, long a resident of the Waiʻanae district, leased the land and the surplus buildings from the Campbell Estate. Manner and his family used the beach site as a recreational area, and this section of Kahe soon became known as "Manner's Beach." Today the two buildings at Manner's Beach are leased by a private concern for its own employees and their guests to use. The beach and water conditions are almost exactly the same as those at the neighboring Hawaiian Electric Beach Park.

The Beaches of Wai'anae District

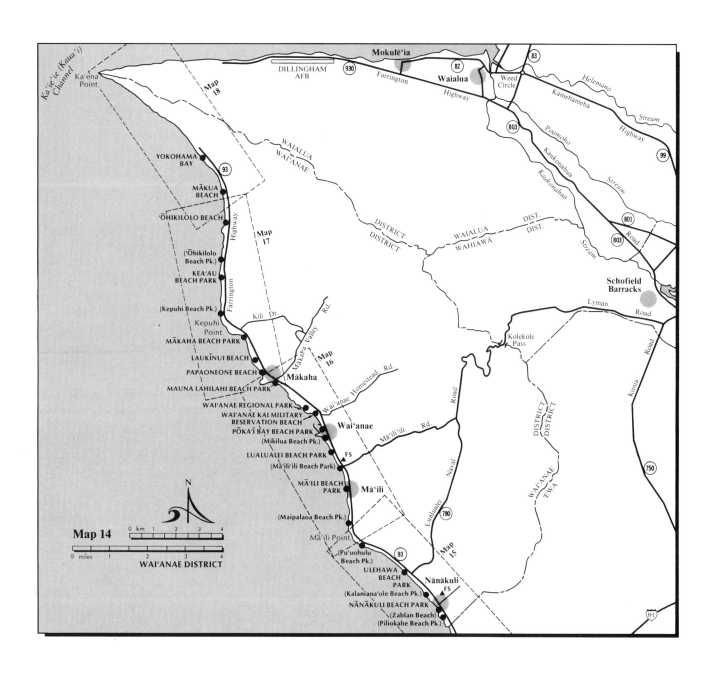

Ka'ie'ie (Kaua'i) Channel

Ka'ena Point

Map 18

Mokulē'ia

DILLINGHAM AFB

Farrington Highway

930

Waialua

Weed Circle

82

83

Helemano Stream

Kamehameha Highway

803

Poamoho

Kaukonahua Stream

99

YOKOHAMA BAY

93

WAIALUA WAI'ANAE

801

MĀKUA BEACH

'ŌHIKILOLO BEACH

Highway

Map 17

DISTRICT DISTRICT

WAIALUA WAHIAWĀ

DIST. DIST.

803

Road

('Ōhikilolo Beach Pk.)

KEA'AU BEACH PARK

Farrington

Schofield Barracks

Lyman Road

(Kepuhi Beach Pk.)

Kili Dr.

Kepuhi Point

MĀKAHA BEACH PARK

Kolekole Pass

LAUKĪNUI BEACH

Makaha Valley Rd.

Map 16

PAPAONEONE BEACH

Mākaha

MAUNA LAHILAHI BEACH PARK

Wai'anae Homestead Rd.

Naval Road

Kunia Road

WAI'ANAE REGIONAL PARK

WAI'ANAE KAI MILITARY RESERVATION BEACH

PŌKA'Ī BAY BEACH PARK

Wai'anae

Ma'ili'ili Rd.

DISTRICT DISTRICT

750

(Mikilua Beach Pk.)

FS

LUALUALEI BEACH PARK

(Ma'ili'ili Beach Park)

WAI'ANAE 'EWA

MĀ'ILI BEACH PARK

Mā'ili

Lualualei

780

(Maipalaoa Beach Pk.)

Mā'ili Point

Map 15

(Pu'uohulu Beach Pk.)

93

N

ULEHAWA BEACH PARK

Nānākuli FS

Map 14

0 km 1 2 3 4

0 miles 1 2 3 4

WAI'ANAE DISTRICT

(Kalaniana'ole Beach Pk.)

NĀNĀKULI BEACH PARK

(Zablan Beach)

(Piliokahe Beach Pk.)

H-1

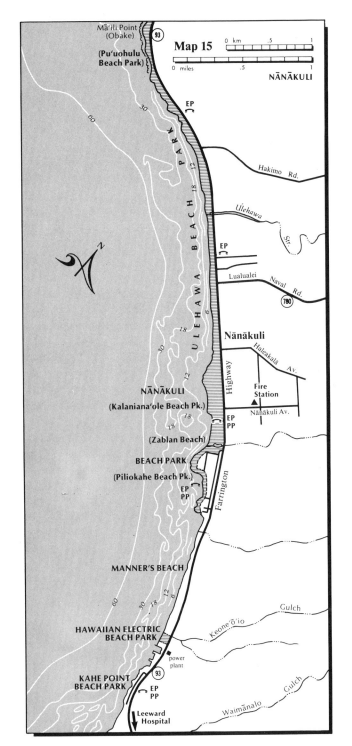

Nānākuli Beach Park

(formerly Kalaniana'ole Beach Park; includes former Piliokahe Beach Park and Zablan Beach)
89–269 Farrington Highway

F: 1 recreation building/pavilion; 1 bathhouse; 3 comfort stations; 2 combination basketball/volleyball courts; 1 softball field; children's play apparatus; camping and picnic equipment; 19 marked camping sites with parking; 2 lifeguard towers; 38 parking stalls
LG: daily service provided by City and County from June through August
EP: 2 in park area
PP: in park area
FS: 84–334 Nānākuli Avenue, Nānākuli
H: Leeward Hospital, 98–1010 Haukapila Road
SS: Farrington Highway
WA: diving; snorkeling; swimming
WC: beach park split into two sections by a beachside housing subdivision, connected along the shoreline by a paved pathway. Eastern section (formerly Piliokahe Beach Park) is situated on low cliff; swimming in cove below park; no lifeguards. Western section (formerly Kalaniana'ole Beach Park) is a pocket sand beach; 2 lifeguard towers in this section; dangerous currents and large shorebreak from October through April; generally calm during summer
PA: unlimited

Nānākuli means "to look at the knee" and recalls a time when many of the areas within the Wai'anae district were named after or referred to parts of the body. The majority of these names, however, were changed or altered under the influence of the Christian missionaries. The missionaries established a station at Waiawa in 'Ewa in 1834. Using that station as a home base, they traveled from Hālawa to Wai'anae with their teachings.

On April 5, 1868, two cousins left their home in San Ignacio, Guam, and joined the crew of the schooner *Daniel Webster*. When the schooner arrived in Hawai'i in 1869, both of the cousins left the ship. Joaquin Zablan married and became the head of one line of Zablans. His cousin, who was probably named Benjamin, also married and became the head of another line of Zablans. Benjamin had three sons, Antony ("Kia"), Silvestre, and Benjamin, and it was from this son Benjamin that Zablan Beach in Nānākuli received its name.

In September 1916, W. D. Holt resigned as district magistrate of the Wai'anae region, and on September

Nānākuli Beach Park. A foam-streaked ocean fronts the deserted beach on a quiet weekday. This particular section of Nānākuli Beach Park was formerly known as Kalaniana'ole Beach Park in honor of Prince Jonah Kūhiō Kalaniana'ole.

29, 1916, Governor Lucius E. Pinkham appointed Benjamin P. Zablan to succeed Holt. Upon receiving his two-year appointment, Zablan moved to Nānākuli, where he made his home on the beach beside Nānākuli Stream. Silvestre and Kia both followed him and lived in the vicinity. In 1918 Governor C. J. McCarthy reappointed Benjamin to his position as district magistrate. In 1920 he resigned from the post that for four years had kept him traveling on horseback from courthouse to village courthouse. Sometime during the 1920s, when some of the Nānākuli lands were opened up for Hawaiian homesteaders, Benjamin moved his family from the beach to a nearby homestead lot, where his descendents have remained to this day.

The eastern end of Nānākuli Beach, where the Zablan home formerly stood, often was safer and calmer than the western end. When other homesteaders began to move into Nānākuli, they often told their children to swim in front of Zablan's. Soon the beach area around the mouth of Nānākuli Stream was known as "Zablan Beach" and it is still called that by local residents.

Eventually the park and beach area (which includes Zablan Beach) was designated as a City and County beach park, initially called Nānākuli Beach Park. In

February 1940, however, the people of Nānākuli petitioned Mayor Crane and the Board of Supervisors to name the park Kalaniana'ole in honor of Prince Jonah Kūhiō Kalaniana'ole, the beloved ''father of the Hawaiian Homesteads Act.'' The request was approved unanimously and the dedication was set for Kūhiō Day of that year. On March 26, 1940, the anniversary of Kūhiō's birthday, a huge *lū'au* and a *hukilau* were held along with the formal opening ceremonies. The event drew many dignitaries from Honolulu, who traveled the long distance to Nānākuli to participate in the festivities.

One of the unpublicized highlights of this *lū'au* was the celebration by the Nānākuli homesteaders of their newly installed suburban water system. When the homestead lots were first opened for occupation, the bulk of Nānākuli's freshwater was transported from either Wai'anae or 'Ewa. When eventually a water pipe was installed it proved to be totally inadequate. During May 1935, for example, there was a very severe water shortage in Nānākuli. None was available even for such basic needs as bathing, cooking, and drinking. Farmers living near the supply tank got the majority of the water, the leftovers going to the homesteaders through a single three-inch pipe. Finally in 1939 the situation was rectified when a suburban water system was installed in the homestead lots. The Kalaniana'ole Beach Park *lū'au* in February of 1940 was held as a dual celebration.

In recent years Kalaniana'ole Beach Park was combined with Piliokahe Park nearby, and both were renamed Nānākuli Beach Park. A small Hawaiian homestead housing area separates the two sections, which are joined by a narrow strip of City-and-County-owned lava forming a shelf along the water's edge. This abandoning of the old names in favor of a general, all-inclusive park name has been evidenced in recent years not only at Nānākuli, but also throughout the entire Wai'anae district. This new policy has not been well accepted by many local residents. To them, the older names reflect the history and culture of their district. Kalaniana'ole is a good example of their trust and pride. In addition, the individual names were convenient for pinpointing small and distinct sections of the very long stretches of beach found all through the Wai'anae district. Helping to solve this latter problem, parkkeepers have put up small signs bearing neatly carved Hawaiian

names of flowers; and now such unofficial titles as *koki'o* (a hibiscus) and *aupaka* (a native violet) can be found in the Nānākuli area to identify a particular comfort station or park section.

The Piliokahe section of Nānākuli Beach Park is situated on a sea cliff above a small cove. A small sandy pocket beach in the cove provides a good swimming area during the summer. The deeper water is almost always clear for skin divers and snorkelers. During the winter, however, the cove can become very dangerous with turbulent surf and strong currents.

The Kalaniana'ole section of Nānākuli Beach Park is the most popular. Situated between two limestone points, the pocket of sandy beach is about 500 feet long and 125 feet wide. The swimming area is relatively calm during the summer, but can be very dangerous during the winter. Large surf creates a steep foreshore that often forms very strong rip currents and a pounding shorebreak. Zablan Beach, at the eastern section, generally is calmer and has become a favorite diving spot for novice SCUBA divers, who follow the sand channel created by the stream to deeper waters. Lifeguard towers along the beach are staffed daily during the summer months, when the number of swimmers is greatest.

Ulehawa Beach Park

(includes former Pu'uohulu and Maipalaoa
Beach parks)
87–1581 Farrington Highway

F: 2 comfort stations; 1 lifeguard tower; camping and picnic areas; 51 parking stalls
LG: daily service provided by City and County from June through August, and on all weekends throughout the year
EP: 2 in park area
PP: Nānākuli Beach Park
FS: 84–334 Nānākuli Avenue, Nānākuli
H: Leeward Hospital, 98–1010 Haukapila Road
SS: Farrington Highway, Nānākuli
WA: diving; shorecasting; bodysurfing; swimming
WC: dangerous currents from October through March; generally calm during summer; long beach; majority of shoreline made of exposed reef and beachrock; small, pocket sand beach fronting lifeguard tower
PA: unlimited

Ulehawa literally means "filthy penis," and is said to have been the name of a chief who once lived in the area. The beach park takes its name from Ulehawa Stream, which empties into the ocean after passing through a section of the park. The long park shoreline stretches from the *makai* boundary of the Nānākuli and Lualualei districts to the area around Maipalaoa Stream. Three separate little parks, Ulehawa, Pu'uohulu, and Maipalaoa, were combined to form Ulehawa Beach Park.

The original Ulehawa section is the most-frequented area of the beach. It centers around the comfort station bearing the name Aupaka. A sandy pocket beach lies between a limestone point on the east and a reef shelf on the west. During the summer, this covelike area is relatively calm and safe for swimming, with its wide sand beach. During the winter, however, much of the beach disappears. The winter surf creates some very powerful rip currents and a good bodysurfing break. There is a lifeguard tower overlooking the cove area that is staffed during the summer and on all weekends. The rest of the original Ulehawa Beach Park is relatively undeveloped. The beach, for the most part, is steep and narrow, with exposed reef and rocks along most of the shoreline. The bottom drops off rather sharply into deeper waters. Swimming is poor and dangerous during the winter. At the mouth of Ulehawa Stream, however, the freshwater runoff has formed a relatively smooth shelf compared with the surface in the rest of the area. Children from Nānākuli often play and bodysurf here.

The Pu'uohulu section of Ulehawa Beach Park lies around the large rocky point located at the base of the mountain Pu'uohulu-kai. No recreational swimming is possible in this area. The entire shoreline at the water's edge is a long low cliff composed of limestone and raised coral reef. The park is not only undeveloped but also is covered with underbrush and *kiawe* trees. Surf pounds the cliffs almost continually, especially during the winter months. The area is frequented primarily by pole fishermen. The lone concrete marker on the point warns fishermen about the dangerous water conditions. Such markers were set up in 1935 in many such hazardous spots by the former Honolulu Japanese Casting Club. Originally the markers, with the word "danger" printed in Japanese on their sides, were placed above an actual spot where a fisherman had been washed away and lost. The Pu'uohulu point area was known to the Japanese fishermen as *"obake,"* or "ghosts," from a feeling that the place was haunted.

The Maipalaoa section of Ulehawa Beach Park, stretching from Mā'ili Point to Maipalaoa Stream, also is undeveloped. The offshore reef in this area forms a shallow, enclosed lagoon which opens into deep water at the Mā'ili end, creating the safest section for swimming throughout the entire Ulehawa Beach Park. The lagoon is protected even when the surf is high. The shallow bottom is a mixture of sand pockets and patches of coral reef. The western end of the fringing reef provides a popular surfing break.

Mā'ili Beach Park
(includes former Mā'ili'ili Beach Park)
87-021 Farrington Highway

F: 3 comfort stations; 2 volleyball courts; camping and picnic areas; 1 lifeguard tower; 68 parking stalls
LG: daily service provided by City and County from June through August and on all weekends throughout the year
EP: 2 in park area
PP: none
FS: 86-230 Farrington Highway, Wai'anae
H: Leeward Hospital, 98-1010 Haukapila Road
SS: Farrington Highway, Mā'ili
WA: diving; board surfing; swimming
WC: dangerous currents and surf from October through March; generally calm during summer; long beach; majority of shoreline made of exposed reef and beachrock; best swimming in front of lifeguard tower
PA: unlimited

Mā'ili Beach Park, extending from Maipalaoa Stream to Mā'ili'ili Stream, is another long stretch of shoreline in the Wai'anae district. It is a combination of the former Mā'ili'ili and the original Mā'ili beach parks. Mā'ili is a contracted form of the word *mā'ili'ili,* which means "lots of little pebbles." The *'ili'ili* stones were used for many purposes, such as net-sinkers, percussion instruments for dances and chantings, and even as jacks by children playing the game of *kimo*. There has been

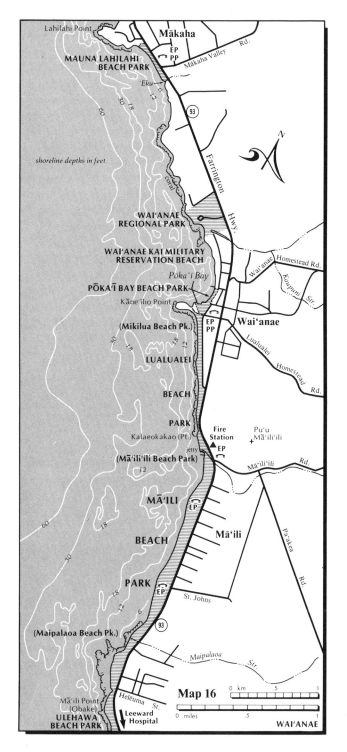

some controversy over this translation of *mā'ili,* however, inasmuch as other interpreters of the name claim that *'ili'ili* were never found in this area.

During the summer the long beach is wide because of the seasonal accretion of sand. During the winter the sand is washed away, sometimes very severely. Almost the entire area of the beach park is undeveloped and is still covered by scrub brush and grass. It is broken into three sections by two separate housing developments near the shoreline. Reef shelves line the entire beach along the water's edge.

The most popular swimming area is in front of the wide sand beach next to the mouth of Mā'ili'ili Stream. The waves here were a much frequented surfing spot at one time, but the construction of the jetty intruded rather seriously into the break. The jetty was completed in August 1966 as part of a major improvement to the stream channel.

The ocean bottom drops off quickly into the deeper offshore waters. During the winter months, when the swells are heavy, there are powerful rip currents and strong backwashes along the entire length of the park. There is only one lifeguard tower here, which is staffed daily during the summer months and on all weekends.

Lualualei Beach Park
86–221 Farrington Highway

  F: 2 comfort stations; 15 marked camping sites with parking; cooking stands and picnic tables; 22 parking stalls
LG: none
EP: in park area
PP: Pōka'ī Bay Beach Park
FS: 86–230 Farrington Highway, Wai'anae
  H: Leeward Hospital, 98–1010 Haukapila Road
SS: Farrington Highway, Wai'anae
WA: diving; pole fishing; board surfing; swimming
WC: dangerous currents and surf from October through March; majority of shoreline fronted by coral reef and beachrock
PA: unlimited

The widest and the most popular section of Lualualei Beach Park was known to Hawaiians as Kalaeokakao, "the point of the goats," because of the numerous wild goats roaming about there during the 1800s. Goats are not indigenous to Hawai'i. They were introduced by Captain Cook in 1778, and additional animals were brought by Captain Vancouver in 1792. Initially, these animals were protected by *kapu,* and they multiplied so rapidly that soon they were running wild on seven of the eight major islands. They began to encroach on cultivated lands and also to destroy plants growing in watersheds and forest areas. The situation grew so critical that it became necessary to kill them off in great numbers. On the Big Island during the late 1920s, for example, George R. Clark organized seven or eight large hunts that killed from 700 to 4,000 goats in each drive. Beginning near the Chain of Craters area, Clark and thirty other *paniolo* would fan out and drive the wild animals toward the seashore at Apua Point, where the goats were rounded up and herded along the shore to Kalapana. There they were slaughtered. The hides were cured, bundled, trucked to Hilo, and finally shipped to the mainland.

On O'ahu, goats were particularly numerous in Wai-'anae. They were often seen in abundance on Pu'u Mā-'ili'ili, the large hill behind the major part of Lualualei Beach Park and Kalaeokakao, "goat point." Today most of the remaining goats in Wai'anae live in the higher mountains, and Kalaeokakao has become part of the City and County beach park.

Lualualei Beach Park stretches from Kalaeokakao to Kāne'īlio Point. The entire park is fronted by low cliffs and raised coral reefs, making recreational swimming almost impossible. The park is used primarily by picnickers and fishermen. It is a combination of two former parks, Mikilua and the original Lualualei.

Pōka'ī Bay Beach

In very ancient times, when the great Hawaiian chiefs and navigators sailed across the vast Pacific between Hawai'i and Kahiki, a legend arose about a voyaging chief named Pōka'ī. It said that he brought and planted at Wai'anae the first coconut tree in Hawai'i, from which grew in time a famous grove, Ka Ulu Niu o Pōka'ī. The grove stretched from the site of the present

police station to that of the Sacred Hearts Church. A few of its trees remain today. The bay *makai* of the grove, formerly known as Mā'alaea, eventually took the name of the legendary planter. The shoreline at the mouth of Kānepūniu Stream was called Keaupuni, another name sometimes applied to Pōka'ī Bay.

Kāne'īlio Point separates Lualualei Beach Park from Pōka'ī Bay. On this point Kū'īlioloa *heiau* was built. Kū'īlioloa, one of the few *heiau* known that was enclosed by water on three sides, must have been a commanding structure and probably was an important site for travelers departing and arriving by canoe on the western end of O'ahu. Kamehameha the Great is said to have stopped here before departing on his first attempt to conquer Kaua'i. He went inland to Kahoa Ali'i *heiau,* at the foot of Pu'u Kahea, and then returned to Kū'īlioloa to hold the final services before he sailed.

Pōka'ī Bay Beach Park
(formerly Nene'u Beach)
85–037 Wai'anae Valley Road

F: 1 comfort station; 1 boat ramp; camping and picnic areas; 1 lifeguard tower; 44 parking stalls
LG: daily service provided by City and County from June to August and on all weekends throughout the year
EP: in park area
PP: in park area
FS: 86–230 Farrington Highway, Wai'anae
H: Leeward Hospital, 98–1010 Haukapila Road
SS: Farrington Highway, Wai'anae
WA: diving; pole fishing; board surfing; swimming
WC: safe all year; shallow, sandy swimming area
PA: unlimited

The beach in Pōka'ī Bay, situated between Kāne'īlio Point and Kānepūniu Stream, is divided by three breakwaters. Pōka'ī Bay Beach Park, the best section and also the only public one, falls between the point and the first breakwater. The rest of the shoreline is controlled by the Wai'anae-Kai military reservation, a twenty-acre tract that was set aside in 1918 for military purposes. Today the reservation is essentially a recreational facility for military personnel.

Christine A. Takata

Pōka'ī Bay Beach Park. The public mooring site in Pōka'ī Bay just offshore from the beach park. Protected by a breakwater, this bay is the only area on the entire Wai'anae coast where boats can tie up safely even during times of heavy surf, and where swimmers can always feel secure even though other beaches nearby are experiencing dangerous wave action and rip currents.

Pōka'ī Bay Beach Park formerly was known as Nene'u, as is evidenced now only by a small store bearing that name to the rear of the parking lot. Nene'u is a wide, flat sandy beach that is well protected by a small boat harbor. The harbor and breakwater were dedicated in October 1953, and since then have protected the bay from the heavy surf during fall and winter months. The inshore waters are shallow, and the sea bottom slopes very gradually into deeper areas. Nene'u is an excellent swimming beach for children and adults alike. The only hazard is the boat traffic in the harbor. Warning signs are posted in the water to make people aware of this danger. A lifeguard tower is located within the beach park, and it is staffed daily during the summer months and on all weekends.

Nene'u is an important recreational beach not only to the town of Wai'anae, but to the entire district. It is the most protected and the most stable beach along this entire coastline. For this reason it is an excellent swimming place throughout the entire year, even when the rest of Wai'anae's shoreline is experiencing seasonal erosion and heavy surf.

Wai'anae Kai Military Reservation Beach
(also Pōka'ī Army Beach or Wai'anae Army Recreation Center)
Army Street, Wai'anae

F: complete recreation center with concessions; 1 lifeguard tower
LG: service provided by military personnel
EP: Pōka'ī Bay Beach Park

88

PP: in beach area
FS: 86–230 Farrington Highway, Wai'anae
 H: Military: Tripler Army Medical Center, Jarrett White Road (off Moanalua Road); Civilian: Leeward Hospital, 98–1010 Haukapila Road
SS: Farrington Highway, Wai'anae
WA: diving; board surfing; swimming
WC: safe all year; good beginner's surf
PA: limited to military personnel

The Wai'anae Kai Military Reservation Beach is moderately steep because of a high seawall running the length of the reservation. Both the beach and the offshore bottom are sandy and have no hazardous water conditions. At high tide there is sometimes a slight shorebreak, but is does not affect the good swimming conditions. The facilities are restricted to military personnel and their dependents and guests.

In the outer waters of the bay, fronting the Army Beach, is a large reef area that attracts many novice surfers. Usually the waves are slow and gentle, providing ideal conditions for beginners.

Wai'anae Regional Park

85–471 Farrington Highway

 F: 4 tennis courts; 1 comfort station; 1 softball field; parking area
LG: none
EP: Pōka'ī Bay Beach Park
PP: none
FS: 86–230 Farrington Highway, Wai'anae
 H: Leeward Hospital, 98–1010 Haukapila Road
SS: Farrington Highway, Wai'anae
WA: diving; pole fishing; swimming
WC: dangerous currents and surf from October through March; entire shoreline is a low sea cliff with sharp beach rock; no easy access to ocean
PA: unlimited

Wai'anae Regional Park is a large, fifty-acre field bordering the ocean on the western side of Pōka'ī Bay. The name Wai'anae is usually translated as "mullet water," the word *'anae* referring to the full-grown mullet. On the Pōka'ī side of the park, Kānepūniu Stream empties into the ocean through a small inlet formerly known as Keaupuni.

The Park has a softball field and four tennis courts, but does not offer a good place for recreational swimming. The entire shoreline is a low sea cliff of sharp coral rocks with a six- to ten-foot drop into the ocean. The feasibility of constructing a new small boat harbor along this section of coast is being studied.

Mauna Lahilahi Beach Park

(formerly Laulauwa'a)
84–1161 Farrington Highway, Mākaha

 F: 1 comfort station; 1 lifeguard tower; cooking stands and picnic tables; roadside parking along Farrington Highway
LG: daily service provided by City and County from June through August
EP: in park area
PP: in park area
FS: 86–230 Farrington Highway, Wai'anae
 H: Leeward Hospital, 98–1010 Haukapila Road
SS: Farrington Highway; Cornet Village
WA: diving; pole fishing; board surfing; swimming
WC: strong currents when surf is big from October through March; majority of shoreline is beachrock
PA: unlimited

Mauna Lahilahi means "thin mountain." The small hill, 230 feet high, is so thin that it almost appears to have been cut with a knife. The mountain divides the shoreline into two separate beach areas. The beach on the west side was called Papaoneone, "sandy shelf," while that on the east side was called Laulauwa'a, "canoe paddle blade." Laulauwa'a is known today as Mauna Lahilahi Beach Park.

The park is fronted by a sandy beach situated between two rocky points. The width of the beach varies seasonally, being narrow during the winter and moderately wide during the summer. There are occasional outcroppings of beach rock and reef along the water's edge, but they are low and pose no problem to swimmers. The bottom drops off fairly abruptly, but very rarely are there any rip currents or strong backwashes, even when the surf is up. The inshore areas can become turbulent, but generally do not present any major hazards. The water is often murky. The City and County maintains a lifeguard tower in the area, which is manned daily during the summer months.

One stream crosses the beach at the eastern end of the park. It was formerly called 'Eku, which means "to root, as does a pig." Legend says that Kamapua'a, the demigod from Hau'ula who could change his form from a man to a pig as he wished, attempted to root inland from the shoreline here. He was trying to conceal himself and approach a village at the same time. As usual, he was engaged in one of his devious escapades. The villagers, however, realized what was happening and beat him back with canoe paddles. The sand-bottom watercourse, 'Eku, today remains dry almost year round, so it presents no danger for wandering children.

Papaoneone Beach

(also Lahilahi Beach, Turtle Beach, Keawaiki Beach, or Crescent Beach)
(borders Lahilahi Street and Farrington Highway, Mākaha)

  F: none
 LG: none
 EP: Mauna Lahilahi Beach Park
 PP: Farrington Highway; Cornet Village
 FS: 86–230 Farrington Highway, Wai'anae
  H: Leeward Hospital, 98–1010 Haukapila Road
 SS: Farrington Highway, Mākaha
 WA: diving; bodysurfing; swimming
 WC: dangerous currents and shorebreak when surf is big from October through April; long, curving sand beach
 PA: public right-of-way on Moua Street

The Waterhouse estate in Māhaka comprises the entire Mauna Lahilahi area. Situated directly on the ocean, Mauna Lahilahi, the "thin mountain," dominates the level regions of the estate and forms a small bay that was formerly called Keawaiki, "the little harbor." Inshore of Keawaiki is a long, wide, curved sand beach that extends from the edge of the Waterhouse estate to a rocky lava shelf. Known variously today as Lahilahi, Crescent, and Turtle beaches, the old Hawaiian name was Papaoneone, "sandy shelf." Papaoneone often has a steep foreshore, but usually the backwash is gentle.

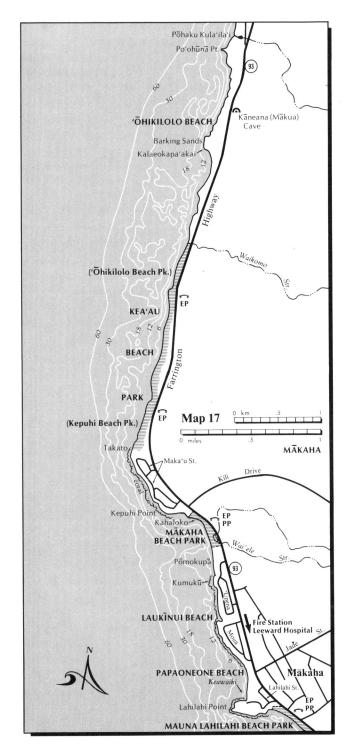

There are no rip currents unless the surf is very big. The sandy bottom, however, drops off quickly and often there are persistent alongshore currents which should be of concern to parents with young children. The surf that wraps around the outermost point of Mauna Lahilahi follows the lava terrace shoreward and strikes the beach first at the eastern end of Papaoneone. There the beach is steepest and usually is scoured down to the underlying rock. The waves washing the sand away form a small but enjoyable shorebreak for bodysurfing. The only public access to Papaoneone is from the right-of-way on Moua Street.

Laukīnui Beach
'Ūpena Street, Mākaha

```
 F: none
LG: none
EP: Mākaha Beach Park
PP: Mākaha Beach Park
FS: 86–230 Farrington Highway, Wai'anae
 H: Leeward Hospital, 98–1010 Haukapila Road
SS: Farrington Highway, Mākaha
WA: diving; swimming
WC: dangerous currents from October through April; tiny
    pocket sand beach
PA: public right-of-way on 'Ūpena Street
```

The ti, or *kī,* was a widely used and valued plant in ancient Hawai'i. The *lau kī,* or ti leaf, was an emblem of divine power: it was worn around the neck as a charm against malign spiritual influences. The *kahuna* often wore a band of *kī* leaves around his neck. The *lau kī* was also a special emblem of the goddess Ha'iwahine, and it was much used as a decoration around a *hālau,* or house of *hula* instruction.

The people used the long green leaves for the wrapping, carrying, and cooking of food. They also used the leaves as plates and to cover food being cooked in the *imu.* The leaves were bound around the head to relieve headaches and to cool the fevered brow. One modern use has made it famous—the making of *hula* skirts. Slit into narrow strips, the *lau kī* is the "grass" in most grass skirts. One of the other well-known uses for the ti leaf is in the method of net fishing known as the *hukilau.* For this, leaves are tied to a rope which is set offshore in a semicircle. When the ends of the rope are drawn together, the fluttering leaves help to scare the fish into the small bag net that is tied to the vertex of the rope.

Laukīnui, the "large ti leaf," was the name of a *heiau* that stood on the Mākaha shoreline and is said to have been the most important one in the district. Nothing remains today of the former temple except its name, attached to a small beach near the *heiau* site. Laukīnui Beach is a small sandy cove situated in the center of the long rocky shoreline separating Papaoneone and Mākaha Beach Park. The beach itself provides a good sunbathing area with limited swimming. There is no convenient public access to the beach. Long before the land adjoining the beach was developed, the Holt family of Mākaha used it as a pasture for cattle. Because of this, the shoreline at Laukīnui was known to many fishermen as Pipi, or "beef."

Mākaha Beach Park
84–369 Farrington Highway

```
 F: 1 comfort station/caretaker's residence; camping area;
    1 lifeguard tower
LG: service provided by City and County daily all year
EP: on beach
PP: in park area
FS: 86–230 Farrington Highway, Wai'anae
 H: Leeward Hospital, 98–1010 Haukapila Road
SS: Farrington Highway, Mākaha
WA: diving; board surfing; bodysurfing; paipo board surf-
    ing; swimming
WC: dangerous rip currents, shorebreak, and backwash
    when surf is big from October through April; some of
    biggest surfing waves in Hawai'i during winter; swim-
    mers must beware of loose surfboards coming into
    shore
PA: unlimited
AI: home of annual Mākaha International Surfing Contest
    since 1952
```

Mākaha, meaning "fierce" or "savage," refers to a notorious community of bandits, who lived far back in the valley and plied their trade just to the rear of the present beach park. Above the Hawaiian Electric boost-

Mākaha Beach Park. Swimmers and spectators stand at the water's edge to watch the surfing action offshore. Mākaha is one of the most famous big-wave surfing beaches in the world and is the home of the Mākaha International Surfing Contest, first held in 1952. Loose surfboards being washed inshore often pose a real hazard for unwary swimmers in this particular area of the beach.

er station at the base of the cliffs is a large upright rock that was known as Pāpale o Kāne, the "hat of Kāne." There bandit lookouts kept watch for travelers on the trail below. If a large group was spotted, the lookout would cry, *"Kai nui"* ("High tide") to his companions hidden below, and this would warn them that the party of travelers was too large or too strong for them to contend with. However, when the lookout cried *"Kai malolo"* ("low tide"), the band would attack, having been informed that the group was a small or weak one.

Although the entire valley from the mountains to the sea was called Mākaha, no single beach was known by this name. All of the shoreline was referred to as Mākaha-kai or Mākaha-on-the-ocean, and each little beach, point, reef, and rock had its own name. The beach and bay that form the major part of today's Mākaha Beach was called Kahaloko. Adjacent to the beach was a large fishpond known as Mākāhā (with the accent on the last syllable). A *mākāhā* was a sluice gate to a fishpond. The pond was fed by the waters of Wai'ele Stream, which now is stagnant, dirty, and often waterless. The waters of Wai'ele were channeled off elsewhere, at the back of the valley, to irrigate sugarcane fields and for other similar purposes. Eventually the pond was cut off from the ocean and partly filled for the construction of a road and of a bed for railroad tracks.

Eric M. Nishida

Mākaha Beach Park. Two surfers wade carefully across the inshore reef into the surf and the afternoon glare on a windy day of small surf.

The beach lying between the mouth of Wai'ele Stream and the lava rocks to the east of it was called Pōmokupā, and the rocky area that borders Pōmokupā was known as Kumukū. Kumukū is a popular bodysurfing area. With the coming of progress and the death of the fishpond, all of the Hawaiian shoreline names fell into disuse. The areas of Kumukū, Pōmokupā, and Kahaloko were called simply Mākaha Beach. The outermost point of the bay, Lae o Kepuhi, was named for the several blowholes found along the lava and reef terrace that circles the point. *Kepuhi* means "to blow." The largest of these blowholes can be found at the end of the public right-of-way at 84–267 Makau Street.

After World War II, the sport of surfing spread beyond Waikīkī. Mākaha Beach eventually became a mecca for board surfing enthusiasts. When big west or north swells are running, the waves here provide some of the most spectacular and dangerous surfing found anywhere in the world. Because of these excellent waves, the Waikīkī Surf Club established the Mākaha International Surfing Championships in 1952. The contest, which has been held every year since its initiation, has made Mākaha one of the most famous surfing beaches in the world.

The long sandy shore at Mākaha Beach Park undergoes considerable seasonal variations in width. During the winter there is a great deal of erosion from the often heavy surf, so usually the foreshore is steep. During the summer the sand returns, forming a beautiful wide beach. The waters are safe for swimming except when the surf is big. Then the shorebreak becomes very dangerous and creates very strong backwashes. The alongshore currents run toward the center of the beach and join to form a very powerful rip current flowing seaward through a wide sand channel. The channel was cut by the former Wai'ele Stream. The hazardous water conditions created by the good surfing waves are complicated further by the numerous surfers in the area. Runaway boards washing toward the shore are very dangerous to unwary swimmers.

Kea'au Beach Park

(includes former Kepuhi and 'Ōhikilolo beach parks)
83-431 Farrington Highway, Kea'au

 F: 2 comfort stations; 55 marked camping sites with parking; cooking stands and picnic tables
LG: none
EP: 2 in park area
PP: Mākaha Beach Park
FS: 86-230 Farrington Highway, Wai'anae
 H: Leeward Hospital, 98-1010 Haukapila Road
SS: Farrington Highway, Mākaha
WA: diving; swimming
WC: dangerous currents and surf from October through April; entire shoreline is a low sea cliff, with reef and beachrock; poor access to ocean; sandy beach at western end of park; rocky ocean bottom
PA: unlimited

The land divisions of Mākaha and Kea'au are separated on the shoreline by Kalae o Mākaha, or Mākaha Point. This rocky, raised reef was much frequented by Japanese pole fishermen who cast their lines from the low sea cliffs. They called the area "Takato," probably after someone once associated with that section. Inland of Kalae o Mākaha, near the present intersection of Lawai'a Street and Farrington Highway, lay a boulder that was commonly known as the "Clapping Rock." People said that if a person standing four or five feet away clapped his hands the rock would produce an echo. The Hawaiian name for this stone was Pōhaku Kīkēkē, the "knocking rock." Residents thought that at one time the ocean had flowed underground through a lava tube and hollowed out a place at the base of Pōhaku Kīkēkē. This would have given the boulder a resonant quality similar to that of the Bell Stone at Wailua, Kaua'i. Whatever its sound, and whatever its cause, Pōhaku

Kīkēkē has not been heard for many years. A similar stone, also called Pōhaku Kīkēkē, is said to have been located on the grounds of the King's Daughters' Home in Kaimukī.

In the upper regions of Kea'au Valley there is one spot, an area of red soil, on which nothing has ever grown. It was said to have been blighted by the *menehune,* but why they did so is unknown. In later years, when the United States military forces made use of the upper part of Kea'au, they renamed it "Happy Valley," but the *haole* title disappeared with the end of the Second World War. At one time pineapples were cultivated in the upper valley, where Kuolo Stream runs into Wa'ikomo, but the venture did not succeed.

The shoreline is made up of three adjoining beach parks, formerly separate but now united under one name, Kea'au Beach Park. Almost the entire improved park area is fronted by sharp lava and raised reef. This improved section is used primarily by campers and picnickers, and on calm days by SCUBA and skin divers, who frequent the offshore waters. The sand beach beginning at the unimproved section of the park is not really suited for recreational swimming. The reef comes up to the water's edge and the bottom drops off abruptly. A surfing break just offshore occasionally attracts a few board surfers, but even they must be careful. The ocean here can become very dangerous with strong currents when the surf is up. Observant residents of Kea'au say that surfers must be especially wary when Kaua'i is visible across the channel. Such a sighting indicates a coming storm, but when Kaua'i becomes visible a second time, after the storm, the turbulent weather is supposed to have ended—for a time.

The major stream crossing the beach from Kea'au Valley is Waikomo. It is located a considerable distance down the beach from the improved park area and usually is dry most of the year. It poses no hazard for wandering children. Formerly the sea off Waikomo was much frequented by commercial fishermen. The large channel carved long ago in the ocean bottom by the waters of the stream provided the only access to the beach from the sea along this entire stretch of shoreline when the surf was high. The fishermen would come in here, unload their catches on the shore, and send them to Honolulu on the train.

94

'Ōhikilolo Beach
Farrington Highway

F: none; roadside parking near Kāneana Cave (Mākua Cave), Farrington Highway
LG: none
EP: Kea'au Beach Park
PP: Mākaha Beach Park
FS: 86-230 Farrington Highway, Wai'anae
H: Leeward Hospital, 98-1010 Haukapila Road
SS: Farrington Highway, Mākaha
WA: diving; swimming
WC: dangerous offshore currents and surf from October through April; entire shoreline is exposed reef and beachrock; swimming possible in large tidal pools
PA: follow trail from Kāneana Cave to ocean and walk east
AI: site of once famous "Barking Sands"

'Ōhikilolo is translated as "prying out brains," but the origin of the name for this small land division is now unknown. The single large lava point along the 'Ōhikilolo shoreline was known as Kalaeopa'akai, the "salt point." The people from the surrounding villages came here to gather *pa'akai,* "hard sea," the crude Hawaiian salt. The black lava at the point has numerous shallow pockets which are filled with ocean water from spraying and splashing waves. The heat of the sun evaporates the water and the crystalized salt remains. Although the salt still forms in Kalaeopa'akai's pans, it is rarely gathered for use. The advances of civilization have touched even this remote point, and most of the depressions that catch the salt water are dirty and fouled with rubbish.

The sand dunes that comprise most of the beach at the rear of Kalaeopa'akai are the once famous "Barking Sands" of O'ahu. Barking Sands also are found near Mānā, Kaua'i, which Baldwin described in these terms:

"When thoroughly dry, this sand becomes resonant whenever its grains are set in motion. While they are called barking sands, they emit a great variety of sounds according to the method of friction. At times the sound will resemble subterranean thunder; again it will be a sighing or a faint groaning as of someone in pain; when the wind forms little cascades there is a resulting sound as from a lady's silk skirt; the act of sliding down the hills produce a sound having cadence periods; they were probably named for this.

"This phenomenon is a rare one, being common to only a few places in the world. It is said that there is a hill of barking sands at Mākua ['Ōhikilolo], O'ahu." (from "A Footpath Journey," by Vaughan MacCaughey, in *Mid Pacific Magazine,* August 1917:188).

The Barking Sands in 'Ōhikilolo have not been heard for many years. The once high sand dunes were mined and were leveled to accommodate railroad tracks. In addition the dunes are almost completely overgrown with brush. All these changes seem to have silenced the once resonant sands.

The major attraction at 'Ōhikilolo is Kāneana, a large cave high above the shoreline that is situated just off Farrington Highway near the border of 'Ōhikilolo and Mākua. Once a gigantic sea cave, Kāneana, the "cave of Kāne," was created by wave action in a fault crack more than 150,000 years ago, when O'ahu's present coastline was underwater. It is also known as Ke'ana'ana, but most frequently is called Mākua Cave.

The huge cavern, 450 feet long, was said to have been the home of Nanaue, a son of the shark god Kamaho-ali'i. Nanaue had a dual nature, being able to assume the form of a shark or of a man. He killed many people in the area and brought his victims into the cave through a secret ocean entrance. His altar was a white rock slab far back in one of the cave's smaller chambers. His reign of terror ended when he was put to death after his duality was discovered.

Almost the entire shoreline of 'Ōhikilolo is rocky, and its waters are deep and often dangerous. The only safe place to swim is a small, secluded cove between Kalaeopa'akai and Kāneana. The shallow inshore pond is protected from the open ocean by a stretch of raised beach rock. There is no convenient public access to the greater part of 'Ōhikilolo Beach except by following the shoreline from below Kāneana Cave.

Mākua Beach
Farrington Highway (Mākua and Kahanahāiki)

F: none; roadside parking along secondary roads throughout beach area
LG: none
EP: Kea'au Beach Park
PP: Mākaha Beach Park
FS: 86-230 Farrington Highway, Wai'anae
H: Leeward Hospital, 98-1010 Haukapila Road
SS: Farrington Highway, Mākaha
WA: diving; pole fishing; bodysurfing (limited); swimming

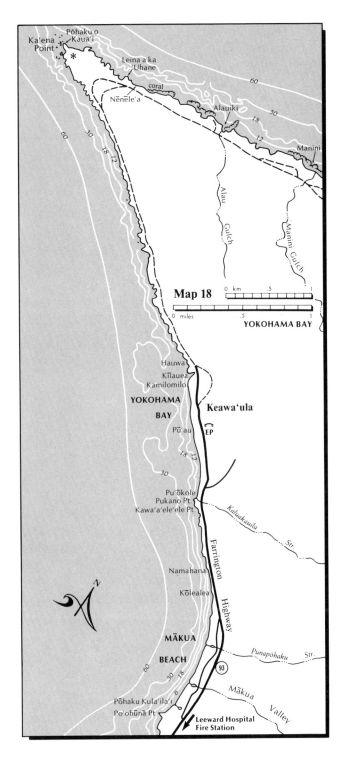

Map 18

0 km   .5   1

0 miles   .5   1

YOKOHAMA BAY

WC: dangerous currents and surf from October through
    April; generally calm during summer; long sandy beach
PA: unlimited
AI: main location site for Lahaina scenes in movie *Hawai'i*

Why the name Mākua, meaning "parent" or "grown to
maturity," should have been applied to this area is not
known. Several possibilities have been advanced. The
Hawaiians may have related the immense valley at the
rear of the beach to maturity. The name could have
been that of a former chief. The term *mākua* also is applied to the leader, or "parent," of certain types of fish
that travel in schools. It designates, for example, the
rare yellow *nenue,* an obvious standout among it grey
followers, and the large *'ō'io* that precedes the rest of its
school.

In the days of old, Mākua was a densely populated
valley with a thriving community. The majority of the
early inhabitants lived inland, in an area called Pu'u
Pa'i. Fruit trees abounded, and freshwater wells and
springs were plentiful. Pigs ran wild throughout the
valley, and often at night they came to the seashore to
root in the sand for *'ōhiki,* sand crabs. Fishermen had
to hide their bait in their canoes so that the scavenging
pigs could not get it. The beach at Mākua, as well as
that at Mākaha, was a landing and departure area for
canoes, at which travelers could spend the night before
resuming their journeys.

On the east side of Mākua is a small valley called
Ko'iahi. In this small place the finest-leafed *maile* on
O'ahu, the *maile lauli'i o Ko'iahi,* was found. Growing
primarily on the cliffs, the *maile lauli'i o Ko'iahi* fell victim to wild goats. *Maile* of any variety, the fragrant
leaves of which are used as decorations or for *lei,* is rarely found today anywhere on O'ahu, although in some
places a few plants have survived.

Mākua Beach is a long, curving sandy shore located
between two rocky points. The point at the eastern end
was called Po'ohūnā, "hidden head." It was and still is
a popular fishing area, especially for *moi.* Running
seaward from Po'ohūnā is an underwater reef shelf
known as Papaloa. It was said that Papaloa had pockets
of air where divers could breathe without coming to the
surface.

At the eastern edge of the sand beach, sitting in front
of the first stream mouth, is a large white rock known as

Pōhaku Kulaʻilaʻi. *Kulaʻi* means "to dash to pieces," and in this instance the reference is to waves pounding against the rock and being shattered into spray. A female *moʻo* who lived here during certain times of the year bathed in a freshwater spring on the *mauka* side of Farrington Highway, at the spot marked today by two large mango trees. After her bath she would come down to the beach and comb out her hair on Pōhaku Kulaʻilaʻi. Legend says that when the spring water was green, the *moʻo* was present; when it was clear, she was gone. This *moʻo* was said to have been a companion of Nanaue, the shark god of nearby Kāneana. Pōhaku Kulaʻilaʻi is used today by swimmers as a diving rock.

During World War II, Mākua Valley was taken over by the armed forces for use as a bombing range. Valley residents who lived inland moved down to the beach, leaving the entire upper regions open for target practice. The Mākua Protestant Church, once situated on the shoreline behind Pōhaku Kulaʻilaʻi, was used by military chaplains as well as by the people of Mākua. The church's roof was marked clearly so that Air Force pilots would realize it was not a designated target. In spite of the precaution, however, the church was bombed and many of the hand-carved headstones in the adjoining graveyard were destroyed. Eventually the Mākua Protestant Church's congregation was awarded $5,000 in compensation, but the building itself was never replaced. Today the graveyard, which is still maintained and used by the congregation, is the sole remnant of the Mākua community. Mākua Valley is still off-limits to the public because the military continues to use it as an "impact area." There are no known maps of the area indicating "dud" or unexploded munition sites.

Although Mākua Beach is a continuous stretch of shore, the beach actually is situated in two adjacent land divisions, Mākua and Kahanahāiki. In the Kahanahāiki section, there is a small reef on the shoreline not far from the western end of the beach. It was called Kōlealea, for a well known fishing shrine that no longer exists. It is different from the rest of the beach because it always remains free of sand.

The beach surrounding Kōlealea was called Laehau and is marked only by a single mango tree growing above the thick underbrush. The Laehau area was the site of Ukanipō *heiau,* which no longer exists. The west-

ern point of the beach, where the sand ends, is Namahana, the "rest" or the "warmth," probably referring to the fact that travelers frequently rested in Mākua. A stone retaining wall that supported the railroad line still exists at Namahana.

The long beautiful beach at Mākua is safe for swimming when the ocean is calm, as it usually is during the summer. But when big swells roll in, the waters become very turbulent and dangerous, the currents very strong. The bottom drops to overhead depths rather quickly, sometimes creating a rough and violent shorebreak. The Mākua shoreline gained new fame in 1965, when it was used as a major location for the Lahaina scenes in the film *Hawaiʻi.*

Yokohama Bay

(also Yokohama Beach; formerly Keawaʻula Beach and
Pūʻau Beach)
Farrington Highway, Keawaʻula

  F: none; roadside parking along Farrington Highway
LG: none
EP: on beach
PP: Mākaha Beach Park
FS: 86–230 Farrington Highway, Waiʻanae
  H: Leeward Hospital, 98–1010 Haukapila Road
SS: Farrington Highway, Mākaha
WA: diving; shorecasting; board surfing; bodysurfing; paipo board surfing; swimming
WC: very dangerous currents, surf, and backwash from October through April; rocky ocean bottom, especially in surfing area
PA: unlimited
AI: Yokohama marks end of improved road; state beach park, undeveloped; Kaʻena Point Satellite Tracking Station on ridge above beach

Yokohama Bay is located in the district of Keawaʻula. This region is said to have been named for the great schools of *mūheʻe,* or squid, that once frequented the offshore waters. The *mūheʻe* are almost invisible when the sun is hidden, but the schools often show a distinctive reddish brown color when the sun is out. The *mūheʻe* came to this area in such great numbers that the water appeared to turn red, so the bay was called Keawaʻula, "the red harbor." The *mūheʻe* is the true,

Eric M. Nishida

Yokohama Bay. A calm day at Yokohama. This particular section of this well-known surfing beach was called Pū'au by the Hawaiians and was a noted grounds for *moi* or threadfish. Japanese pole fishermen frequenting the area were the source of the beach's popular name, Yokohama.

free-swimming squid, as opposed to the *he'e,* the day octopus, and the *pūloa,* the night octopus, both of which are commonly if erroneously called squid in Hawai'i.

From the beginning of the Hawaiian sugar industry during the 1830s and 1840s, one of the greatest problems was the shortage of workers. To increase the number of laborers, plantations began to look abroad for help. From 1852 on, people from many nations came to work on Hawai'i's plantations, and to make their contributions to the fascinating admixtures of features, complexions, and customs that are unique to today's

Hawai'i. The first group of contract workers consisted of 195 Chinese who were imported to the islands in 1852. The first Japanese immigrants arrived in 1868, followed by Portuguese in 1878, and Norwegians and Germans in 1881. Members of at least a dozen other nationalities came at different times to work for the sugar and pineapple plantations.

Today Filipinos, who began arriving in 1904, provide the largest group of workers, but for a long time Japanese immigrants were the major source of labor for the plantations. The Japanese men who worked for the Wai'anae sugar plantation discovered the excellent pole-fishing grounds off the many rocky ledges and beaches in the Wai'anae district. Because one of the places they frequented consistently was the beach at Keawa'ula, the area was nicknamed "Yokohama Bay."

Until the late 1940s, trains of the O'ahu Railway and Land Company ran from Honolulu to Hale'iwa by way of Wai'anae and Ka'ena Point. Often the winter surf in the Mākaha, Mākua, and Keawa'ula areas was so devastating that it undermined and tore up the tracks that had been laid above the shoreline. Because of this problem the railroad station in Mākua, "Section House 6," was manned by a small group of troubleshooters. It is believed that these Japanese men were the first non-Hawaiians to fish in Keawa'ula.

Yokohama, the name of the famous port city in Japan from which most Japanese immigrants to Hawai'i had sailed, probably was applied to the beach area beyond Mākua because of the many Japanese fishermen who used it for sport.

Yokohama Bay is the last sandy stretch of shore on the northwestern coast of O'ahu. It is a moderately wide beach situated between two rocky lava points. The eastern point, located just *makai* of the Ka'ena Point Satellite Tracking Station access road, was called Pukano. It was once the site of a fishing shrine with the same name. On the Ka'ena side of Pukano is a small reef that is never covered with sand. It was known as Pu'ōkole. Usually *'ōkole* means anus, but in this instance the name refers to a small anemone whose shape was thought to resemble an anus. The little sea creatures, called *'ōkole,* were plentiful in this area. They adhere to the sides of overhanging rocks at the water's edge and are gathered for food. Pu'ōkole was also a favorite place for catching *pai'ea,* a *limu* crab; *nāholoholo,* a brown crab with white spots; and the common *'a'ama,* the black rock crab.

The beach around the well-known surfing spot in Yokohama Bay, where the middle stream crosses the sand, was called Pū'au. The reason for this name is forgotten now. At one time Pū'au was an excellent *moi* ground, and attracted many fishermen. The eastern end of the beach was known as Kamilomilo, ''the whirling water.'' This area is where the famous ocean cave Kīlauea is supposed to be located. Kīlauea is said to run underground beneath O'ahu and to connect with the cave of Pohukaina in Ka'Ō'io Point at Ka'a'awa on the windward coast.

Yokohama Bay today is part of a state park complex that will remain relatively undeveloped, at least for a while, and eventually will include shorelines on both sides of Ka'ena Point.

Generally, the beach is wide during the summer and narrow during the winter. The foreshore is not made up entirely of sand, but rather is a line of large boulders and smaller beach rock which are exposed when the beach sand is washed. The popular surfing break at Pū'au in the center of the beach is a dangerous spot. The waves break on a shelf of larger rocks and raised reef which have caused many serious injuries and at least one death. The surf is steep and fast, and the bottom conditions are especially hazardous at low tide. When the waves are up the white water comes all the way to shore, creating a dangerous shorebreak, a strong backwash, and very severe rip currents. Loose surfboards washing ashore also pose a danger for inshore swimmers. Recreational swimmers should be very cautious unless the ocean is completely calm. This very popular park is entirely undeveloped. There are no lifeguards in the area. Ka'ena Point, the westernmost tip of O'ahu, is visible from the entire Keawa'ula shoreline.

In addition to the dangers in the sand beach section of Keawa'ula, those of one other nearby shoreline should be mentioned. Kawa'a'ele'ele, ''the black canoe,'' is the next-to-the-last lava point before reaching Yokohama Beach. It is used occasionally by youngsters from the Wai'anae area as a diving and jumping rock. They stand high upon the point and time their jumps to coincide with the waves rushing into the narrow cove below them. As easy as the sport seems to be, it can be very dangerous for anyone not familiar with the wave movements and the special timing needed in making a successful jump. A similar problem exists at Makapu'u Beach Park. Experienced bodysurfers enter the water by standing on the lava point below the comfort station and diving into a wave washing across the sharp rocks. Inexperienced persons attempting to imitate these entries have suffered broken bones and severe lacerations, even though the height of the rocks is not very great. Kawa'a'ele'ele does not by any means attract the crowds that Makapu'u does, but the possibility of getting hurt there is just as great.

The Beaches of Waialua District

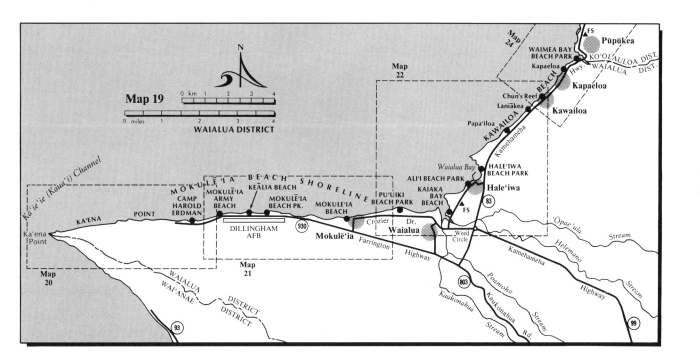

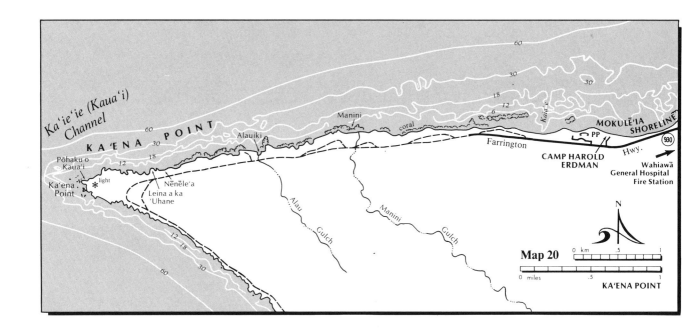

Map 20
0 km .5 1
0 miles .5 1
KA'ENA POINT

Ka'ena Point

Farrington Highway
(westernmost tip of O'ahu)

 F: 1 unmanned Coast Guard lighthouse; roadside parking
LG: none
EP: Mokulē'ia Beach Park, 68–919 Farrington Highway
PP: Camp Erdman, Farrington Highway
FS: 66–420 Hale'iwa Road, Waialua
 H: Wahiawā General Hospital, 128 Lehua Street
SS: Farrington Highway, Waialua or Hale'iwa towns
WA: diving (limited); shorecasting
WC: currents dangerous all year; biggest waves on O'ahu during big winter surf; the break on the Wai'anae side of the point has never been surfed; entire shoreline in point area is fronted by beachrock and reef
PA: unlimited

The dry and barren lands of Ka'ena Point make up the westernmost extremity of O'ahu. Ka'ena means "red hot" or "glowing," and probably refers to the spectacular sunsets so commonly seen over the vast expanse of waters surrounding the point. Ka'ena also is the name of a brother of Pele, the goddess of fire. The Ka'ena area once supported several *heiau*, a number of fishing shrines, and a small fishing village called Nēnēle'a. The

entire region was steeped in legend, three of the most well-known being the stories of Pōhaku o Kaua'i, Kākā-he'e, and Ka Leina a ka 'Uhane.

At Ka'ena Point, the demigod Maui attempted to bring together the islands of O'ahu and Kaua'i. Taking his wonderful hook, *mana i ka lani,* "divine power of heaven," (which had raised so many other islands from the sea), he cast it across the Ka'ie'ie Waho Channel and snagged Kaua'i, visible from Ka'ena on clear days. Giving a tremendous tug, Maui pulled loose only a huge boulder, which fell into the waters very close to the present lighthouse at Ka'ena. The rock is still known as Pōhaku o Kaua'i, "the stone from Kaua'i." The towline Maui used was made of 'ie'ie root, so the channel connecting the two separated parts of Kaua'i, the isle and the rock, was called Ka'ie'ie Waho, "the outer 'ie'ie."

Pi'ikoi, another demigod in many Hawaiian legends, was especially well known for his feats in archery. On one occasion Alāla, Pi'ikoi's father, decided to visit his daughter in Mānoa Valley, so he and Pi'ikoi sailed for O'ahu from their home on Kaua'i. Midway across the channel the great squid god Kākāhe'e tried to seize them. In the ensuing battle Kākāheʻe was killed near Lae o Kaʻena. To commemorate the confrontation, the land inshore was called Kākāheʻe.

Kaʻena was best known as the main place on Oʻahu from where souls departed this earth. When a person lay on his deathbed, his soul left the body and wandered about. If all earthly obligations had been fulfilled, the soul eventually found its way to Kaʻena. There it was taken by minor gods and at that moment actual death came to the individual's body. The exact place at Kaʻena was called Ka Leina a ka ʻUhane, "the soul's leap." Located on the Mokuleʻia side of the point, the place was known also to railroad men as "White Rock," for the overhanging mass of limestone lying between the tracks and the sea.

The sea cliffs on the Mokuleʻia side of Kaʻena Point were called Nēneleʻa. Fishermen attracted to the point to catch the fish, present in abundance in the deep off-shore waters, built a small village that they named Nēne-leʻa. On calm days their canoes were launched and brought ashore over the rocks.

The entire Kaʻena shoreline is edged by lava and reef. Almost always the waters around the point are turbulent, and even on seemingly calm days the offshore currents are very powerful. There are no sand beaches anywhere near the point, the only sandy region being the dunes around the lighthouse. There are several small, partly protected coves near the point where determined people can go into the water to get wet when the ocean is not rough, but these inlets cannot accommodate recreational swimming. During the winter months, when a big north swell is running, Lae o Kaʻena has the largest, most perfectly shaped big waves found anywhere in Hawaiʻi. The break, situated on the Keawaʻula side of the point, has never been ridden, or even attempted, although among island surfers there has been a great deal of speculation on the possibility of making such an attempt. The waves, which reach average heights of thirty to forty feet, are utterly awe-inspiring.

Mokuleʻia Beach Shoreline

Mokuleʻia Beach is the general name given to the six-mile stretch of shoreline that runs approximately from Camp Erdman to Puʻuiki. Although the beach passes through four land divisions in the Waialua district, Kaʻena, Keālia, Kawaihāpai, and Mokuleʻia, it is known only by the name of Mokuleʻia, the longest, widest, and most populated section. The first beach lot subdivision in the Waialua district was established at Mokuleʻia, and soon the shoreline of the entire district was known by this name, especially among people who lived in Honolulu. Very few people realize that the land division of Mokuleʻia includes only one portion of the long beach.

Camp Harold Erdman

YMCA camp; Farrington Highway, Kaʻena

 F: extensive private camping facilities: swimming pool, tennis courts, cabins
LG: service provided by volunteers
EP: Mokuleʻia Beach Park
PP: on the premises
FS: 66–420 Haleʻiwa Road, Waialua
 H: Wahiawā General Hospital, 128 Lehua Street
SS: Waialua or Haleʻiwa towns
WA: diving; snorkeling; swimming
WC: strong currents from October through April; generally calm during summer
PA: limited to YMCA use
AI: most well-known camp facility on Oʻahu

To residents of Oʻahu probably the best-known site on Mokuleʻia Beach is Camp Erdman, located in Kaʻena. Harold Randolph Erdman, for whom the camp is named, was born of missionary parents in Kobe, Japan, in 1905. His mother was born in Hawaiʻi, and when the family returned to the islands Harold began his formal education. After graduating from college on the mainland, he returned to Hawaiʻi in 1928 and was employed by the Oʻahu Railway and Land Company. A member of the Oʻahu polo team, Harold was killed in a fall from a horse in Kapiʻolani Park during the summer of 1931. Oʻahu's polo matches were moved from Kapiʻolani Park to Mokuleʻia in 1964.

Before Erdman's fatal accident, the directors of the local YMCA had long been trying to establish a permanent camping facility on Oʻahu. They had leased a small tract of beach-front property in Kaʻena from Walter Dillingham for one dollar a year, and had obtained substantial donations from other *kamaʻāina* families for the facilities and related equipment. Camp Mokulēʻia was first used in 1926. Soon after Harold's death the problem of establishing a permanent site was resolved: Marion Dillingham Erdman, Harold's mother, and Mary Dillingham Frear, her sister (as well as Walter's) wrote a letter to the officers of the Honolulu YMCA, expressing the wish to have Camp Mokulēʻia renamed in memory of Harold. They also declared that they would assist the YMCA to achieve ownership of the camp. In February of 1932, Camp Harold Randolph Erdman was formally dedicated.

During World War II, the campsite was leased by the 14th Naval District as a rest and recreation center for officers, and camping was suspended for YMCA members from 1943 to 1946. When the facilities were reopened after the war, islanders again began to frequent the area. Today Camp Erdman is heavily used, not only as a summer camp for children, but also as a year-round center for leadership training, retreats, conferences, and similar activities.

Mokulēʻia Army Beach

Farrington Highway, Kaʻena
(across from Dillingham Airfield)

  F: 3 lifeguard towers; 1 comfort station; 1 gravel parking lot
LG: service provided by military personnel
EP: Mokulēʻia Beach Park, 68–919 Farrington Highway
PP: Camp Erdman
FS: 66–420 Haleʻiwa Road, Waialua
  H: Military: Tripler Army Medical Center, Jarrett White Road (off Moanalua Road); Civilian: Wahiawā General Hospital, 128 Lehua Street
SS: Waialua or Haleʻiwa towns
WA: diving; swimming
WC: dangerous currents from October through April, especially when surf is big; long sand beach
PA: facilities limited to military personnel

The Kaʻena section of Mokulēʻia Beach also includes the part known as Mokulēʻia Army Beach. This shoreline recreational facility for the armed forces had been located in Haleʻiwa, but when the old lease expired in June 1970 the present site was acquired on an Air Force permit which began in July 1970.

Camp Erdman marks the end of the improved road

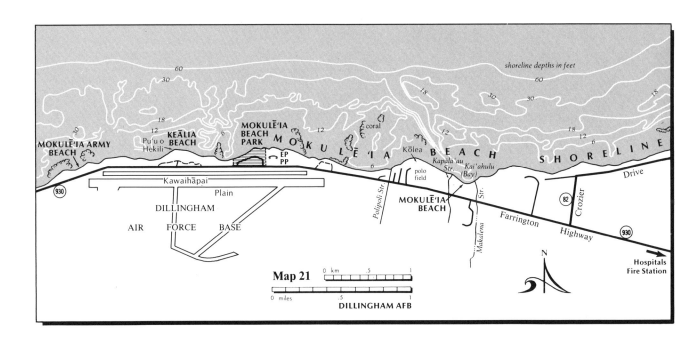

Map 21

DILLINGHAM AFB

from Haleʻiwa, the end of the sand beach, and also the end of the fringing reef. The Hawaiian name of this area is Kaiaʻe. The shoreline from Camp Erdman around Kaʻena Point to Yokohama Bay is rocky, with the deep and open ocean immediately offshore. The sandy beach areas that include Camp Erdman and Mokuléʻia Army Beach are the widest and cleanest sections of the entire Mokuléʻia stretch. These areas, however, are exposed to very severe rip currents and alongshore currents during the winter months, especially when the surf is up. The offshore reef is broken and affords little protection to the beach inshore. Both Camp Erdman and Mokuléʻia Army Beach provide water safety service for the personnel under their charge, but the unsupervised general public is advised to be very cautious: over the years, this particular section of Mokuléʻia Beach has been the scene of many serious and fatal swimming incidents.

Keālia Beach

Farrington Highway, Keālia

  F: none; roadside parking along Farrington Highway
LG: none
 EP: Mokuléʻia Beach Park, 68–919 Farrington Highway
 PP: Camp Erdman or Mokuléʻia Beach Park, 68–919 Farrington Highway
 FS: 66–420 Haleʻiwa Road, Waialua
  H: Wahiawā General Hospital, 128 Lehua Street
 SS: Waialua or Haleʻiwa towns
WA: diving; swimming; shorecasting
WC: strong currents from October through April
 PA: unlimited

Keālia means "the salt bed," or a "self-encrusted area," but if there was a specific reason for applying the name to this place it is now unknown. The most popular section of the beach is the Puʻu o Hekili area, the site of a former fishing shrine. The wide sand beach here is reached by following any of a number of unimproved roads through the brush to the shoreline. The area is frequented by fishermen and occasionally by campers.

For recreational swimming, the shoreline is relatively safe on calm days, but even then sometimes the alongshore currents are insistent. During the winter, when the surf is big, the offshore reef provides little protection for the beach, so extreme caution should be observed before any water activity is considered.

Mokuléʻia Beach Park

68–919 Farrington Highway, Kawaihāpai

  F: 1 comfort station; cooking stands and picnic tables; children's play apparatus; 65 parking stalls
LG: none
 EP: in park area
 PP: in park area
 FS: 66–420 Haleʻiwa Road, Waialua
  H: Wahiawā General Hospital, 128 Lehua Street
 SS: Waialua or Haleʻiwa towns
WA: diving; shore casting; swimming
WC: dangerous currents from October through April, especially when surf is big; ocean bottom is a combination of coral patches and sand pockets
 PA: unlimited

In ancient times the plains of Kawaihāpai, "the lifted water," were thickly populated with Hawaiian fishermen. The area today is comparatively deserted except for Dillingham Air Field, a small U.S. Air Force landing strip, the major portion of which is located in Kawaihāpai. The many ironwood trees found along the shoreline, as well as most of those growing throughout the rest of the Waialua district, were planted as windbreaks to protect the sugarcane fields that once extended along this coast.

The major attraction in Kawaihāpai is Mokuléʻia Beach Park, the only developed public portion of the entire stretch of beach. The twelve-acre park has a comfort station, a large grassy playground, and picnic facilities. It attracts many campers and fishermen. The beach fronting the park lies on the leeward side of a sandy point. It is moderately wide, but steep, and is somewhat protected by the broken offshore reef. There are several sand pockets at the water's edge where inshore swimming is safe, but only on calm days. All too often the currents in this region are strong, especially when the tides are changing or during the winter, when the surf is up.

Mokulē'ia Beach Park. Family members hunt shells and other treasures in the high-tide debris line on a day overcast by the ocean's spray. This region of the Waialua district once housed a large Hawaiian fishing community, but today is sparsely populated.

Mokulē'ia Beach

Farrington Highway, Mokulē'ia

  F: none; roadside parking along Farrington Highway
LG: none
 EP: Mokulē'ia Beach Park
 PP: Mokulē'ia Beach Park; Waialua or Hale'iwa towns
 FS: 66–420 Hale'iwa Road, Waialua
  H: Wahiawā General Hospital, 128 Lehua Street
 SS: Waialua or Hale'iwa towns
WA: diving; shorecasting; swimming; beachcombing

WC: dangerous currents from October through April, especially when surf is big
 PA: follow shoreline from Mokulē'ia Beach Park

Mokulē'ia is most commonly translated as "district of abundance," probably referring to the time when this large land division in the district of Waialua easily supported several substantial Hawaiian settlements. *Mokulē'ia* is also another name for a youthful stage of the *kāhala,* the amberjack fish. A little-known fact about the area is that it once housed a school for the Hawaiian art of *lua,* a semireligious form of self-defense. During the 1840s the school was suppressed, along with all related institutions throughout the islands. Knowledge of the art gradually diminished to the point where today very few individuals know anything at all about the *lua,* and even fewer are willing to talk about it.

A form of *lua* was practiced by almost all groups of the widespread Polynesian race, from the Maoris in New Zealand, through the Tongans, Samoans, and Tahitians, to the people of Hawai'i. All the systems were similar: an opponent's strength was used against him in the art of resistance.

Ku'i-a-lua was the patron god of Hawaiian *lua* fighters. Ku'i means "to strike" or "to injure," so Ku'i-a-lua can be translated as the *lua* strike style. *Ku'i,* however, also means "to join," and *lua* also means "two." According to one authority, the alternate definition of these words, "the joining of two," gives an insight into the truest objective of the art. The Hawaiians recognized the spiritual and physical duality of man, and the *lua* in its highest form was an attempt to attain harmony within this duality. This purpose was accomplished by participating in self-defense exercises, breathing exercises, proper diet, chanting, and a study of the *hula* to develop rhythm and coordination. Students also were given intensive instruction in the anatomy and physiology of the human body. The *lua* initially was a defensive art, not an aggressive one, as is popularly believed. The art was so highly developed that, when it was used, it could inflict every type of bodily damage imaginable, including death. The most complete form of *lua* was taught only to the *ali'i* and their immediate families, who served as personal bodyguards to the kings. A version also was taught to the royal women.

King Kalākaua, recognizing the tremendous value of the *lua* system as an aid to individual defense and discipline, attempted to revive the art based on a greater regard for human life. The few people who know any of the *lua* forms today were taught for the most part by students who attended Kalākaua's school.

To help them gain success in war, all Hawaiian men were given some instruction in the basic defense forms of the *lua.* In addition to the technique of the *lua,* the curriculum of the Mokulē'ia school also included training in spear throwing, wrestling, swimming, and gymnastics, in order to make a fighter's body strong and effective.

The section of Mokulē'ia Beach that actually lies in the land division of Mokulē'ia was the first and largest shoreline residential area to be developed in western Waialua. The popularity of this section and its subsequent growth led to the entire coast, from Camp Erdman to Pu'uiki, being called Mokulē'ia Beach.

The part of Mokulē'ia, where the first of the three streams meets the ocean was called Polipoli. *Polipoli,* those soft, porous stones used for polishing wood surfaces and as sinkers for squid lures, were found in the region. East of Polipoli, now fronting the Mokulē'ia Beach Colony, was the site of a fishing shrine called Kōlea, after the Pacific golden plover. In later years Japanese shorecasters also erected their own shrine in the vicinity, which was similar in purpose to the statue of O-Jizōsan at Hālona Point near Koko Crater.

The large bay located *makai* of the Mokulē'ia Polo Field was called Kai'ahulu, "the foamy sea." Two streams flow into Kai'ahulu, Kapālā'au, "the wooden fence," and Makalena, meaning "to look about in wonder or admiration." Near the sandy point that forms the eastern boundary of Kai'ahulu is a recreational area for the business firm of Castle and Cooke. The land was bequeathed to the company by Edward Tenney, an employee for many years, and was set aside for the use of Castle and Cooke's personnel. Executives of the company cannot use the facilities there.

The entire shoreline of Mokulē'ia Beach situated within the land division of Mokulē'ia is private property, and no convenient public access is available. The inshore waters here, as at the rest of the beach, are relatively safe when the ocean is calm, but are exposed to strong currents during the winter months, especially when there is big surf along the North Shore.

Pu'uiki Beach Park
Waialua Beach Road, Mokulē'ia

F: 1 bathhouse/pavilion; picnic area; 1 unmarked parking
   lot
LG: service provided by volunteers

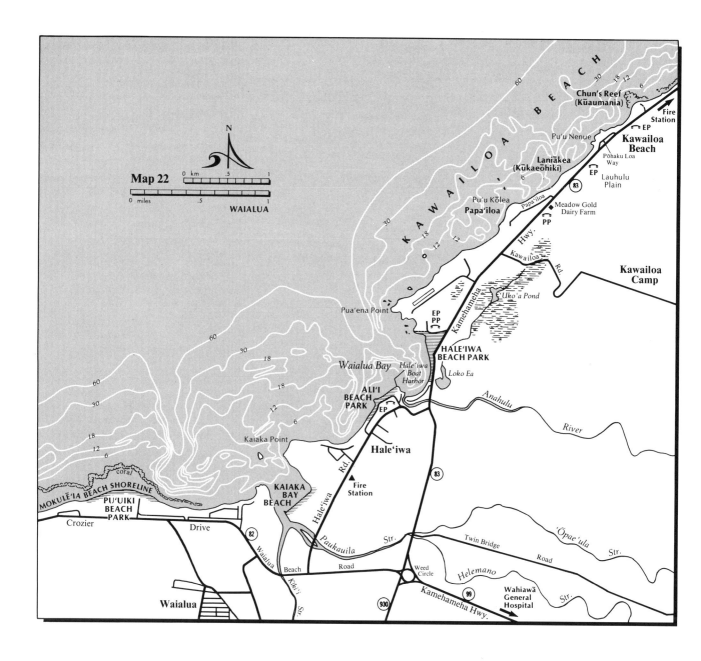

Map 22

WAIALUA

KAWAILOA BEACH

Chun's Reef
(Kūaumania)

Fire
Station

Pu'u Nenue

EP

Kawailoa
Beach

Laniākea
(Kūkaeōhiki)

Pōhaku Loa
Way

EP

Lauhulu
Plain

Papa'iloa

Pu'u Kōlea

Papa'iloa

Meadow Gold
Dairy Farm

PP

Kawailoa
Rd.

Kawailoa
Camp

Pua'ena Point

'Uko'a Pond

Kamehameha

EP
PP

HALE'IWA
BEACH PARK

Waialua Bay

Hale'iwa
Boat
Harbor

Loko Ea

Anahulu

ALI'I
BEACH
PARK

EP

River

Kaiaka Point

Hale'iwa

83

MOKULĒ'IA BEACH SHORELINE

coral

PU'UIKI
BEACH
PARK

Fire
Station

Hale'iwa Rd.

Crozier

Drive

82

Waialua Beach

Kīki'i Str.

Paukauila Str.

Twin Bridge

Road

'Ōpae'ula Str.

Weed
Circle

Helemano

Road

Waialua

930

99

Kamehameha Hwy.

Wahiawā
General
Hospital

Str.

EP: Waialua Beach Park, Hale'iwa
PP: none
FS: 66–420 Hale'iwa Road, Waialua
 H: Wahiawā General Hospital, 128 Lehua Street
SS: Hale'iwa or Waialua towns
WA: diving; swimming
WC: safe all year except when ocean is extremely rough;

shallow and rocky ocean bottom; shoreline protected by offshore fringing reef
PA: limited to employees of Waialua Plantation

Pu'uiki, "little hill," is situated between Mokulē'ia, and Kaiaka Bay in the land division of Kamananui.

108

Pu'uiki Beach has a relatively steep shore with coarse sand and many pebbles. It is well protected by a fringing reef immediately offshore, but provides only fair recreational swimming. The sea bottom is primarily rocky, with only occasional sand pockets that can easily accommodate swimmers at high tide. The inshore currents can become strong during periods of high surf.

Pu'uiki Beach Park, privately owned, is located on Waialua Beach Road. Maintained by the Waialua Sugar Company for its employees, the beachside facility is not open to the public. There is no convenient access for the general public to any part of Pu'uiki Beach.

Kaiaka Bay

(former site of Fresh Air Camp)
Fresh Air Camp Road, Hale'iwa

F: none
LG: none
EP: Waialua Beach Park, 66–167 Hale'iwa Road
PP: none
FS: 66–420 Hale'iwa Road, Waialua
H: Wahiawā General Hospital, 128 Lehua Street
SS: Kamehameha Highway, Hale'iwa
WA: crabbing; pole fishing; swimming; throw-netting
WC: safe all year; narrow, brown sandy beach that slopes abruptly to deeper bay waters; water almost always murky from river runoff
PA: unlimited

James A. Rath arrived in Honolulu in 1905 and, at the request of the Hawaiian Board of Missions, he took charge of a chapel in Kapālama on Pua Lane. In 1906 Mr. Rath, having realized that there was a great need for an institution to offer educational, recreational, and other social services to the community, disassociated himself from the mission board and formed the Pālama Settlement in Honolulu.

As part of the settlement's program to aid underprivileged children in poorer parts of Honolulu, Mr. Rath took them on camping trips to the windward and north shores of O'ahu. In 1917 he leased from the Bishop Estate eighteen acres of land on the northern point of Kaiaka Bay to form a permanent campsite. Besides a home for the Rath family, carpenters from Pālama built a pavilion, a kitchen, and twelve cottages. At first, Mr.

Rath attempted to bring entire families to the camp, but this plan did not prove to be workable. He decided, instead, to bring out only children, usually fifty or sixty at a time, to whom he taught many basic aspects of ordinary healthful living, such as personal hygiene, in addition to numerous recreational activities.

Mr. Rath named his place "Fresh Air Camp" simply because he wanted to get the Honolulu children into the sunshine and fresh air of the country. Later, stories claiming that the old Hawaiians had believed this region to be especially healthy circulated about the area. These, however, were only unfounded rumors. Before the Fresh Air Camp was built, the Kaiaka Point area was dry and barren, covered only by lantana which was as profuse then as *koa haole* is now. The Waialua Sugar Plantation supplied the equipment to clear the land, and Mr. Rath and other men planted the ironwood trees still plentiful in the area. During the months when children from Honolulu were not using the camp, it was rented by companies in town for employees' picnics and parties. The cabins were also rented to the Waialua community, and the camp's baseball field was the Waialua team's home field for many years. The only evidence of the former campsite today is Fresh Air Camp Road, the access road to the point.

Kaiaka Point was also the site of a balancing rock called Pōhaku o Lana'i, which was said to have floated ashore from the distant land of Kahiki. Pōhaku o Lana-'i, obvious among all the other rocks in the immediate vicinity, was a single boulder situated on a somewhat broader base of limestone.

Kaiaka, "shadowy sea," is a small, pretty bay located on the outskirts of Hale'iwa. The beach is a narrow strip of shoreline about five hundred yards long. The sand is always brown from the continual flow of silt into the waters of the bay. Two large streams join just to the rear of Kaiaka and empty into the southern portion of the bay. The wave action near shore generally is mild, allowing the silt to accumulate along the shoreline. The bottom drops off rather abruptly immediately offshore. The beach and bay waters are used primarily by children from the neighborhood and by fishermen. Often during the winter, when heavy rains fall in the uplands above Hale'iwa, the entire bay is flooded with very muddy water. The Kaiaka Point area is presently an undeveloped public park.

Ali'i Beach Park

(part of Waialua Beach)
66–167 Hale'iwa Road, Hale'iwa

F: 1 comfort station; 1 lifeguard tower; 88 parking stalls; 1 boat ramp in nearby small boat harbor

LG: service provided by City and County on weekends and holidays all year and daily throughout the summer

EP: in park

PP: Hale'iwa Road

FS: 66 420 Hale'iwa Road, Waialua

H: Wahiawā General Hospital, 128 Lehua Street

SS: Kamehameha Highway, Hale'iwa

WA: diving; pole fishing; board surfing; swimming

WC: dangerous currents and surf from October through April; shallow inshore ocean bottom made up of coral reef with sand pockets; abrupt drop from reef shelf in western end of park into deep channel

PA: unlimited

The area generally referred to as Waialua Beach is situated between Kaiaka and Kūpaoa points. The southern half of the beach toward Kaiaka is the better section for recreational swimming. Here there is a small bay fairly well protected by the offshore reef. A large sand-filled channel provides excellent swimming grounds. This area was the former site of the Hale'iwa Army Beach before it was moved to the Ka'ena section of Mokulē'ia Beach.

The northern half of the beach, centering around Kūpaoa Point, includes the twenty-acre Ali'i Beach Park stretching from Ka'ena Point to Waimea Bay. The park is located on the *makai* side of Hale'iwa town.

On August 5, 1899, the Hale'iwa Hotel opened. It was located just to the rear of the present beach park, on the site now occupied by the Sea View Inn. The hotel's planners, or perhaps its staff, probably gave the name "Ali'i Beach" to the shoreline fronting the hotel.

Christine A. Takata

Ali'i Beach Park. A family fishes off the rocky point in the middle of the park. The surfing break offshore from these rocks, known simply as "Hale'iwa," is one of the most popular on the North Shore. The Wai'anae Mountain Range is in the background.

110

No references to this name can be traced beyond the hotel's founding.

The primary attraction of Aliʻi Beach is its surfing waves. Surfers frequented the area long before the beach was ever developed, and to them the break was simply known as Haleʻiwa. Aliʻi or Haleʻiwa has some of the best waves on the North Shore, but the break is very dangerous. The inside lineup breaks on an extremely shallow reef shelf that becomes even shallower as waves pass over it toward the shore. The area is especially hazardous at low tide. Surfing accidents have caused numerous injuries and at least one fatality. Swimming shoreward of the surfing area generally is safe in the shallower regions at the Kaʻena side of the beach, even when the waves are big. The deeper waters around the breakwater, however, often have very strong rip currents that run seaward into Waialua Bay. Surfers often find themselves swimming out to sea after their loose boards. City and County lifeguard service is provided throughout the summer and on weekends and holidays during the winter.

Haleʻiwa Beach Park

(formerly Māeaea)
62–449 Kamehameha Highway, Haleʻiwa

F: 1 comfort station/pavilion; 1 food and beverage concession; 2 basketball courts; 2 volleyball courts; 1 baseball field; 2 softball fields; 1 lifeguard tower; 97 parking stalls
LG: service provided by City and County daily from June through August
EP: in park area
PP: in park area
FS: 66–420 Haleʻiwa Road, Waialua
H: Wahiawā General Hospital, 128 Lehua Street
SS: Kamehameha Highway, Haleʻiwa
WA: pole fishing; board surfing (offshore at Puaʻena Point); swimming
WC: safe all year; shallow, sandy bottom
PA: unlimited

During the 1830s, American Protestant missionaries began establishing stations in the rural areas of Oʻahu. The first such station was begun in July 1832 by John S.

Emerson and his wife, who built their mission home on the banks of the Anahulu Stream in the district of Waialua. Emerson's area of responsibility extended initially from Waiʻanae on the west to Kaʻaʻawa on the east coast, a vast region which he covered on horseback. The people from Waiʻanae who traveled to Waialua to attend services used a trail that ran over the mountains from the head of Mākaha Valley. In 1834, Emerson established a school in Waialua. During that same year other mission stations were set up in Kāneʻohe, Koʻolauloa, and Waiawa in ʻEwa. Emerson continued his missionary work until 1864, when he retired from his pastorate because of ill health. He died at his home on the Anahulu Stream in 1867.

When John Emerson resigned, a young man named Orramel Hinckly Gulick was appointed to succeed him. Earlier, in 1860, Gulick had opened a family school on Printer's Lane in Honolulu, with eleven Hawaiian girls for students. Two years later he was stationed at Waiʻōhinu on the Big Island, where he was principal of the Kaʻu Female Seminary. Then in 1865 Gulick was sent to Waialua on Oʻahu, to head the Waialua Female Seminary, which was built just across the river from the Emerson mission homestead. Students in the seminary (the common name at the time for a secondary school) were taught entirely in Hawaiian. The school was supported completely by the Hawaiian Evangelical Association until 1872, when the kingdom's Board of Education allotted the institution $1500. In 1869 the school was temporarily discontinued because of the illness of the founder, the Reverend Gulick, but it reopened in 1870 under a new principal, Miss Mary Green. The seminary continued for twelve more years before finally closing. The failing health of Miss Green, the deteriorating condition of the dormitory building, and community difficulties all contributed to the demise of the school.

The importance of the missionaries and of the Waialua Female Seminary to the present community stems from the name of the school's two-story dormitory: it was called Haleʻiwa, "house of the frigate bird." On August 5, 1899, a beautiful new hotel opened across the river from the ruins of the former seminary. Adopting the name of the school, the owners appropriately called it the Haleʻiwa Hotel. For many years it was a flourishing resort of the O.R. & L. Co.'s (Oʻahu Railway and

111

Haleʻiwa Beach Park. A lone beachcomber walks through the rubble, seaweed, and litter strewn at the water's edge by unusually high surf the day before. At the far end of the beach are the breakwaters that mark the Haleʻiwa Boat Harbor, the only boat harbor on Oʻahu's North Shore.

Land Company's) train line, even though Hawaiians felt the hotel would never bring luck to its owner because it was constructed on the ruins of Kamani *heiau*. Water for the hotel was supplied from Kawaipūʻolu, a spring adjacent to the nearby Emerson homestead. Curtis P. Iʻaukea, who had served as royal chamberlain to the Kalākauas at ʻIolani Palace, was the hotel's first manager.

In 1943 the run-down hotel and its beach were acquired as a recreational facility for army officers, and in 1947 it was purchased by the Army for $84,000, for use as a training area as well. Today the hotel site, no longer owned by the Army, is occupied by the well-known Sea View Inn. During the height of its popularity with islanders, the hotel made the name of Haleʻiwa famous. Eventually the community surrounding the resort was called Haleʻiwa.

Over the years there has been a great deal of speculation on the correct interpretation of Haleʻiwa, "house of the frigate bird." One theory is that the *ʻiwa* builds a very beautiful nest, the name, therefore, being symbolic of a beautiful home. This interpretation sounds reasonable, but it is not based upon fact: the nest of the *ʻiwa*, like that of most seabirds, is simply a crude, unattractive pile of sticks. Another suggestion is that the *ʻiwa* once nested in the area, but this, too, is unlikely. The

112

wing span of the adult *'iwa* generally is about seven feet, making it impossible for the birds to take off unless they are standing on a cliff or a high rocky place where they can launch themselves into the wind. The only known area around O'ahu where the *'iwa* lands is on Moku Manu, an islet off Mōkapu.

Besides its usual English name, the frigate or man o'war bird, the *'iwa* is also known locally as the storm bird. Often it will approach land when the sea suddenly becomes stormy. At such times many *'iwa* can be seen gliding effortlessly above the shoreline areas. Their very light bodies and their great wing spread allow the birds to stay aloft almost indefinitely with no apparent effort. Probably it was the grace, and the beauty, of the *'iwa* in flight that appealed to the early missionaries and gave rise to the name Hale'iwa. In the light of the seminary's basic moral teachings, among them the commandment "thou shalt not steal," it is a bit amusing to note that among Hawaiians the term *'iwa* was a slang expression for thief. The birds occasionally obtain their food by robbing boobies returning to their breeding colonies. The *'iwa* forces the booby to disgorge its catch in flight and seizes the spoils in midair, or picks it off the ocean's surface.

Hale'iwa Beach Park was formally dedicated in October 1939 by David Akana, then acting mayor of Honolulu, as Waialua Beach Park, but residents of the area preferred to use the name Hale'iwa. In 1948 the name was changed officially to Hale'iwa Beach Park. The old name for the beach fronting the park was Māeaea, "stench." When 'Elani, a chief of the area, died, his body was placed on a ledge near Pua'ena Point and allowed to decompose. The odor came to the sands of Hale'iwa, so the shoreline was named Māeaea.

The present thirteen-acre beach park has many recreational facilities, including a long, safe, and sandy swimming beach. There are no particularly hazardous water conditions in the inshore areas. City and County lifeguard service is provided daily during the summer.

Kawailoa Beach

The shoreline comprising Kawailoa Beach extends from Pua'ena Point just north of Hale'iwa Beach Park all the way to the tiny Wānanapaoa Islands in Waimea Bay. Kawailoa means "the long water" and refers to the stream in this land division, which was thought to be the longest stream on O'ahu. At one time the lands of Kawailoa were the property of Princess Victoria Kamamalu, the sister of Kamehameha IV and Kamehameha V.

Kawailoa Beach is several miles long and includes about half of the famous surfing areas on O'ahu's North Shore. It consists of stretches of sandy beach interrupted by outcroppings of lava and reef rock. The beach changes with the seasons and experiences up to forty feet of erosion in some sections during the winter months. Because of the great length of the beach, its proper name is not much used except on official maps. Since the rise of interest in board surfing throughout the area that began in the late 1950s, the different sections of the beach have become better known by the names given to the corresponding offshore surfing breaks, such as Chun's Reef, Laniākea, and so on.

Papa'iloa Beach
fronting Papa'iloa Road

  F: none; roadside parking along Kamehameha Highway at Laniākea Beach area
LG: none
 EP: pole #132, Kamehameha Highway at Laniākea Beach
 PP: Meadow Gold Dairy Farm, 61–657 Kamehameha Highway
 FS: 59–719 Kamehameha Highway, Sunset Beach
  H: Wahiawā General Hospital, 128 Lehua Street
WA: diving; shorecasting; board surfing; swimming
WC: strong currents from October through April, especially when surf is big
 PA: follow shoreline from Laniākea Beach

Papa'iloa, or "long hut," referring to a temporary shack such as is put up near a fishing grounds, is the first section of Kawailoa Beach that offers a place suitable for swimming. Papa'iloa takes its name from a nearby road. The shoreline from Pua'ena Point to Papa'iloa is primarily rocky, and is ill suited for recreational activity except for diving on calm days. The wide sandy point at

Papa'iloa Beach. Two surfers make their way back up the beach following a long swim after their surfboards, carried away by the well-known Laniākea rip current, which often carries off surfers as well as their boards. Experienced surfers and Honolulu Fire Department personnel make many rescues in this area every year.

the end of Papa'iloa Road was called Pu'u Kōlea, "hill of the golden plover." The beach and reef fronting the entire length of Papa'iloa Road were known as Kaha'a-kolu, "the three marks." The significance of this name is unknown. Pu'u Kōlea and Kaha'akolu, or Papa'iloa Beach as they are better known, have several good sand pockets where swimming is safe. The reef, however, is broken and low, offering little protection to the inshore areas. As a result the inshore currents are often strong, even on calm days. When the surf is high, the currents are very powerful. The foreshore becomes steep, sometimes creating dangerous backwashes and rip currents.

Laniākea Beach

(formerly Kūkae'ōhiki)

Kamehameha Highway (between Papa'iloa and Pōhaku Loa Way)

 F: none; roadside parking along Kamehameha Highway
LG: none
EP: pole, #132, Kamehameha Highway
PP: Meadow Gold Dairy Farm, 61–657 Kamehameha Highway
FS: 59–719 Kamehameha Highway, Sunset Beach
 H: Wahiawā General Hospital, 128 Lehua Street
SS: Kamehameha Highway, Hale'iwa

Laniākea Beach. This beach that surfers call Laniākea was known to the Hawaiians as Kūkaeōhiki. Laniākea was originally the name of the freshwater springs located on the far side of the lava point in the center of the picture.

WA: diving; shorecasting; board surfing; swimming
WC: strong currents from October through April, especially when surf is big; powerful rip current in channel outside of Lauhulu Bridge; entire shoreline is fronted by beachrock
PA: unlimited

Pu'u Nenue, "hill of the pilot fish or rudder fish," is the wide, rocky lava point seaward of Pōhaku Loa Way. It was so named because in years past the *nenue* were found in abundance in those waters. On the Waimea side of the point there is a small freshwater spring among the rocks at the sea's edge. The spring, which is still flowing, was called Laniākea. A former Honolulu sheriff, one of the first persons to build a house in the Pu'u Nenue area, named his home "Laniākea" after the spring below it. The side of his old residence still displays a sign bearing the name.

When board surfers first began to frequent the North Shore in the late 1950s, the name Laniākea somehow was transferred from its original site at the spring to the surfing break on the Hale'iwa side of Pu'u Nenue. Today Laniākea Beach is the long stretch of shoreline between Papa'iloa Road and Pōhaku Loa Way. The native name for this beach was Kūkae'ōhiki, "excrement of the sand crabs." Such sand pellets can still be found around the large holes the *'ōhiki* dig in the sand when they come ashore at night. The wide plains to the rear of Kūkae'ōhiki were called Lauhulu. This old name is preserved on the bridge at the Hale'iwa end of the beach.

Laniākea is not a particularly good swimming beach. Most of the shoreline is fronted by a low reef, and the offshore bottom is rocky. The only sandy swimming area is near the Lauhulu Bridge. This area is not always

115

safe for swimming because often the alongshore currents are strong, even on calm days. When the surf is high, Laniākea has some of the best waves along the North Shore. During big winter swells, the wide channel on the Hale'iwa side of the break develops a very powerful rip current running straight out to sea. This rip has swept many surfers away from shore and necessitated innumerable rescues. Laniākea is an undeveloped City and County park.

and the name stuck. In earlier times, the wide, sandy point and shallow reef inside the present Chun's Reef were known as Kū'aumania, "inactive sea slug."

Today Chun's Reef is one of the most popular surfing places on the North Shore. Recreational swimming is not particularly good there, because the very shallow reef comes right up to the beach. When the surf is big, the inshore currents can be very strong, generally pulling toward the rocks of Pu'u Nenue.

Chun's Reef Beach
(formerly Kūaumania)
Kamehameha Highway
(Waimea Bay side of Pōhaku Loa Way)

 F: none; roadside parking along Kamehameha Highway
LG: none
EP: pole #142, Kamehameha Highway
PP: Meadow Gold Dairy, 61–657 Kamehameha Highway
FS: 59–719 Kamehameha Highway, Sunset Beach
 H: Wahiawā General Hospital, 128 Lehua Street
SS: Kamehameha Highway, Hale'iwa
WA: diving; board surfing; swimming
WC: strong currents from October through April, especially when surf is big; shallow ocean bottom of coral reef
PA: unlimited

John Chun, a well-known, long-time resident of Hale'iwa, formerly owned a two-story house on Kamehameha Highway across from the old dairy camp at Kawailoa. Mr. Chun's children and others from the neighborhood frequently went surfing in front of the house and at the other breaks in the immediate vicinity. A close family friend, Miss Edna Reese, called the area "Chun's Reef," and the North Shore surfing community soon picked up the name. Formerly the beach and reef fronting Chun's home was called Kūmakani, "to stand against the wind." The general name for the entire surrounding area was Hūkamakani, "the wind whistles or roars," because of a wind peculiar to this area that sometimes blows from the mountains rather than from the ocean as is usually the case.

When mainland surfers began frequenting the North Shore, they mistakenly gave the name "Chun's Reef" to the surfing break on the Waimea side of Pu'u Nenue,

Kapaeloa Beach
(shoreline fronting Kamehameha Highway between Chun's Reef and Waimea Bay)

 F: none; roadside parking along Kamehameha Highway
LG: none
EP: Waimea Bay Beach Park, 61–031 Kamehameha Highway
PP: Waimea Bay Beach Park
FS: 59–917 Kamehameha Highway, Sunset Beach
 H: Wahiawā General Hospital, 128 Lehua Street
SS: Kamehameha Highway, Hale'iwa
WA: diving; board surfing
WC: strong currents from October through April, especially when surf is big; entire shoreline rocky; no sand beach
PA: unlimited

Kapaeloa is the last section of Kawailoa Beach. On the shoreline it stretches from the point of Ka'alaea, past Moku Manu, and ends just before the Wānanapaoa Islands in Waimea Bay. The entire stretch is rocky, with only a few small sand pockets. There are several offshore breaks that board surfers can ride, but possibilities for recreational swimming do not exist. The place is frequented primarily by fishermen and divers.

Waimea Bay Beach Park
61–031 Kamehameha Highway, Waimea

F: 1 comfort station; 1 lifeguard tower; picnic area; 44 parking stalls
LG: service provided by City and County daily all year

EP: in park area
PP: in park area
FS: 59–917 Kamehameha Highway, Sunset Beach
 H: Wahiawā General Hospital, 128 Lehua Street
SS: Kamehameha Highway, Pūpūkea or Paumalū
WA: diving; snorkeling; board surfing; swimming
WC: extremely dangerous rip currents and shorebreak from October through April, especially when surf is big; surfing for experts only as Waimea has biggest ridable waves in Hawai'i
PA: unlimited

Waimea means "reddish water," such as is caused by the erosion of red soil. Like its namesake on Kaua'i, Waimea has the distinction of being the first place on O'ahu where contact was made between foreigners and Hawaiians. After Captain Cook was killed at Kealakekua Bay on February 14, 1779, his two ships, the *Discovery* and the *Resolution,* touched at Waimea, O'ahu, for water on their way to Kaua'i. Cook's officers described the bay as being picturesque, beautiful, well-cultivated, and heavily populated. Some years later, in 1793, Captain Vancouver's store ship, the *Daedalus,* brought the second group of foreigners to Waimea. After anchoring the ship in the bay, a detail rowed ashore in a small boat to search for water. They landed at Kaluahole, the beach at the foot of Kēhu-o-Hapu'u, the bluff on the Hale'iwa side of the bay. While the crew

Christine A. Takata

Waimea Bay. Youngsters at the water's edge watch cautiously as an incoming wave crashes into the receding backwash of another in Waimea's often spectacular shorebreak. Waimea Bay is probably the most famous big-wave-riding area in the world. During the winter months, waves breaking seaward of Waimea Point often reach heights of 20 to 30 feet. The tower of Sts. Peter and Paul Mission rises in the background.

was drawing water from the stream, two of their number were killed in an attack by some Hawaiians who wanted their weapons. Later, at Waikīkī, Vancouver demanded that the murderers be punished. The king of Oʻahu thereupon ordered two Hawaiians to be shot, but no one was certain that they were the actual murderers from Waimea.

A relatively large Hawaiian population lived in Waimea until 1894, when a great flood destroyed many homesites and fields in the valley. After that, people began leaving the area and moving to other parts of Oʻahu. Today no descendants of the old-time residents live anywhere in the valley. The devastating flood of 1894 also washed thousands of tons of mud and silt into the lowlands around the mouth of Waimea River. This deposit of soil gave the sands of the bay a firm foundation, and within a short time the beach had been built up high enough to block the course of the river. Before the great flood, the river flowed uninterruptedly into the ocean and canoes passed freely between ocean and river. Today the river breaks through the barrier beach only following very heavy rains in the mountains above. The well-known waterfall in Waimea Valley was called Waihī, "dripping water," because even when the water level in the river above was very low, a continual trickle flowed over the falls. In former times the river below the falls was much narrower and much cleaner than it is at present. After the flood it was often dammed up for months at a time by the wide sand beach piled up at its mouth. In this way, an excellent fishpond was formed. Awa, ʻoʻopu, and mullet were plentiful in the pond waters. In the old days the lower regions of the valley, as well as the surrounding cliffs, were relatively free of vegetation. This lack of plant life made it possible for voices to echo from cliffs far back into the valley and, of course, in the reverse direction as well. Often children could be heard amusing themselves by calling across the distances. The phenomenon has since disappeared as foreign plants have spread across Waimea's hills and dells.

The beautiful barrier beach at the head of the bay was much wider in the past than it is today. On the Haleʻiwa side of the bay is a high islet, universally known as "the Rock," that many swimmers use as a jumping-off place. Beneath this rock is a fairly large underwater tunnel. In earlier times, when the beach sand covered the bay floor around the rock, it formed a cave out of this tunnel. Fishermen, after laying their nets offshore during calm summer days, would sleep in the cave to insure that they would be back in the water at sunrise. In this way the fish were still fresh when they were taken out of the nets, and the possibility that sharks would steal some of the catch was reduced. Unfortunately, the sands of Waimea were mined extensively for many years until the winter of 1961/62, thereby considerably reducing the natural deposit of sand.

The beach at Waimea was also used as a burial site, as were the numerous caves found all through the valley and in its cliffs. This practice was discouraged, and the last beach burial here was performed in 1938.

The so-called haunted house of Waimea Bay, located on the turn just past the entrance to the road leading into the valley, was built in 1912 by one of the first homesteaders in the area. He never lived in the house, however, because his wife died about the time the building was completed. The house was constructed on the site of a former fishing *heiau* and old burial ground, and that fact gave rise to the many "haunted house" stories told by people living on the North Shore. Some skeptics claim that there are lava tubes beneath the house, and that these fill with water from the ocean when the surf is high. The water washing in and out of these underground tunnels supposedly creates many of the strange noises heard in the vicinity of the house.

Just past the "haunted house," on the *mauka* shoulder of the road, is an inconspicuous tongue of rock. It was called Kaʻahakiʻi and was said to be one of the original boundary markers between the districts of Waialua and Koʻolauloa. When the road was improved in 1930 workmen left the stone untouched, although the earth on either side of it was cut away. The stone can still be seen when the roadside vegetation is cut low.

On the cliffs above Kaʻahakiʻi, a number of sisal plants are growing. They have thick, bluish green, overlapping spiked leaves and very tall central flower stalks. These plants, found scattered throughout the North Shore area, are descendants of those grown in a business endeavor earlier in this century. Sisal leaves provide hemp fibers, used for making ropes, sacking, twine, cable insulation, and sailcloth, and the tall stalks can be used as fencing material. In 1907, the newly organized Hawaiian Fibre Company tried to establish a new industry in Hawai'i, the exportation of sisal hemp. Proceeds from the venture never matched the expectations. The plants escaped the bounds of commerical fields and now grow wild throughout the islands.

Probably the best-known landmark at Waimea is the high tower located just inshore from the northern point of the bay. The tower is one of the remnants of a rock-crushing plant established by C. W. Winstedt. In 1929, Winstedt won the contract to build the section of Kamehameha Highway from Waimea to Kahuku. In 1930 he set up temporary quarry operations to speed his work. Winstedt originally intended to make the Waimea Rock Quarry a permanent facility, but the site was abandoned in 1932 after the road project was completed. Shipping quarried materials out of Waimea Bay by barge would have been impossible during the long months of the huge winter surf, and moving them by truck or train was too expensive. In April 1953 the Catholic mission transformed the storage bins and machine sheds into a church named the Saints Paul and Peter Mission. The lower sheds were converted into a patio and a chapel. Services are performed here by a priest who drives over to Waimea from Saint Michael's Church in Waialua.

Waimea Bay is famous internationally as the home of the biggest ridable surfing waves in the world. Hawaiians called this surf *nalu po'i*. During winter months the waves here provide some of the most exciting and dangerous surf imaginable. When a big swell is running, surfers and spectators from all over O'ahu crowd the shoreline to watch the board riders in those seemingly murderous waves. Besides the break beyond the point, the inner shorebreak also is devastating, sometimes reaching heights of ten to twelve feet. A tremendously strong rip current runs seaward straight out through the middle of the bay. Needless to say, Waimea has been the site of untold numbers of heroic rescues, uncountable surfing injuries, and occasional fatalities. The waters of this bay should not even be approached by the average person if a sizable swell is running. Even extremely experienced surfers think twice before paddling out into that turmoil. To see Waimea during the summer months, when often it is as calm as a swimming pool, unfortunately gives swimmers a confidence which they extend to the winter season. City and County lifeguards are stationed at the beach daily all the year around, to try to insure the safety of incautious and unsuspecting enthusiasts.

The Beaches of Ko'olauloa District

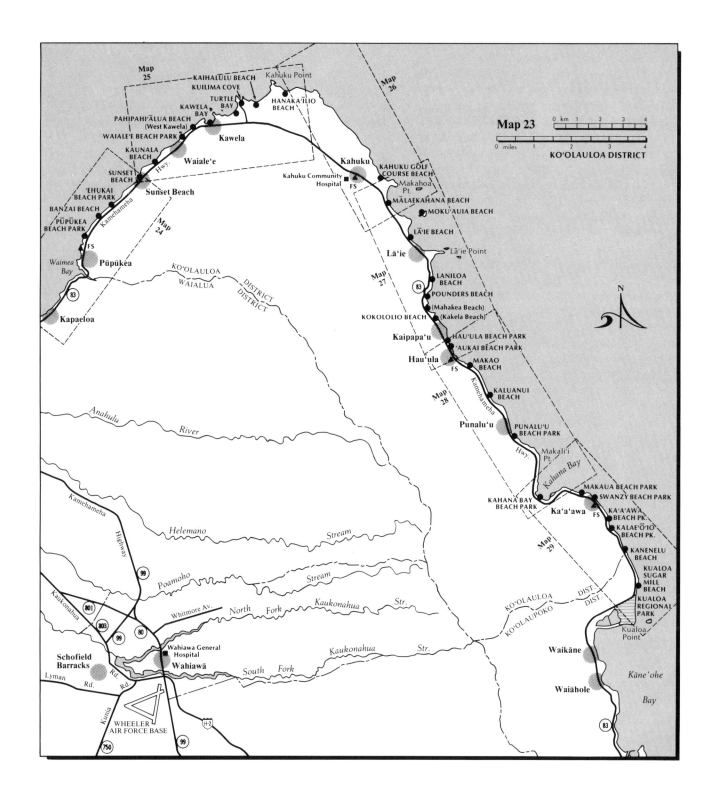

Map 23

KO'OLAULOA DISTRICT

0 km 1 2 3 4

0 miles 1 2 3 4

Map 25

KAIHALULU BEACH
KUILIMA COVE
Kahuku Point
TURTLE BAY
KAWELA BAY
PAHIPAHI'ĀLUA BEACH (West Kawela)
WAIALE'E BEACH PARK
KAUNALA BEACH
SUNSET BEACH
'EHUKAI BEACH PARK
BANZAI BEACH
PŪPŪKEA BEACH PARK

HANAKA'ĪLIO BEACH

Kawela
Waiale'e

Sunset Beach

Kamehameha Hwy.

Map 24

FS

Waimea Bay

83

Pūpūkea

Kapaeloa

Map 26

Kahuku

Kahuku Community Hospital
FS

KAHUKU GOLF COURSE BEACH
Makahoa Pt.
MĀLAEKAHANA BEACH
MOKU'AUIA BEACH
LĀ'IE BEACH

Lā'ie
Lā'ie Point

Map 27

83

LANILOA BEACH
POUNDERS BEACH
(Mahakea Beach)
(Kakela Beach)
KOKOLOLIO BEACH

Kaipapa'u

Hau'ula
FS

HAU'ULA BEACH PARK
'AUKAI BEACH PARK
MAKAO BEACH

KALUANUI BEACH

Kamehameha

Map 28

Punalu'u

PUNALU'U BEACH PARK

Hwy.

Makali'i Pt.

Kahana Bay

KO'OLAULOA DISTRICT
WAIALUA DISTRICT

KAHANA BAY BEACH PARK
Ka'a'awa
FS

MAKAUA BEACH PARK
SWANZY BEACH PARK
KA'A'AWA BEACH PK.
KALAE'Ō'IŌ BEACH PK.

Map 29

KANENELU BEACH

KUALOA SUGAR MILL BEACH

KUALOA REGIONAL PARK

Kualoa Point

KO'OLAULOA DIST.
KO'OLAUPOKO DIST.

N

Anahulu River

Kamehameha Highway

Helemano Stream

Poamoho Stream

Whitmore Av.
North Fork Kaukonahua Str.

Kaukonahua Str.

South Fork

Schofield Barracks

Lyman Rd.
Kunia Rd.

Kaukonahua

801
803
99
80

99

Wahiawa General Hospital
Wahiawā

H-2

WHEELER AIR FORCE BASE
750
99

Waikāne

Waiāhole

Kāne'ohe Bay

83

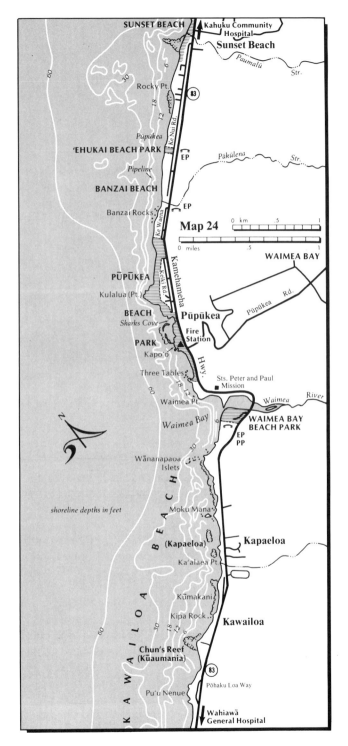

Map 24

0 km   .5   1
0 miles   .5   1

shoreline depths in feet

Pūpūkea Beach Park

59–727 Kamehameha Highway

- **F:** 1 recreation building; 2 comfort stations; 1 basketball court; 1 volleyball court; children's play apparatus; camping facilities; 26 parking stalls
- **LG:** none
- **EP:** in park area
- **PP:** in park area
- **FS:** In middle of park
- **H:** Kahuku Community Hospital, Hospital Road, Kahuku
- **SS:** Kamehameha Highway, Pūpūkea
- **WA:** diving; snorkeling; swimming
- **WC:** extremely dangerous currents and surf from October through April; generally calm during summer; almost entire park is fronted by coral shelf and reef
- **PA:** unlimited

The pecten, or scallop, is a marine bivalve with two thin but tough shells. Most adult scallops live as free swimmers, without attaching themselves to any fixed surface, and occasionally they congregate in large numbers. These sea mollusks have acquired the art of jet propulsion: by opening and closing their valves, they can send a jet of water out through a small groove and glide several feet through the water. Sixteen species have been recorded from the Hawaiian Islands, five of which have white or translucent shells. Most pectens are very small, being less than half an inch in length. Although apparently they live outside the reef, at some times of the year they are found in abundance on certain beaches. One of these places in former times was the Waimea coast on O'ahu's North Shore, and probably it was for these little creatures that Pūpūkea, or "white shell," was named. Pūpūkea is also noted in Hawaiian legend as being the brother of the god Lono.

Pūpūkea Beach Park, comprising eighty acres, is narrow and long, with a primarily rocky shoreline. There are two popular swimming sites within the park, "Three Tables" at the Waimea end, and "Shark's Cove" at the Kahuku end. At one time Three Tables was commonly called Avocado Beach. During the early 1900s, Frederick Haley, Sr., established a 400-acre avocado farm in the Pūpūkea highlands. At the height of its production the farm had more than 11,000 trees, of many varieties. The avocados were hauled in wagons pulled by mules down the steep road along the cliffs to the Maunawai train stop at the foot of the present Pūpūkea Road. Be-

Pūpūkea Beach Park. Heavy winter surf pounds against the outer edge of the large tidal pool in the middle of the beach park. This area, called Kapoʻo by the Hawaiians, is very dangerous when the waves are big.

cause of Haley's venture people soon referred to the shoreline area as "Avocado Beach." Appropriately, the first subdivision established between the train stop and Waimea Bay was called the Avocado Beach Lots.

In 1912, Haley sold most of his farm to Libby, McNeil, and Libby, who used the area for growing pineapples. The fruits produced in the Pūpūkea highlands were judged by many people to be the best of all those grown on Oʻahu. From the highlands to the railroad station at the foot of the cliffs, the pineapples, like the avocados, were hauled in wagons pulled by mules. Because of this use of mule power, the cliffside was called "Jackass Hill."

The name "Three Tables" for the Waimea end of Pūpūkea Beach Park is a relatively recent invention. The small sandy inlet there is protected somewhat by a short stretch of raised coral reef. The flat reef is broken into three sections, thus inspiring the name Three Tables. During the winter months, especially when the surf is heavy, powerful rip currents run between the beach and the tables. These currents have caught many unsuspecting inshore swimmers, necessitating numerous rescues. Three Tables has also been the site of several fatalities, when swimmers have been swept into the surf pounding against the rocks off Waimea Point. Swimming in this area should be restricted to the calmer summer months.

Situated in the middle of Pūpūkea Beach Park is an area once known as Kapoʻo, "the loud," because of the echoing sound from crashing waves. During a large winter swell the reason for this name becomes obvious, as the waves thunder against the rocky shoreline. Just inland from Kapoʻo is the Sunset Beach Fire Station, a primary rescue base for the North Shore. The firemen at this station, as well as those at all other City and County shoreline stations, respond to water emergencies as well

124

as to fires and other critical situations. The rescuers of Sunset Station, working in conjunction with those from Waialua Station, are called upon every year to make innumerable rescues along the North Shore.

"Shark's Cove" is located on the northern side of the Sunset Beach Fire Station. The cove with its adjoining tidal pools is undoubtedly one of the most beautiful sections of shoreline of O'ahu's entire coast. During the summer months Shark's Cove is used heavily by amateur SCUBA divers. These divers, needing a common reference among themselves, gave the inlet its popular name, although sharks are not any more abundant in this area than they are elsewhere around the island.

When the ocean is calm, the cove provides excellent swimming and snorkeling grounds. The large tidal pools nearby attract many children, fishermen, and beachcombers. During the winter, however, the serenity of the area quickly changes. Heavy surf pounds into the cove and washes violently across the tidal pools. At such times there is an extreme danger in even approaching the water's edge.

The park area north of Shark's Cove is primarily a wide, flat, rocky point that was once known as Kulalua. Sitting on Kulalua is a conspicuous group of large lava boulders. These rocks were said to have been followers of Pele, the goddess of the volcano, whom she immortalized by turning them into stone.

Sunset Beach

Late in 1919, a new real estate development called the Pūpūkea-Paumalū Beach Tract opened for sale to the public. It included the entire fetch of beach from Kulalua (in the present Pūpūkea Beach Park) to 'O'opuola Street (on Sunset Point). On the first day, eighty-six lots were purchased. Further sale was postponed until January 8, 1920, when the rest of the lots were sold. In the light of today's real estate prices, it is interesting to note that the total amount received for all lots was $46,124.25. As with many other shoreline tracts in the rural areas of O'ahu, the homes built here originally were essentially country houses for people who lived in Honolulu. Later, this new development, the Pūpūkea-Paumalū Tract, was renamed Sunset Tract because of the spectacular sunsets so often seen there. Naturally, the shoreline was referred to as Sunset Beach.

Sunset Beach, extending well over two miles along the shore, is the longest stretch of wide beach on O'ahu. Outcrops of lava rock and raised sections of reef at the waterline are exposed seasonally. The sand is continuous and the beach averages 200 feet in width. During winter months the beach experiences a severe erosion that often creates a steep, narrow foreshore. During the winter surf season, approximately from September to April, recreational swimming here is extremely dangerous. Strong alongshore currents and powerful rip currents occur almost everywhere. During such times even spectators on the beach must be wary of waves surging across the sand. The Sunset area has been the site of countless rescues and injuries, and of many drownings.

During the summer the beach is at its widest and has a gentle slope to the water's edge. The inshore waters generally are safe for recreational swimming, but even on calm days the alongshore currents can be quite strong. There are very few places where the beach is protected by a reef. The bottom at the water's edge drops off rather abruptly, so children especially must be carefully watched.

With the rise in popularity of board surfing during the late 1950s, many sections of the long beach were given specific names to designate favored surfing sites. Today the name Sunset Beach refers only to one particular surfing spot in Paumalū, although most maps still label the entire stretch of shore as Sunset.

Banzai Beach
(shoreline between Ke Waena and Ke Nui Roads, Pūpūkea)

 F: 1 lifeguard tower; roadside parking available on Ke Waena Road, Ke Nui Road, and on Kamehameha Highway
LG: daily service provided by City and County from June to August and on all weekends throughout the year
EP: on beach at northern end of Ke Waena Road
PP: none
FS: 59–719 Kamehameha Highway, Sunset Beach
 H: Kahuku Community Hospital, Hospital Road, Kahuku
SS: Kamehameha Highway, Pūpūkea or Paumalū
WA: diving (limited); bodysurfing; swimming
WC: extremely dangerous currents and surf from October through April; occasional strong currents during calmer

Banzai Beach. Whitewater boils across the Banzai Rocks located at the intersection of Ke Waena and Ke Nui roads. A "Dangerous Currents" sign posted at the water's edge by a lifeguard warns swimmers to be extremely cautious in this area. The famous surfing spot, the Banzai Pipeline, is located between this beach and ʻEhukai Beach Park. Kaʻena Point, the western end of the Waiʻanae mountain range and the westernmost point on Oʻahu is visible in the background.

summer months; many outcroppings of beachrock along shoreline; ocean bottom slopes quickly to deeper offshore waters
PA: public right-of-way on Ke Waena Road or follow beach from ʻEhukai Beach Park, Ke Nui Road

Banzai is a Japanese word meaning "Ten Thousand Years" that is used on occasions calling for a "Hurrah" or a wish for "Long Life," as, for example, during a toast at a party. It also been used as a war cry. The *banzai* charge, a go-for-broke, death-inviting attack by Japanese soldiers was familiar to many American servicemen in the Pacific Theater during World War II.

During the late 1950s, film maker Bruce Brown produced *Surf Safari,* one of the first movies ever made about surfing. On one especially rough winter day, Brown filmed a bodysurfer riding some tremendous waves on the Kahuku side of the rocks between Ke Waena and Ke Nui roads. During the narration accompanying the film, as the bodysurfer began to drop in on a particularly vicious wave, Brown called out "Banzai!"

much to the amusement of the audience. The name caught on among surfers, and this part of Sunset Beach has been known ever since as Banzai Beach.

The Pipeline

(shoreline fronting Ke Nui Road, approximately 100 yards to the left of ʻEhukai Beach Park)

  F: none
 LG: none
 EP: ʻEhukai Beach Park, 59–337 Ke Nui Road
 PP: none
 FS: 59–719 Kamehameha Highway, Sunset
  H: Kahuku Community Hospital, Hospital Road, Kahuku
 SS: Kamehameha Highway, Paumalū or Pūpūkea
 WA: diving (limited); board surfing; bodysurfing
 WC: extremely dangerous currents and surf from October through April; occasional strong currents during calmer summer months
 PA: from Banzai Beach or ʻEhukai Beach Park

126

Between the Banzai Rocks and 'Ehukai Beach Park is a very shallow coral shelf that extends about fifty yards into the ocean. When a strong winter swell hits the North Shore, particularly one from the west, the waves passing through the deep offshore waters rise up to tremendous heights in a matter of seconds as they strike the shelf. The waves are so steep and so powerful that the thick crest of each one is thrown forward as it breaks, often forming an almost perfect tube. Because of this characteristic of its waves, the break here was named the "Pipeline." It is also known as the "Banzai Pipeline" because of its proximity to Banzai Beach.

The first recorded attempt to ride the Pipeline was made in 1957. Bob Shepard and Bill Coleman paddled out to it and each caught one wave. Both were wiped out and cut up on the shallow reef. After that the break was left pretty much alone until the early 1960s, when Phil Edwards, who was considered by many to be the best surfer in the world, finally rode the Pipeline successfully. From then on the Pipeline has been surfed regularly and occasionally even bodysurfed. The devastating waves, breaking so furiously upon the shallow reef, have caused numerous cases of lacerations and broken bones and several fatalities. Undoubtedly it is one of the most spectacular surfing spots in the world.

'Ehukai Beach Park

59–337 Ke Nui Road, Pūpūkea

 F: 1 comfort station; 1 lifeguard tower; roadside parking along Ke Nui Road
LG: daily service provided by City and County
EP: in park area
PP: none
FS: 59–719 Kamehameha Highway, Sunset
 H: Kahuku Community Hospital, Hospital Road, Kahuku
SS: Kamehameha Highway, Paumalū
WA: diving (limited); board surfing; bodysurfing; paipo board surfing; swimming
WC: extremely dangerous currents and surf from October through April; occasional strong currents during calmer summer months
PA: unlimited
AI: The Pipeline (Banzai-Pipeline), the famous surfing break, is approximately 100 yards to left of beach park; surfing break called Pūpūkea is to right

'Ehukai means "reddish-tinged water," and refers to the trailing spray of a breaking wave. As most surfers know, the sun shining through the spray of a curling wave often gives it a reddish or rainbow hue. Probably for this reason Hawaiians called sea spray 'ehukai.

'Ehukai Beach Park, only one acre in size, is located at 59–337 Ke Nui Road. It is not visible from Kamehameha Highway because of the tall bushes on the medial strip between Ke Nui Road and the highway. This strip was formerly the bed for the O. R. & L. railroad tracks that ran all the way from Honolulu to Kahuku. The park is developed and has a comfort station and a lifeguard tower. Swimming is good during the spring and summer months, but is hazardous during the fall and winter. The park provides the most convenient access for spectators who wish to see the Pipeline in action. The breaks in front of the park are popular with bodysurfers as well as with board surfers. When the beach erodes severely, however, large boulders are exposed, which have figured in several fatalities in the area. 'Ehukai, like the rest of this stretch of shoreline, can be extremely dangerous.

Up along the shore, to the right of 'Ehukai Beach Park is the popular surfing break called Pūpūkea. Besides Sunset itself, Pūpūkea was the first spot in the 1950s to be surfed consistently along this entire length of Sunset Beach. Just past Pūpūkea is a wide projection of the shore known as Rocky Point. It was named that in 1960 by the first Australian surfers to come to the islands. They were also the first to surf and bodysurf in the area. Several public rights-of-way lead to Pūpūkea and Rocky Point. This surfing break called Pūpūkea should not be confused with the beach park of the same name.

Sunset Beach Park

59–100 area of Kamehameha Highway, Paumalū

 F: 1 lifeguard tower; roadside parking along Kamehameha Highway
LG: daily service provided by City and County from June to August and on all weekends throughout the year
EP: in parking area
PP: none
FS: 59–719 Kamehameha Highway, Sunset

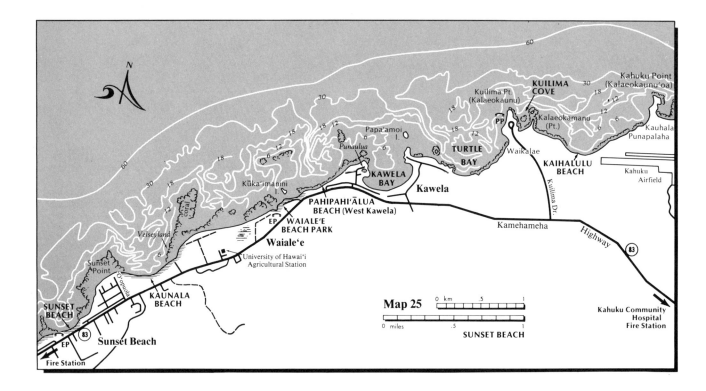

Map 25 SUNSET BEACH

H: Kahuku Community Hospital, Hospital Road, Kahuku
SS: Kamehameha Highway, Paumalū
WA: diving (limited); board surfing; swimming
WC: extremely dangerous currents and surf from October through April; generally calm during summer
PA: unlimited
AI: famous surfing beach

The surfing break and the section of shoreline known to the surfing community as Sunset Beach is located in the land division of Paumalū. At one time a woman lived on Oʻahu who was noted for her ability to catch octopus. One day a chief asked her to go to a particular reef and get some octopus for a *lūʻau* he was planning. Before she entered the water at the designated place, she was met on the beach by an old man. He explained to the woman that there was a limit upon the number of octopus to be caught at this reef, and that she must not catch more than that number. The woman agreed, but once in the water she disregarded the warning, catching more octopus than she could handle. Suddenly, a large shark appeared and attacked the woman, taking off both her legs. Later, when her body was examined, the people saw the marks left by the shark's teeth. They knew that she had been punished by the guardian of the reef. After that incident, the place was named Paumalū, "taken by surprise."

During the late 1940s, some of the better surfers from the Waikīkī area found their way to Sunset. They were the first modern wave riders to surf in this break, although they were still using the old heavy boards made of redwood. One of those surfers was Woody Brown who, with Alfred Kumalae, in 1946 constructed the first modern catamaran based on the old double canoes the Hawaiians used in crossing the Pacific. Other than Brown and his friends, very few surfers rode the waves anywhere on the North Shore. The focus of attention for big wave riding was at Mākaha, especially after the annual Mākaha International Surfing Championships were established in 1952. During the early 1950s, however, one man left the waves of Mākaha and made his

Eric M. Nishida

Sunset Beach. Offshore from the beach park is the famous Sunset surfing break, which provides some of the most dangerous and demanding surfing waves found anywhere on O'ahu's North Shore, and which in recent years has become the annual site of several professional surfing contests. Probably just as well known in this area is the notorious Sunset Rip, an extremely powerful rip current that is the cause of numerous near-drownings every winter.

way to the North Shore. The surfing world had just made the transition from the old redwood surfboards to the new, light-weight, and highly maneuverable balsa boards. Bob Simmons was the first person to ride Sunset with a modern balsa surfboard. Simmons, somewhat of a recluse, was well known among the local residents as "a crazy *haole* surfer," not only because he kept to himself, but because he tackled the tremendous waves all alone. Not until 1957 and 1958 did other riders of the big waves go to the North Shore, to see what had kept Simmons happy there for so long. Surfers like Jose Angel, Buzzy Trent, and Peter Cole, who are still ranked with the best riders of the North Shore's big waves were among the first to experience the thrill of riding the tremendous surf—and to understand the reason for Simmon's affinity for Sunset Beach. Ironically, Simmons was killed in a surfing accident at Wind-and-Sea in La Jolla, California, not in the dangerous waves of O'ahu's North Shore.

Sunset has some of the most spectacular winter surf found anywhere on O'ahu. The outside peaks are steep and shifty, often reaching heights of fifteen to twenty feet. The reef midway to shore, where the bottom is comparatively shallow, is often referred to as Val's Reef for Val Valentine who lived inshore; it has taken its toll of many surfers in the years since the explorers from Waikīkī first brought their boards to this challenging break.

129

On the Waimea side of the surfing break, a large channel runs out to sea where Paumalū Stream once flowed into the ocean. The shorebreak and rip currents in this channel are extremely powerful when a big swell is running. The famous "Sunset rip" has necessitated numerous rescues and has delivered many surfboards to lucky people on Kaua'i or beyond. The only safe time to swim at Sunset is during the calm summer months.

Sunset Point, the housing area and shoreline on the Kahuku side of the surfing beach, is better protected by a wide, fringing reef, but even there the inshore currents are strong when the waves are big. There are two public rights-of-way in the Sunset Point area.

but the reason for this name is unknown. Kaunala Beach is long, curving, and sandy, but along almost its entire length it is lined by sections of reef and rock. The only small pocket where swimming is feasible is found at the mouth of Kaunala Stream, just inside the Velzyland surfbreak. The rest of the offshore bottom is rocky. The area attracts beachcombers and fishermen in addition to surfers. The surf at Velzyland breaks on a very shallow reef shelf that has taken its toll of both surfers and their boards. The currents are strong when the surf is big. There is no convenient public access to the beach other than the right-of-way at the end of 'O'opuola Street on Sunset Point. Velzyland is the last in the line of famous surfing breaks on O'ahu's North Shore.

Kaunala Beach

(offshore surfing break called Velzyland)
58–100 area of Kamehameha Highway, Kaunala

F: none; parking available at end of 'O'opuola Street, Sunset Point
LG: none
EP: end of 'O'opuola Street, Sunset Point
PP: none
FS: 59–719 Kamehameha Highway, Sunset
H: Kahuku Community Hospital, Hospital Road, Kahuku
SS: Kamehameha Highway, Paumalū
WA: beachcombing; diving; board surfing; swimming
WC: dangerous currents and surf from October through April; occasional strong currents during calmer summer months; almost entire shoreline is fronted by beachrock and reef
PA: public right-of-way at end of 'O'opuola Street, Sunset Point

During the early 1960s, Dale Velzy, one of the first commercial manufacturers of surfboards in California, sponsored the visit of a group of surfers to Hawai'i to make a promotional film. Heading the project was Bruce Brown, a well-known producer of surfing movies. One day, when no waves could be found at any of the regular spots on the North Shore, Brown and his crew went exploring. They located some surf just past Sunset Point, in the land division of Kaunala. Recognizing the advertising potential of this unnamed break, they called it "Velzyland" after their sponsor. The movie they made was entitled *Slippery When Wet*.

Kaunala means "the plaiting," or "the weaving,"

Waiale'e Beach Park

58–100 area of Kamehameha Highway, Waiale'e

F: none; roadside parking along secondary road paralleling beach
LG: none
EP: in park area
PP: none
FS: 56–674 Kamehameha Highway, Kahuku
H: Kahuku Community Hospital, Hospital Road, Kahuku
SS: Kamehameha Highway, Paumalū
WA: diving; pole fishing; swimming
WC: strong currents from October through April; generally calm during summer; ocean bottom is rocky and shallow; shoreline fronted by patches of beachrock
PA: unlimited
AI: Kūka'imanini Island offshore

Waiale'e means "rippling or stirring water." At one time, on calm days when the tide was low, people on shore could see freshwater bubbling up in small fountains above the offshore reef. Possibly this upwelling of freshwater in the ocean influenced Hawaiians in naming the area. The small island just offshore was called Kūka'imanini, "*manini* fish procession."

Waiale'e Beach is a long, moderately wide, and sandy beach. Swimming is only fair because beach rock and sections of coral reef are exposed along the entire shoreline. The ocean bottom is also rocky, with only a few sand pockets that can accommodate most recreational swimmers. The alongshore currents can become very strong when the surf is big. Kūkaʻimanini Island is completely rocky and covered with sparse vegetation and a few small ironwood trees. The island is used occasionally by children as a base for water games. The beach area is completely undeveloped.

Pahipahiʻālua Beach

Pahipahiʻālua, "to clap the hands twice," was said to have been the name of a fishing shrine in this area, but now its exact location is lost. Pahipahiʻālua Beach, located between Waialeʻe and the nearby point of Kawela Bay, is more commonly referred to as West Kawela. The area is made up primarily of private beach homes. On the shoreline there is no discernible separation between Pahipahiʻālua and Waialeʻe. The water and bottom conditions of both are almost identical. There is no convenient public access to this beach.

Kawela Bay
Hanopu Street, Kamehameha Highway, Kawela

   F: none
  LG: none
  EP: Waialeʻe Beach Park
  PP: Kuilima Hotel, Kahuku
  FS: 56–674 Kamehameha Highway, Kahuku
   H: Kahuku Community Hospital, Hospital Road, Kahuku
  SS: Kamehameha Highway, Paumalū
 WA: diving; board surfing; swimming
 WC: safe all year; dangerous offshore currents during heavy surf
  PA: only from ocean

The shoreline of Kawela, "the heat," passes through the three land divisions, Pahipahiʻālua, ʻŌpana, and Kawela. The bay waters were a favorite lobster grounds of the ancient kings of Oʻahu, and they held the fishing rights directly, instead of granting them to the chief of the district as was the custom in other places. Beach homes and cottages were constructed in the area beginning in the early 1900s. One of the most luxurious of the

Christine A. Takata

Kawela Bay. A fisherman casts leisurely into the calm waters of the bay. The solitude and tranquility of this area have long made it a favorite retreat of many of Oʻahu's residents.

131

original homes was called "Trentino." It was described as "a super summer cottage for special outings," and was designed especially for the employees of the Trent Trust Company. Completed in 1918, Trentino was considered to be the most complete and comfortable camping-out spot on O'ahu.

Probably the natural feature best known in Kawela Bay is the freshwater spring known as Punaulua. The water from the spring forms a pond some distance inland from the bay. At one time the spring waters ran underground and came to the surface in the sea near the shoreline. This meeting of the salt and fresh waters attracted the *ulua,* the crevalle or jack. Frequently two or three large *ulua* could be found lazing about in these waters. Seemingly insensitive to danger and lulled into inactivity, they were easily surrounded and caught by a careful net fisherman. The coming of the *ulua* to this area gave the pond its name Punaulua, or "*ulua* spring."

Kawela Bay is very safe for swimming. Sometimes strong trade winds or heavy surf in the outer bay may create a slight inshore current which runs along the beach. This current is not dangerous. Big surf also produces small gentle waves in the inshore waters. The sandy beach runs almost the entire length of the bay's shoreline. The ocean bottom is primarily sand, with scattered coral heads and mud sediment in some spots. During the summer months the bay waters are very clean, except when incoming tides stir up the bottom sediment and cloud the water. During the winter months Kawela Bay is almost continuously dirty because of the rains that fill the river. Water circulation within the bay is not active enough to clean it quickly. A relatively rock-free, sand-filled channel in the bay's bottom on the Punaulua side comes all the way in to the beach.

Turtle Bay
(also called Wild Beach)
(Sunset Beach side of Kuilima Hotel, Kahuku)

F: none; parking area available in Kuilima Hotel area
LG: none

EP: Waiale'e Beach Park
PP: Kuilima Hotel, Kahuku
FS: 56-674 Kamehameha Highway, Kahuku
H: Kahuku Community Hospital, Hospital Road, Kahuku
SS: Kamehameha Highway, Kahuku
WA: beachcombing; diving; board surfing; paipo board surfing; swimming
WC: dangerous currents and surf from October through April; occasional strong currents during calmer summer months
PA: from Kuilima Hotel area

Turtle Bay, both long and wide, is situated between the eastern point of Kawela Bay and the Kuilima Hotel. It was named for the *honu,* the common green sea turtles, that once frequented these waters and laid their eggs in the sand along the bay's shoreline. Although the turtles are not as abundant as they once were, they can still be seen surfacing for air on calmer days, especially in the early mornings when they come in to feed.

Within Turtle Bay is a small island with a reef, both were known as Papa'amoi. This area was noted for its large schools of *moi,* or thread fish. *Moi* are considered by many islanders to be the best eating of all the inshore fish, and are much sought by throw-net fishermen and shore-casters. The shoreline inside of Papa'amoi was called Wakiu, which also was the name of a former fishpond located just inland from the beach. At the Kahuku end of the bay, where the Kuilima cottages are presently located, the beach was called Waikalae, meaning "divided water." The name referred to a time when 'Ō'io Stream split, with the main branch running into Kuilima Cove and the secondary branch emptying into Turtle Bay.

The beach lining Turtle Bay is long and curving. It is fairly steep, especially during the winter. Almost the entire beach is fronted by rock and raised coral reef, making it a poor area for recreational swimming. During the winter the currents in the bay are very powerful and pull steadily along the shore. Even on calm days the inshore currents can be very insistent and dangerous. The sea bottom is primarily rocky and drops off rather abruptly into the deeper waters. Surfers and fishermen who frequent the place call it "Wild Beach," because of the huge waves that cross the reefs in erratic patterns during the winter months.

Kuilima Cove

(formerly Kalokoiki)
Kuilima Hotel, Kahuku

F: 1 food and beverage concession; marked parking stalls available in beach area
LG: service provided by hotel daily all year
EP: Waialeʻe Beach Park
PP: Kuilima Hotel, Kahuku
FS: 56–674 Kamehameha Highway, Kahuku
H: Kahuku Community Hospital, Hospital Road, Kahuku
SS: Kamehameha Highway, Kahuku
WA: snorkeling; swimming
WC: safe all year; strong currents offshore and where cove water runs through channel in reef to open ocean; small, protected cove; shallow bottom with patches of coral and pockets of sand
PA: private beach owned and maintained by Kuilima Hotel; however, access is extended to general public

The Kuilima Hotel is situated on a point that was once known as Kalaeokaunu. An *unu* was a crude altar used especially by fishermen, so Kalaeokaunu is translated as "the point of the altar." Among the Hawaiians' beliefs in the supernatural, their reverence and regard for sharks were both prominent and widespread. Shark gods and goddesses were numerous along the coasts of all the islands, with each island having a king or a queen shark. The name, the history, and the appearance of each patron shark were well known to everyone in an area. A *kahu,* or guardian, took care of the shark, and the shark in turn watched over the people while they were in the ocean. When the ocean was rough and stormy in the Kahuku area, the *kahu* would perform a ceremony at Kalaeokaunu which included making offerings of food to the guardian shark. If the offerings were acceptable, the ocean would calm down, allowing fishermen to go safely to sea. The smaller point on the northern side of Kalaeokaunu was called Kalaeokamanu, "the point of the bird," but the reason for the name is unknown.

Kuilima Cove is the sandy inlet situated between Kalaeokaunu and Kalaeokamanu. It was formerly called Kalokoiki, "the little pool," and was a favorite swimming place of the old Hawaiian community in the neighboring land division of Kahuku. One of the traditional responsibilities of the ruling family on each island was to make a periodic journey around their domain. During these trips around Oʻahu the village in Kahuku often was designated as one of the overnight stopping places. On one such occasion, the entourage included Lydia Kamakaeha Kapaʻakea, a young woman who was destined to become the only ruling queen and the last reigning monarch of Hawaiʻi. During the brief stay at Kahuku, Liliʻu (as she was affectionately known to her people) was said to have gone swimming in Kalokoiki with others in the party. In later years she was known formally as Queen Liliʻuokalani.

The lands of Kuilima were the large plains *mauka* of the hotel that are presently covered by the golf course. Kuilima means "to go arm in arm," and refers to a story about three men who once crossed these plains walking in such a manner. The name was adopted by the hotel, and today Kalaeokaunu, the promontory on which the hotel was constructed, is known as Kuilima Point.

During the late 1950s, Donald Wolbrink and Associates, Inc., did a study in the Kahuku area for the Campbell Estate. Kalokoiki was described as being "a quiet, sandy, and intimate cove." The Del Webb Corporation's engineering section, in preparing their plans for the area, apparently picked up the adjective "intimate" and labeled Kalokoiki "Intimate Cove" on their blueprints. After the hotel opened in May 1972, however, the name Intimate Cove was changed to Kuilima Cove.

Before the hotel's construction ʻŌʻio Stream emptied directly into Kuilima Cove. The freshwater runoff left a great deal of silt and mud in the cove, making it almost continually dirty, especially during the winter months. The circulation of waters in the protected cove was not strong enough to cleanse the area quickly. To solve the problem, the mouth of the stream was relocated several hundred yards down the beach, past Kalaeokamanu. Some of the coral in the cove was bulldozed to make a better swimming area. When the sites for the cabanas at the rear of the cove were graded, the excess sand from them was used to restore and improve the beach. Today Kuilima Cove is one of the nicest and safest swimming beaches in the Kahuku area. The shallow bottom is rather rocky inshore, but sandy at the water's edge. The cove is protected from the open sea by a reef that is joined to Kalaeokamanu and extends toward the hotel. The only dangerous spot in the inlet is the channel running toward the open ocean alongside Kalaeokaunu. The channel was cut through the reef by the former watercourse of 'Ō'io Stream. Even on calm days a respectable current pulls seaward through the channel, and during periods of heavy surf a strong rip current runs through the opening. Kuilima Hotel provides daily lifeguard service to assure the safety of its guests. The public also is invited to use the swimming area in the cove.

Kaihalulu Beach

(between Kalaeokamanu Point and Kahuku Point, formerly called Kalaeokauna'oa Point)

  F: none; parking area available in Kuilima Hotel area
 LG: none
 EP: Waiale'e Beach Park
 PP: Kuilima Hotel, Kahuku
 FS: 56–674 Kamehameha Highway, Kahuku
  H: Kahuku Community Hospital, Hospital Road, Kahuku
 SS: Kamehameha Highway, Kahuku
 WA: beachcombing; diving; pole fishing; swimming; throw-netting
 WC: dangerous currents and surf from October through April; almost entire shoreline is fronted by raised reef or beachrock
 PA: from Kuilima Hotel only; access from Kahuku Airport Road is limited to residents of Marconi

Kaihalulu, "roaring sea," is the long, curving bay between Kalaeokamanu and Kalaeokauna'oa. It takes its name from the huge, thunderous waves that break on the offshore reefs during the winter months. Kalaeokauna'oa, the northernmost point of the bay, was named for the *una'oa,* a mollusk which in the adult stage attaches itself to seaside rocks. The animal has a small, sharp, hard point that causes intense pain to persons who step upon it. These protrusions can also break off and become embedded in the skin, causing a nasty wound. Hawaiians believed that wounds caused by stepping on the *una'oa* were poisoned. *Una'oa* are found in abundance on the point.

Kalaeokauna'oa, the northernmost point on O'ahu,

is identified as Kahuku Point on most maps. Beginning with the first geodetic survey of the islands, done by the U.S. Navy in 1840, the native terms for many points of land were changed in favor of the more familiar district names, or simply were given English names. On O'ahu, for example, Laniloa became Lā'ie Point, Kawaihoa became Portlock Point, Kūpikipiki'ō became Black Point, Kalaeloa became Barber's Point, and so on. Fortunately, many of the original Hawaiian names were remembered by the people who lived near these several points and were recorded before they could be forgotten.

The section of Kaihalulu Beach just before Kalaeokauna'oa was called Punapalaha, or "slippery spring," because of the slippery rocks found here at the water's edge. Although Punapalaha was not actually a point of land, it was often referred to as "John Jack Point" for John McCandless, who once had a country home near this area. The last section of Kaihalulu just before the point was called Kauhala, "to move up and down, as waves."

Kaihalulu Beach, curving and sandy, is a little more than a mile long. Almost all of its shoreline is fronted by beach rock and coral reef. The offshore reef is broken along the entire length of the beach, affording the inshore waters little protection from strong currents. The ocean bottom is almost completely rocky. About midway down the beach one small ocean pool at the water's edge provides a convenient and comfortable place to get wet. The rest of the beach is relatively poor for recreational swimming, especially during the winter season, when the inshore currents are very strong. The only access to Kaihalulu is from the Kuilima Hotel. The area is frequented primarily by beachcombers and fishermen.

Hanaka'īlio Beach

(between Kahuku Point, formerly called Kalaeokauna'oa Point, and Kalaeuila Point, Kahuku)

  F: none; parking area available in Kuilima Hotel area
 LG: none
 EP: Waiale'e Beach Park
 PP: Kuilima Hotel, Kahuku
 FS: 56–674 Kamehameha Highway, Kahuku

H: Kahuku Community Hospital, Hospital Road, Kahuku
SS: Kamehameha Highway, Kahuku
WA: beachcombing; diving; pole fishing; swimming; throw-netting
WC: dangerous currents and surf from October through April; most of area is high sand dunes; beachrock along most of shoreline
PA: from Kuilima Hotel only; access from Kahuku Airport Road is limited to residents of Marconi

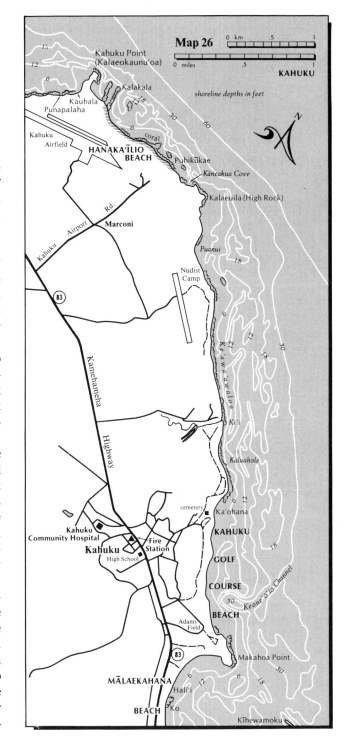

Hanaka'īlio Beach is located between the two points once known as Kalaeokauna'oa and Kalaeuila "the lightning point." Several hundred yards inland of Hanaka'īlio is a small cluster of homes and farms. This little community at the end of Kahuku Airport Road was once the site of a large Hawaiian settlement. In former times the now barren plains of Kahuku were covered with a great variety of trees. The region was very fertile and highly cultivated. Sources of freshwater were plentiful. In 1889, for example, a study of the area was made by James D. Schuyler and G. F. Allardt to determine the water supply available for irrigation. Their report stated that all of the lands of Kahuku Ranch, twenty thousand acres extending from Waimea Bay to Kalanai Point in Lā'ie, were "bursting with freshwater." A tract of 150 acres near the ranchhouse, a short distance from the village, was so full of springs that it was completely fenced in to prevent cattle from becoming mired in it. In the ensuing years, however, the lush, wooded areas gradually disappeared as the waters were channeled and the lands were cleared for agricultural purposes. With these changes, the Hawaiian settlement slowly broke up, and the people dispersed to other parts of the island. Today only a handful of people live in the vicinity of the former village, few of whom are actual descendants of the early Hawaiians. This small community and the neighboring shoreline area are commonly called "Marconi."

Before 1900, Fred J. Cross, an electrician of considerable repute in Hawai'i, had been keeping track of the different experiments in wireless telegraphy that were being conducted in Europe and America. He realized the great potential value that wireless communication represented for the islands. In 1899, when Guglielmo Marconi journeyed to the United States to demonstrate his system of wireless telegraphy, Cross went to New York to confer with Marconi. Cross obtained the franchise of the Marconi system for Hawai'i and made arrangements to have the American Marconi Company construct the necessary installations. In 1902 the Hawaiian branch of the company opened for business with wireless communication established among O'ahu, Maui, and Hawai'i.

Marconi's great dream was to connect all parts of the world by wireless. During the early 1900s he initiated one part of his plan by constructing on O'ahu the world's two largest stations for radio telegraphy. By 1915 both stations were in operation. The sending unit, located at the base of Koko Crater (the present site of the Lunalilo Home), dealt solely with Bolinas, California, its mainland counterpart. The receiving unit, built on the sand dunes at Kahuku, dealt only with its counterpart in Marshalls, California. The entire local operation was coordinated by a central office in Honolulu.

During the late 1920s, the Radio Corporation of America, better known as RCA, bought the American Marconi Company's operations in Hawai'i. Later the extensive premises and buildings at Koko Crater were acquired by the trustees of Lunalilo Home, a residence for aged Hawaiians. In 1928 the main structure of the station was remodeled, and Lunalilo Home was moved there from its former site in Makiki (where Roosevelt High School now stands). The receiving unit at Kahuku was retained and is still used by RCA for ship-to-shore communication for civilian vessels. The old name "Marconi" is still the one by which the community is best known.

Hanaka'īlio Beach, located between Kalaeokauna'oa and Kalaeuila, is the largest section of sand beach in the Marconi area. On the Lā'ie side of Kalaeokauna'oa is a cove similar to the one at Kuilima, but not as sheltered and protected as the hotel's inlet. Kalakala, the finger of reef that makes up the sister point forming the cove, is broken and irregular, allowing a free flow of current through the area. The sand beach of Hanaka'īlio begins at Kalakala and extends for about half a mile to the reef and rocks of Puhikūkae. Hanaka'īlio is a wide, steep, sandy beach fronted by occasional outcroppings of beach rock and reef. Once upon a time it was well used as a nesting place by the *honu,* the green sea turtles, which frequently came ashore at night to lay their eggs in the sand. The sea bottom is rocky and inshore cur-

rents are strong, especially when the surf is big. Today the area is frequented almost exclusively by fishermen, who usually camp next to the two large *naupaka* bushes growing on one of the high sand dunes.

Puhikūkae, "eel excrement," the end of the beach, is marked by an old drainage pipe at the water's edge that was installed by the American Marconi Company. The shoreline from the pipe to Kalaeuila, "the lightning point," is completely rocky. Just inside the point is a small cove, Kāneakua, that is protected enough to allow divers to enter the water.

The rest of the long Kahuku shoreline from Kalaeuila, past the nudist colony, and ending at the Kahuku Golf Course, is very similar to the Hanaka'īlio and Kaihalulu sections of the coast, except that the indentations are not as pronounced: here the shoreline is much straighter. The beach areas consist of reaches of sand with beach rock and reef interspersed. Swimming is possible on calm days at several scattered places. The currents are often strong, especially when the waves are big. The offshore reef is broken and irregular, affording little protection to recreational swimmers. This stretch of shoreline includes the fishing grounds of Puanui, Ke'awa'awaloa, Ki'i, and Kaluahole.

Kahuku Golf Course Beach

(formerly Keone'ō'io Beach; includes Adam's Field, a
public park adjacent to the golf course)
(between Japanese Graveyard and Makahoa
Point, Kahuku)

 F: Kahuku Golf Course; 1 public golf course; 1 clubhouse; Adam's Field; 1 baseball field; 2 softball fields
LG: none
EP: Pounders Beach, Lā'ie
PP: none
FS: 56–674 Kamehameha Highway, Kahuku
 H: Kahuku Community Hospital, Hospital Road, Kahuku
SS: Kamehameha Highway, Kahuku
WA: beachcombing; diving; board surfing; swimming
WC: very dangerous currents from October through April; entire beach fronted by raised reef and beach rock except for one small, sandy channel
PA: unlimited; from Adam's Field or golf course

The beach fronting the Kahuku Golf Course Beach begins at Ka'ohana, the area *makai* of the Japanese Cemetery, and stretches east to Makahoa Point. The long, wide beach has an average width of one hundred feet and consists primarily of sand and bedrock. There are many high sand dunes in the area. The foreshore is covered by rather profuse growths of vegetation, mainly *naupaka* bushes and scrubby ironwood trees. The only feasible swimming place along this shoreline is a small, sandy pocket near the middle of the beach. This pocket is the end of a large channel that cuts through the offshore reef and comes all the way in to the shore. A very strong rip current often runs seaward through this channel, so even on calm days swimming should be restricted to inshore waters. The residents of nearby Kahuku town are well aware of this rip and rarely swim in the area. The channel was once known as Keone'ō'io, "the 'ō'io sands," because 'ō'io fish were very plentiful in this region.

Just inland of Keone'ō'io, at the eastern end of the golf course, is a six-acre public park called Adam's Field. Named for Andrew Adams, the Kahuku Plantation Company's manager from 1904 to 1921, the park land is leased by the City and County. It is undeveloped except for baseball and softball fields. The beaches near Adam's Field and the Kahuku Golf Course are frequented primarily by beachcombers, fishermen, and surfers.

Mālaekahana Beach

(between Makahoa Point and Kalanai Point, Mālaekahana)

F: none; roadside parking along Kamehameha Highway
LG: none
EP: Pounders Beach, Lā'ie
PP: none
FS: 56–674 Kamehameha Highway, Kahuku
H: Kahuku Community Hospital, Hospital Road, Kahuku
SS: Kamehameha Highway, Kahuku
WA: diving; swimming; throw-netting
WC: safe all year; infrequent strong currents; occasional small surf in shorebreak
PA: none (walk around Kalanai Point from Lā'ie Beach)

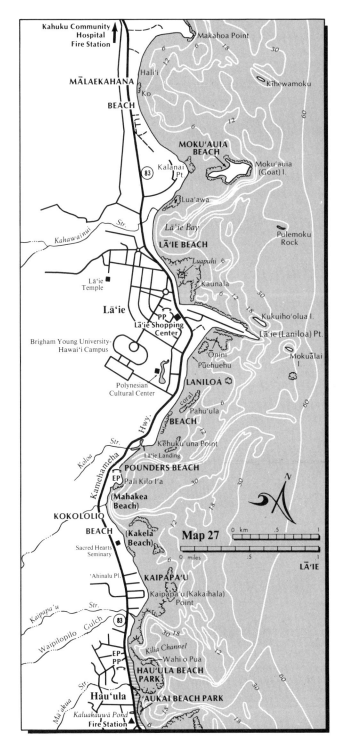

Christine A. Takata

Mālaekahana Beach. Looking across the shallow channel separating Mokuʻauia (Goat Island) from the beach at Mālaekahana. The entire shoreline of the Mālaekahana district has for many years accommodated the private beach homes of many of Oʻahu's more affluent families. The forested area is known by its Hawaiian name, Kalanai (Point), and its English name, Cooke's Point.

The naming of Mālaekahana is said to be connected with the romantic legend of Lāʻie-i-ka-wai, a beautiful young woman, who was hidden as a child in a chamber beside a pool in Lāʻie. Although she was well guarded from mortal men, many princes of the day, having heard of her beauty, attempted to woo her. In the traditional version of the legend, this place was named for Mālaekahana, the mother of Lāʻie.

Mālaekahana Beach is situated between Makahoa, "friendly point," and Kalanai Point. Makahoa is a very well-known place among older Hawaiian fishermen. Formerly the ʻanae-holo, the ocean-going mullet that lived in Pearl Harbor, made an annual journey around the eastern end of Oʻahu, passing through the waters off each district till they reached Mālaekahana. For some unexplained reason, the ʻanae-holo always stopped at Makahoa and then reversed their direction, following the same path back to Pearl Harbor.

Along the shoreline of Mālaekahana are two flat reefs that were also well known to fishermen from the area.

The first was called Kō. This flat reef, or *papa,* has a sandy hole on one side and a channel on the other, and here fish and *limu* were found in abundance. The second spot was called Hali'i, "to spread, as a sheet." This *papa* was an inshore area where the *moi,* a highly esteemed food fish, congregated at night.

Mālaekahana Beach, long, curving, and sandy, is well over a mile in length. It is widest at the Makahoa end and narrows toward Kalanai Point, with some exposed beach rock along its shoreline. The inshore waters provide a safe swimming area with a gently sloping sand bottom. Very small surf breaks close to the beach when the prevailing trade winds are blowing. The Mālaekahana area has long been the site of many country beach homes for O'ahu's more affluent families. There is no convenient access to the beach for the general public, but a portion of the beach will eventually become a public park.

Some people know Kalanai Point as "Cookes' Point," because that prominent Honolulu family leased a piece of property here in the early 1900s, and built a large country house upon it.

Moku'auia Beach

(also Goat Island Beach)
Moku'auia Island (Goat Island), Lā'ie Bay, Lā'ie
(offshore from Kalanai Point)

F: none; roadside parking along Kamehameha Highway
LG: none
EP: Pounders Beach, Lā'ie
PP: none
FS: 56–674 Kamehameha Highway, Kahuku
H: Kahuku Community Hospital, Hospital Road, Kahuku
SS: Kamehameha Highway, Lā'ie
WA: beachcombing; diving; pole fishing; snorkeling; swimming
WC: occasional strong currents from October through April; small, protected, crescent sand beach on leeward side of island; coral rubble beach on windward side
PA: to reach island, wade across narrow strait of water between Kalanai Point and island; water waist-deep for average adult; best to cross on calm day at low tide
AI: Moku'auia is an official state bird refuge; no restrictions on camping, picnicking, fishing, or exploring as long as birds and island are left undisturbed

Goat Island is located in Lā'ie, just offshore from Kalanai Point. Its Hawaiian name is Moku'auia, "island to one side." Moku'auia was well known in the mid-1800s because of a man named Kauahi who lived on the island. Apparently Kauahi, a native lawyer who was noted for his quick wit, kept two mistresses on Moku'auia in violation of the kingdom's marriage laws. When King Kamehameha V heard about the situation, he ordered Kauahi arrested. However, when the warrant was served Kauahi declared that he was king of his island and above prosecution, inasmuch as Moku'auia was not recorded on any official government map at that time.

The town of Lā'ie is a Mormon settlement established in 1864, when the church acquired land in the area and colonized it. Before the establishment of Lā'ie sugar plantation, the colonists raised watermelons and cotton, in addition to keeping their own gardens. An attempt was made to raise goats also, but because of the destructive nature of these animals, especially if they are allowed to run wild, they were moved to Moku'auia. Since that time it has been called Goat Island. It was said to have harbored a large guinea pig population at one time, after some children let loose a few of these little animals there, but none survive at present.

Today Goat Island is a state bird refuge. Permits are not required for camping, picnicking, or fishing as long as the birds are unmolested and the island itself is not despoiled in any way. The beautiful little sandy bay on the leeward side of the island probably is one of the most picturesque swimming beaches on O'ahu. The shallow sand-bottom beach, an ideal place for children to swim, is well protected by a section of offshore reef. There is also a short beach of coarse sand on the windward side of the island.

Goat Island is reasonably easy to reach from Kalanai Point. The short stretch of water between the island and the point can easily be waded at low tide on calm days. Be sure to adequately protect your feet against the sharp coral. When the tide is high or the ocean is rough, the crossing is not quite as simple, especially for children, but it is not impossible. Although there is some low vegetation on Goat Island, along with a few coconut palms and ironwood trees, there is no source of freshwater other than rainfall.

Lā'ie Beach

(also Hukilau)
(between Kalanai Point and Laniloa Point,
Kamehameha Highway, Lā'ie)

 F: none; roadside parking along Kamehameha Highway
LG: none
 EP: Pounders Beach, Lā'ie
 PP: none
 FS: 56–674 Kamehameha Highway, Kahuku
  H: Kahuku Community Hospital, Hospital Road, Kahuku
 SS: Kamehameha Highway, Lā'ie
WA: diving; board surfing; bodysurfing; swimming; throw-netting
WC: strong currents along shore from October through April in areas where beach is unprotected by fringing reef
 PA: none (follow stream at Lā'ie-i-ka-wai Bridge near Lā'ie Shopping Center)

The land division of Lā'ie was named for a beautiful legendary princess, Lā'ie-i-ka-wai, who was said to have been raised in the district. Many princes of the realm attempted to win Lā'ie, who was guarded from the eyes of mortal men. To assure her seclusion, she was often hidden in the secret chamber of a freshwater pool in Lā'ie. The pool, Waiapuka, can still be seen in the vicinity of the Lā'ie dump. Until about 1900, it was still possible to reach the hidden chamber by swimming through an underwater entrance, but mud and other debris have long since filled much of the pool, closing off access to the cave. Lā'ie's name is a shortened form of the two words *lau 'ie,* the "*'ie* vine leaf," and Lā'ie-i-ka-wai, her full title, means "Lā'ie of the water."

Lā'ie was colonized as a Mormon settlement in 1864, fourteen years after the first ten Mormon missionaries arrived in Hawai'i. Today the Lā'ie community pro-

Eric M. Nishida

Lā'ie Beach. This section of Lā'ie Beach is called Hukilau by most island residents because for many years it was the scene of numerous *hukilau* put on for the public by the Mormon community. The small shorebreak in this area is occasionally good enough for bodysurfing. The sand beach ends at Lā'ie (Laniloa) Point.

140

bably is best known as the site of the famous Mormon Temple, the Polynesian Cultural Center, and Brigham Young University-Hawai'i, which, until 1974, was called the Church College of the Pacific.

Before 1970, Lā'ie was also famous for its monthly *hukilau.* The *hukilau* were started in 1947 as a money-raising venture, to help replace the old wooden chapel which had burned down. A *hukilau,* literally "to pull a leaf," actually a rope with many ti leaves attached to it, is an ancient method of fishing in which a group of relatively inexperienced people can pariticipate. Ti leaves are affixed to two long ropes that in turn are attached to either end of a long net. A fine mesh bag is secured to the center of the net. The ropes and the net are fed over the side of a moving boat in a semicircle, finally forming a horseshoe with the ends of the two ropes held on shore. Swimmers are stationed in the water at intervals around the perimeter of the net to *pa'i pa'i,* "splash the water," while the rest of the participants stand on the beach to haul in both ropes simultaneously. The flutterings of the ti leaves, the noise of the weights dragging on the bottom, the humming of the ropes, and the splashings of the swimmers all serve to scare the fish into the net and finally into the finely woven bag as it is pulled up on the shore. The Lā'ie *hukilau* proved to be so popular that the Hawaii Visitors Bureau and many tour agencies asked the Mormons to continue the attraction. For many years the *hukilau* was a very successful event. In 1970, however, the State determined that the *hukilau* was a commercial venture and that the proceeds from it should be taxed. This move made the further production of *hukilau* financially unprofitable, so they were discontinued. Although the events are no longer performed, the center of Lā'ie Beach where they were held is still known island-wide as "Hukilau."

Lā'ie Beach stretches for about a mile and a half from Kalanai Point to Laniloa Point. The entire foreshore of the beach is relatively steep, averaging about seventy feet in width. About four hundred yards from Kalanai is a small reef that was called Luaawa, "*awa* fish hole." From Luaawa to Hukilau the shoreline is open and unprotected by any fringing reef. Alongshore currents in this area can be very strong. A wide sand-bottom channel comes in to shore in this section of the beach. It occasionally attracts bodysurfers who find the small shorebreak ridable.

The shoreline from Hukilau to Laniloa is fronted by a wide, shallow reef, so the inshore waters are safe and protected for swimming. In the old days, a section of sand dunes in this area was known as Pu'uahi, "hill of fire," because of cooking fires that were built in anticipation of fishermen returning with their catches. Now the dunes have been leveled for homesites, but the name has been retained in Pu'uahi Street, just inland from the former hill of fire.

Laniloa Beach

(between Laniloa Point and Kēhuku'una Point, Lā'ie)

  F: none; roadside parking along Kamehameha Highway
 LG: none
 EP: Pounders Beach, Lā'ie
 PP: none
 FS: 54-064 Kamehameha Highway, Hau'ula
  H: Kahuku Community Hospital, Hospital Road, Kahuku
 SS: Kamehameha Highway, Lā'ie
 WA: diving; snorkeling; swimming; throw-netting
 WC: safe all year, except during periods of high or stormy surf; almost entire beach is fronted by shallow coral reef; two sandy channels in shoreline area for recreational swimmers
 PA: public right-of-way next to 55-479 Kamehameha Highway, Lā'ie

Laniloa Beach takes its name from Laniloa Point, a wide, elevated protrusion of coraline rock thrusting into the sea. Laniloa is the old name for this area, although on most maps it is labeled Lā'ie Point. The particular section of shoreline is said to have been guarded by two *mo'o.* These large, dragonlike animals were slain by Kana, the stretching demigod, and his brother Nīheu, the trickster demigod. Their carcasses were chopped up and thrown into the ocean, forming the five islets still to be seen around the end of the point. The hole where Kana severed the head of one of the *mo'o* can be seen in Kukuiho'olua, the island closest to Laniloa. Until 1946 only a large cave existed on the seaward side of Kukuiho'olua, but the devastating tsunami that struck the Hawaiian chain on April 1 of that year broke through the cave and formed the arch in the islet. A mural of the *mo'o* legend was donated to the Hawai'i Campus of Brigham Young University by the Cooke family of Ho-

Lā'ie (Laniloa) Point. Fishermen and tourists step carefully on the cliffs of this rugged promontory known to Hawaiians as Laniloa. This very picturesque area can be reached by turning off Kamehameha Highway onto Anemoku Street at the Lā'ie Shopping Center.

tions. The places where these tributary channels touch the shoreline are the only good swimming spots along the entire beach. The larger of the two sandy pockets was called Pūehuehu, "scattering sea spray." The word *"puehu"* also referred to the feeding habits of the 'ō'io fish, which root in sea sand like pigs do on shore. The turbid, stirred-up water they caused was called *"puehu."*

Farther down the beach from Pūehuehu is a large drainage pipe at the water's edge. The reef in this area, marked by three rocks that protrude above the surface of the ocean, was called Pahu'ula, "lobster box," because at one time traps with live lobsters were kept here. This allowed the fishermen access to a continuous supply of lobsters. From Pahu'ula to Kēhuku'una the beach has been severely eroded by heavy surf. This eastern end of the Laniloa shoreline once was known as "Scott's Beach," for Alvah Scott, a former president of Hawaiian Telephone Company, who had an estate on the bluff near Wailele Stream.

Laniloa is a long sandy beach well over a mile in length. With the exception of the two sand-bottom pockets at 'Ōnini and Pūehuehu, the entire shoreline is covered by shallow sections of raised coral reef. The inshore waters, although primarily rocky, are well protected by the outer fringing reef, making the entire beach safe for swimming. There is one public right-of-way to Laniloa at 55–470 Kamehameha Highway. It meets the beach between 'Ōnini and Pūehuehu.

nolulu, who kept a country home for many years at nearby Kalanai Point. The painting, which inaccurately portrays the *mo'o* as serpents, can be seen by the public at the university campus.

Laniloa Beach begins on the eastern side of the point and continues along the shoreline to Kēhuku'una, where Pounders Beach begins. The inshore reef that makes up the section of the beach closest to the point was called 'Ōnini, "slight breeze." 'Ōnini is remembered by older residents in Lā'ie as the place where a light plane crashed while its passengers were observing effects of the tsunami of 1957.

On the Hau'ula side of 'Ōnini, a shallow, sandy channel runs shoreward through the reef. About halfway into the beach the channel branches into two smaller sec-

Pounders Beach

(also Lā'ie-malo'o, Lā'ie-lohelohe, and Kikila; formerly Pahumoa Beach)
(between Kēhuku'una Point and Pali Kilo I'a Point, Lā'ie)

F: 1 landscaped park; roadside parking along Kamehameha Highway
LG: none
EP: in park area
PP: none
FS: 54–064 Kamehameha Highway, Hau'ula
H: Kahuku Community Hospital, Hospital Road, Kahuku
SS: Kamehameha Highway, Hau'ula

Christine A. Takata

Pounders Beach. Bodysurfers ride the shorebreak waves on a small day next to the sea cliff known to the Hawaiians as Pali Kilo I'a, the fish spotter's cliff. In former times, spotters would direct the movements of surround-net fishermen in ca-noes from this elevated position. The first students at the Hawai'i campus of Brigham Young University named the beach Pounders for the pounding action of the surf.

WA: beachcombing; pole fishing; shore casting; bodysurfing; swimming
WC: very strong currents and dangerous, pounding shorebreak from October through April; generally calm during summer; shallow sand shelf inshore that drops off abruptly to deeper waters at surf line
PA: park area is owned and maintained by local island family; however, use of park area and access to beach is open to public; overnight camping not permitted
AI: Pounders is one of the most popular shorebreak bodysurfing beaches on O'ahu

"Pounders" is a popular bodysurfing beach located in Lā'ie-malo'o between the points of Kēhuku'una and Pali Kilo I'a. Once upon a time the beach was well known as Pahumoa, in tribute to a highly respected fisherman who lived near Koloa Stream. Pahumoa arranged many *hukilau* in this area and, following Hawaiian custom, gave fish to everyone who helped him draw in the nets. He also put aside a portion of his catch for the older people of Lā'ie who were unable to assist him or to fish for themselves. Because of his generosity and kindness he was much respected throughout the community. To honor him the beach was called by his name. Pahumoa's descendants, members of the Kamake'e-'āina family, still live near the beach. They frequently fish in the area, and often their nets can be seen drying near the mouth of Koloa Stream.

During the late 1800s, a large area, including the beach front where Pahumoa maintained his fishing rights, was purchased by Cecil Brown, a prominent resident of O'ahu. Mr. Brown's beach estate, located on the *mauka* side of Kamehameha Highway, was named Kikila, Hawaiian for Cecil. Kikila and Pahumoa Beach are still owned by Mr. Brown's descendants. Except for the beach home at Kikila, the family left the entire property undeveloped. The beach park, still private property, is maintained at the owners' expense for use by the general public. Brown's heirs have no plans to develop this prime beach frontage. It will become a public park when the negotiations are completed.

The name "Pounders" is fairly new. It came from the first students at the Church College of the Pacific, who began attending classes near there in 1955, several years before the present campus (now called Brigham Young University-Hawai'i) was completed. The students who frequented the beach called it "Pounders" for the enjoyable, but often crushing, shorebreak that attracted them. Among fishermen who come from other parts of O'ahu, Pounders is known also as Lā'ie-malo'o, after the section of Lā'ie in which the beach is located.

The limestone bluff that forms the eastern boundary of Pounders was known as Pali Kilo I'a, "fish watcher's cliff." From this elevated place, spotters would direct net fishermen in the waters offshore as they tried to surround a school of fish. Kēhuku'una, the small hill at the opposite end of the beach, also was used as an observation point. This method of spotting and directing the operations of fishermen from shore was employed at many other places around O'ahu.

Probably the best-known landmark at Pounders is the remnants of a former pier that once received interisland steamers and schooners that stopped in Lā'ie. Before the railroad line was brought into the district from Kahuku, sugarcane and other local crops were shipped to Honolulu by boat. The pier was used also as a landing for other vessels transporting supplies and travelers. It was at Pounders, for example, that King Kalākaua landed to attend the dedication of the first Mormon chapel built at Lā'ie.

Pounders is a long, wide beach extending for almost a quarter of a mile between the points of Kēhuku'una and Pali Kilo I'a. The western end of the beach around the old landing usually is calm and safe for swimming. The eastern end, around the limestone bluff, has a shorebreak that, because of its tremendous force, can be dangerous to inexperienced bodysurfing enthusiasts. The bottom is sandy, but it is very shallow, often producing devastating surf conditions when the waves are big. At the edge of the surf line, the bottom drops off abruptly into the deeper offshore waters, sometimes causing strong but short-lived rip currents. Because of its easy accessibility and its good bodysurfing waves, Pounders is one of the most popular beaches in this part of O'ahu. Fishermen also frequent this section of shoreline to fish for *moi, 'ō'io , pāpio,* and other fish good for eating.

Kokololio Beach
(includes Mahakea and Kakela [Castle's] beaches)
(between Pali Kilo I'a Point and boundary separating the districts of Kaipapa'u and Lā'ie-malo'o)

 F: none; roadside parking along Kamehameha Highway
LG: none
EP: Pounders Beach, Lā'ie
PP: none
FS: 54–064 Kamehameha Highway, Hau'ula
 H: Kahuku Community Hospital, Hospital Road, Kahuku
SS: Kamehameha Highway, Hau'ula
WA: beachcombing; shorecasting; bodysurfing; swimming
WC: dangerous currents from October through April; occasional strong shorebreak; generally calm during summer; bottom slopes quickly to deeper offshore waters where beach is unprotected by fringing reef
PA: none (follow trail across Pali Kilo I'a from Pounders Beach)

Kokololio, the land between Lā'ie-malo'o (Pounders) and Kaipapa'u (Hau'ula Kai Shopping Center), takes its name from a peculiar wind that blows from the mountains in this region. Rather than blowing steadily, this wind rushes down upon the shoreline in very sharp, vigorous gusts. This characteristic reminded the Hawaiians of a high-spirited, prankish horse, one that would amble along at a walk and then suddenly run off at a gallop, much to the consternation of its rider. They named the wind Kokololio, "creeping horse," because of the humorous relationship they noted between such a horse and the changeable, undependable, unpredictable wind.

Kokololio Beach lies between Pali Kilo I'a and the rocky shoreline that marks the boundary between Lā'ie and Kaipapa'u. Although the beautiful sand beach is continuous and unbroken, Kokololio Stream divides it into two parts, each of which has its own name. Mahakea, on the Kahuku side, was the name of one of the men who obtained an original land court award to a *kuleana* in this region of Lā'ie. His name remained attached to the land, and today "Mahakea" identifies the beach estate now owned by the Hawaiian Electric Company. The utility company purchased the land in March 1952 from W. W. Monyhan, a former vice president of American Factors. At the time of the purchase the Reverend Henry Judd, an authority in the Hawaiian language, was consulted on the definition of Mahakea, and he translated the name to mean "fallow fields." Located at 55–135 Kamehameha Highway, the small estate is reserved for the use of top-level executives of Hawaiian Electric. Mahakea's existence for so many years has given its name to this section of Kokololio Beach.

The eastern half of the beach, on the Hau'ula side of Kokololio Stream, is known as Kakela. The long, undeveloped field to the rear of the beach was for many years part of an estate owned by the prominent Castle family of Honolulu. Sometimes called "The Dunes," because of the large sand dunes that were a feature of the area, their beautiful two-story home was set amid extensive gardens filled with statuary. The most famous of all the statues was a copy of "La Carita," depicting a mother and two children, originally done by Bartolini, an Italian Renaissance artist. After making the original statue (now in the Pitti Palace in Florence), Bartolini sealed in a secret room the casts of "La Carita" and other works. When, hundreds of years later, his hiding place was uncovered, several copies of "La Carita" were made. The Castle family acquired one and placed it on a knoll overlooking the ocean where it stood for many years in company with copies of the Venus de Milo and the little mermaid of Copenhagen.

Following the sale of the Castle estate in 1953 to the Zion Securities Company, the business branch of the Mormon Church, "La Carita" was left in place on her knoll. Vandals, using the statue for target practice, shot the hip and robe off the mother and the genitals off the little boy. The statue was removed to the Church College of the Pacific. Ortho Fairbanks, a professional worker in marble who had made the copy of the bronze statue of Kamehameha the Great now exhibited in the United States Capitol, was asked to repair "La Carita." He restored much of the statue of the mother to its original condition, but decided to change the little boy into a little girl. Today the repaired sculpture stands in a courtyard within the college's administration building. Visitors can see it there during regular business hours.

The prominence of the Castle family in Kokololio for so many years gave rise to the name "Kakela" for this section of the beach. Kakela is the Hawaiian pronunciation for castle. A surfing spot offshore from the estate was most commonly known as "Statues," for obvious reasons.

The long, curving sand beach of Kokololio, including Mahakea and Kakela, probably is one of the most beautiful shorelines on this side of O'ahu. The only reef in the Mahakea section is a small ledge next to Pali Kilo I'a that was called Papa'a'ula. Except for the part protected by Papa'a'ula, the entire shoreline here is exposed to the open sea. The inshore currents are often swift and very powerful when the ocean is rough. A strong shorebreak also forms when the surf is big, but it is not as suitable for bodysurfing as is its neighbor, Pounders, because the bottom drops off too sharply. The only area of Kokololio that is protected by a fringing reef is the eastern half of Kakela beginning at Haleweke, the sand dune where "La Carita" stood for so many years. From Haleweke to Kaipapa'u, the inshore waters are shallow and suitable for recreational swimming, but even in these protected sand pockets the alongshore currents can be very strong, especially with an incoming tide. The waters along the entire stretch of Kokololio should be approached cautiously, especially during winter months. There is no convenient public access to any part of the beach from Kamehameha Highway.

Kaipapaʻu Beach

(Kamehameha Highway fronting Hauʻula Kai Shopping
Center)

F: none
LG: none
EP: Hauʻula Beach Park
PP: Hauʻula Kai Shopping Center
FS: 54-064 Kamehameha Highway, Hauʻula
H: Kahuku Community Hospital, Hospital Road, Kahuku
SS: Kamehameha Highway, Hauʻula
WA: diving; snorkeling
WC: rocky shoreline and shallow, rocky ocean bottom
PA: no convenient public access

To Hawaiian fishermen, a *papa* is a flat section of ocean bottom that is somewhat smooth, such as a shelf or reef. A *papaʻu* is just the opposite, being a rough, uneven reef area with many pockets and a rocky bottom. The land division of Kaipapaʻu, meaning "ocean of shoals," was named for its shallow, rocky offshore bottom. There is very little sand beach along the Kaipapaʻu shoreline, which stretches from the Sacred Hearts Seminary to Waipilopilo Stream. The area is frequented by skin divers and fishermen. The rocky shoreline and shallow bottom attract few recreational swimmers.

The *makai* region of Kaipapaʻu, the area surrounding the Hauʻula Kai Shopping Center, formerly was known as Kakaihala. Papapiapia, Papaʻakea, and Kaʻo were the popular fishing grounds fronting Kakaihala. There is no convenient public access.

Hauʻula Beach Park

54-135 Kamehameha Highway, Hauʻula

F: 1 comfort station/pavilion; 1 lifeguard tower; 1 volley-
ball court; camping and picnic equipment
LG: daily service provided by City and County from June to
August
EP: in park area
PP: in park area
FS: 54-064 Kamehameha Highway, Hauʻula
H: Kahuku Community Hospital, Hospital Road, Kahuku
SS: Kamehameha Highway, Hauʻula
WA: diving; snorkeling; surfing (limited); swimming
WC: safe all year; strong currents outside protective fringing

reef from October through April or when ocean is stormy; entire park is fronted by shallow coral reef
PA: unlimited

The town of Hauʻula was named for the flowers of the *hau* trees that are abundant in the area. During the summer months of July and August, the *hau, Hibiscus tiliaceus,* blossoms profusely every morning. The bright yellow petals change color as the day progresses until they are a reddish gold by dusk. During the night the flowers turn dark red and fall to the ground. The cycle is repeated each day, as along as the plant blossoms. The degrees of redness in the petals vary with locality and seem to be responses to weather and terrain.

In former times the entire village of Hauʻula was full of *hau* trees. People said that the yellow flowers changed to a bright red by the end of each day, created a brilliant scene in the setting summer sun. This spectacular change, combined with the profusion of *hau* trees, led to the name Hauʻula, or "red *hau*." Although today the few remaining *hau* trees continue to blossom during the summer, the spectacle that gave rise to the naming of the town can be seen no longer.

The *hau* was an important tree to the Hawaiian people. The flowers were used to make a tea given to soothe certain catarrhal diseases and for other medical purposes. The strong fibrous bark of the *hau* frequently was used to make lashings, ropes, and cables as well as for nets and tapa. When fishing restrictions were in effect, *hau* branches were stuck in the sand all along the shore by the *konohiki,* the chief's administrative officer. During such times only deep-sea fishing was permitted. When an army went into battle a priest walked at its head, bearing a branch of *hau* which he set upright in the ground and guarded as an insignia favorable for his side. Each battling force respected this *mīhau* of the other and left it alone. The *mīhau* was allowed to fall only if the battle was being lost. This gave rise to the expression *"Ua puali ka hau nui i ka hau iki,"* The great *hau* is broken by the smaller one.

One of the best-known legends about Hauʻula centers around the hill called Lanakila, across the highway from Hauʻula Beach Park. In ancient times two brothers, *kupua* both, landed at Kawaihoa on Oʻahu. They had the ability to change from their human form to that of a *hilu* fish. In their fish guises, the younger brother journeyed through the waters along the leeward or *kona*

146

Hauʻula Beach Park. Tall ironwood trees dominate the shoreward edge of the park. The ruins of historic Lanakila Church are located on the low hill across Kamehameha Highway from the beach park. The point of land to the left of the picture is Kalaeokapalaoa, the point of the whale, which derives its name from a legend of the Hauʻula area.

side of the island and the older brother followed the windward or koʻolau coastline. As they traveled, both of them increased the number of *hilu* in the waters around Oʻahu. When the older brother reached Hauʻula of Koʻolauloa in his fish form, he was caught in the nets of the fishermen. The younger *kupua,* after missing his brother, traveled in his human form through the *koʻolau* side of Oʻahu. His search proved to be unsuccessful until he reached Hauʻula. There an old couple who lived on a hill near the ocean told him that not long before his arrival a large *hilu* had been caught and killed. The *kupua* realized that his brother was dead. He told the old couple to mark the four corners of their land and to stay in their home. There were five streams in Hauʻula— Hanaimoa, Kawaipapa, Maʻakua, Pāpale, and Punaiki—but only Maʻakua flowed all the way down to the shore. The younger *kupua* followed Maʻakua Stream into the mountains and dammed its waters above the vil-

lage. When he released the pent-up waters, all the people in the entire village were drowned except for the old couple who had befriended the young man. Because of this incident the hill was called Lanakila, "to rise to a high place," and by extension, a victory or triumph.

In 1853 a Congregational church was completed on Lanakila hill, overlooking the sea. Many of the stones for the church walls were obtained from Wahi o Pua, the shallow semicircle of reef fronting the present beach park. Also pieces of coral removed from this area were burned in *umu,* the furnaces constructed for converting the coral to lime. The lime produced in this way was mixed with sand to make the mortar to set up the church's stone walls and the frames of the twelve large windows and three panel doors.

By the late 1890s there was a shift in population. Many people had moved from Hauʻula down the coast to Kaluanui and Punaluʻu. About 1897 the wood taken

147

from Lanakila Church was hauled by mules to Hale'aha in Kaluanui, where it was used to construct a smaller church. Since that time the original Lanakila Church has been in ruins.

In 1921 an executive order set aside the shoreline *makai* of Lanakila for public use, as Hau'ula Beach Park. The large reef that enclosed the new park's beach and inshore waters was known then as Wahi o Pua, "place of young fish." In former times Wahi o Pua provided the entire village of Hau'ula with most of its food from the sea. Today those natural resources have been rather depleted. In 1947 the bath house and pavilion were completed.

The beach fronting Hau'ula Beach Park is fairly straight and narrow. It is about 1,000 feet long and has a moderately steep foreshore. The waters of Wahi o Pua directly *makai* of the park are safe and protected, but are not attractive for recreational swimming. The bottom is shallow and primarily rocky.

There are two dangerous spots in the area, one at each end of the beach. On the Kahuku end, a large sand-bottom channel, once known as Kilia after a type of wave, crosses the reef and comes in to the beach. The currents in Kilia are often strong and, combined with its deep waters, make it a potentially hazardous area for unknowing swimmers. At high tide, Kilia is a popular surfing spot among the young people of Hau'ula.

At the eastern end of the beach park, Ma'akua Stream comes down to the ocean. As with many Hawaiian streams, a bar of sand often separates Ma'akua from the sea, thereby forming a *muliwai,* a pond of brackish standing water. The *muliwai* can be a dangerous place for wandering children. City and County lifeguard service is provided in this beach park during the summer months.

'Aukai Beach Park

54–071 Kamehameha Highway, Hau'ula

F: none; roadside parking along Kamehameha Highway
LG: none
EP: Hau'ula Beach Park
PP: Hau'ula Beach Park
FS: 54–064 Kamehameha Highway, Hau'ula

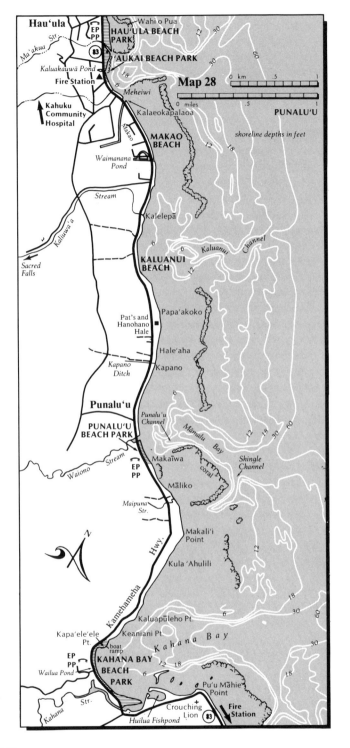

148

H: Kahuku Community Hospital, Hospital Road, Kahuku
SS: Kamehameha Highway, Hau'ula
WA: diving; paipo board surfing (limited); swimming
WC: very strong currents when surf is big or ocean is stormy; waves breaking on shelf at high tide can safely accommodate paipo board surfers; entire beach park is fronted by shallow coral shelf
PA: unlimited
AI: named after Alfred 'Aukai 'Āluli, last private owner of this park's land

'Aukai Beach Park is a 0.2–acre bit of land in Hau'ula located in front of the *muliwai* once called Kaluakauwā. The small park was named for Alfred 'Aukai 'Āluli, once the owner of this land and of the large homestead across the highway from it. 'Aukai was born in Ke'anae on Maui and came to Hau'ula in 1910. He built a grass shack on the property at first; it was followed in 1912 by a wooden house, part of which is still standing. This Hau'ula land was given to him by an uncle. In December 1932, the Territory of Hawai'i bought all rights to the beach and road area of 'Aukai's property for $87.35, in its plan to realign and improve Kamehameha Highway. In 1940 ownership of the beach strip was transferred to the City and County, to make it a public park. Eventually it was named 'Aukai Beach Park in honor of the last private owner of the land. Mr. 'Aukai is well remembered among the older residents of Hau'ula. He was a very kind and friendly man who was well known to the children. He spent a great deal of time on his beach before he died in the early 1950s. He was buried in the graveyard of the historic Lanakila Church.

To the rear of 'Aukai's homestead was a large pond, now a swamp, that once housed a *luamo'o,* a dragon hole. When the yellow *hau* flowers were blooming profusely, the pond and *muliwai* waters of Kaluakauwā would turn cloudy or greenish, signifying that the *mo'o* was living in that home. When the *hau* trees stopped blooming, the water would become clear once again, and the people would know that the *mo'o* was gone. The pond, fed originally by streams from Kapoho Valley to the rear of Makao, drained into the ocean through the *muliwai.* Today the former pond is a swamp, most of which has been filled. The *luamo'o* was destroyed when the foundation for a sugar plantation railroad running from Kahuku to Kahana Valley was constructed.

The shoreline of 'Aukai Beach Park is fronted by a raised coral reef that makes recreational swimming impossible at any time. At high tide, small waves wash across the shelf, creating a fairly strong alongshore current. The tiny park, however, borders upon a small bay with a sand bottom and a very narrow but sandy beach. It is easily accessible from the park and provides a good swimming area. When the ocean is rough, however, some very strong alongshore currents in the bay can form fast-moving rip currents in its offshore waters.

The small bay adjoining 'Aukai Beach Park ends at Kalaeokapalaoa, "the point of the whale," where the *muliwai* Meheiwi meets the ocean. The point takes its name from a legend about Hau'ula, the story of Makuakaumana, a *kahuna* who had come from the distant land of Kahiki.

Makuakaumana lived in the nearby valley of Kaipapa'u. One day his son, who had long been searching for his father, located the *kahuna*'s home. He entreated his father to return to Kahiki with him, but Makuakaumana refused. Disappointed and angered by his father's refusal, the son made a prophecy and left. He prophesied that one day Makuakaumana would go down to the beach and never return. Some time later, a large whale was washed ashore at Meheiwi. Thinking it dead, the people of Hau'ula played on its back and jumped from it into the ocean. Makuakaumana, hearing the shouts of laughter, left his home and joined in the play. As he climbed upon the great creature to make his third jump, the whale suddenly came to life and carried Makuakaumana off to Kahiki. From then on, the point was known as Kalaeokapalaoa.

There is one public right-of-way to the point.

Makao Beach
Kamehameha Highway, Hau'ula (across from Makao Road or Pokiwai Street)

F: none; roadside parking along Kamehameha Highway
LG: none
EP: Hau'ula Beach Park
PP: none
FS: 54–064 Kamehameha Highway, Hau'ula
H: Kahuku Community Hospital, Hospital Road, Kahuku
SS: Kamehameha Highway, Hau'ula

WA: beachcombing; diving; pole fishing; snorkeling; swimming

WC: safe all year; infrequent strong currents when surf is big or stormy; narrow sandy beach; shallow coral bottom

PA: unlimited

The name Makao was given to this section of Hau'ula because of many Chinese rice farmers who once lived and worked in the area. Ships traveling from China to Hawai'i often sailed out of Macao near Canton, and the name was associated with the local Chinese farming community.

Makao probably is best known as the original homestead of the Lanes, a once-prominent island family. William Carey Lane was born in Cork County, Ireland, in 1821. It was a time of religious turmoil and persecution in Ireland and William's father, a staunch Catholic, electing to give up his lands rather than compromise his principles, moved his family to New York. At the age of eighteen, young William went to sea. After roaming the Pacific for several years, he settled in the Hawaiian Islands. He married a beautiful Hawaiian chiefess of Ko'olauloa, Mary Kukeakalani Kaho'oilimoku. Kukeakalani's father Kukanaloa was a high chief who had been attached to the court of Kamehameha the Great. Kukanaloa's closeness to the Conquerer was proved by the fact that he was in charge of Kamehameha's personal war canoe.

William and Kukeakalani Lane had twelve children, six sons and six daughters. During the reign of Queen Lili'uokalani, four of the Lane boys were personal aides to the queen. After the overthrow of the monarchy, all six brothers took part in the counterrevolution that attempted to restore the queen to her throne. Their father reminded them never to forget the loyalty and the fighting spirit gained from both their Hawaiian and Irish heritages. The failure of the royalist insurrection meant imprisonment and some difficult years for the Lane brothers, as well as for others who had participated in the attempt at restoration. In time however, the family once again resumed its prominent place in island society.

The Lane homestead was located in Makao, where Kukeakalani owned 176 acres of land. In addition to sheep ranching, William raised blooded horses for himself and Kamehameha V. Because he was the only *haole* living permanently on this side of O'ahu, he was appointed to many public offices, such as district magistrate, tax collector, and surveyor. The Lane homestead was the stopping place in Hau'ula for members of the Hawaiian nobility and their escorts who rode horseback into the country. The only evidence today of the once splendid Lane estate is a small family graveyard near the end of Makao Road.

The shoreline of Makao and Kapaka, a small district bordering Makao, is composed of a narrow sand beach, well protected by an offshore fringing reef. The ocean bottom is shallow and rocky all the way out to the reef and primarily attracts fishermen and skin divers. At high tide very little of the beach is not covered by water. Inshore currents are almost negligible. Access to the area is easy, as the entire beach is bordered by Kamehameha Highway.

Kaluanui Beach

53–500 area of Kamehameha Highway, Kaluanui (between Hau'ula and Punalu'u)

  F: none; roadside parking along Kamehameha Highway
 LG: none
 EP: Hau'ula Beach Park or Punalu'u Beach Park
 PP: none
 FS: 54–064 Kamehameha Highway, Hau'ula
  H: Kahuku Community Hospital, Hospital Road, Kahuku
 SS: Kamehameha Highway, Hau'ula
 WA: beachcombing; diving; snorkeling; swimming
 WC: safe all year, except when surf is big or stormy; strong rip currents in channels through outer reef
 PA: public right-of-way at Kaliuwa'a Stream (Kaluanui Bridge)

The Kaluanui district of Ko'olauloa abounds in legends, the outstanding character in most of them being Kamapua'a, the demigod who could assume the form of a pig as well as that of a man. Kamapua'a's exploits took him to all of the islands in the Hawaiian chain. He was the foremost rogue among Hawaiian deities and usually caused trouble and destruction wherever he went. As a rooting hog, he mischievously ruined the cultivated lands of the chiefs; and as a handsome man he played havoc with the affections of high-born women. One of his most famous escapades took place in Kaluanui.

Kamapua'a, in his pig form, had been harassing the people of Hau'ula and spoiling their fields. One day, in anger, they chased him from the village and surrounded him near the mouth of Kaliuwa'a Valley above Kaluanui. Kamapua'a broke through the barrier and raced up the narrow, steep-walled gorge. Upon reaching the head of the valley he realized that he was trapped. Calling upon his superhuman powers, he reared up on his hind legs and scaled the sheer mountain wall. His hooves gouged into it an immense groove or fluting. Because of this feat the people realized that the pig was really Kamapua'a the demigod. After that time no one entered Kaliuwa'a without making an offering, usually a rock placed on a ti leaf. The long upright groove was called Kaliuwa'a, "the canoe hull," for its resemblance to the belly of a Hawaiian canoe. Because of the practice of making offerings, the foreign people who came later called the valley "Sacred Falls."

The land division of Kaluanui stretches from Kaliuwa'a Stream at the Kamehameha Highway bridge marked "Kaluanui" to Waiono Stream, at the western end of Punalu'u Beach Park. Kaluanui means "the large pit," and probably refers to a place where the legendary Kamapua'a once relieved himself in a hole he had dug, in accordance with the *kapu* governing such acts. The district of Kaluanui also includes the smaller shoreline areas of Kalelepā, Papa'akoko, Hale'aha, Kapano, and Waiono.

The most popular swimming and fishing section of Kaluanui Beach is found almost at its center, where Kaluanui Channel cuts through the reef into a large sandy bay. Many divers and surround-net fishermen, as well as recreational swimmers, frequent these waters. Almost the entire length of Kaluanui Beach is sandy, shallow, and safe for swimming. Occasionally the alongshore currents are strong, but they do not cause a serious problem. The dangerous currents run offshore through Kaluanui Channel and the outer regions of the fringing reef. There is one public right-of-way in Kalelepā alongside Kaliuwa'a Stream. The only other convenient public access to the beach is the open stretch of Kamehameha Highway at the mouth of Kapano Stream.

Punalu'u Beach Park
53–309 Kamehameha Highway, Punalu'u

 F: 2 comfort stations; cooking stands and picnic tables; roadside parking along Kamehameha Highway
LG: none
EP: in park area
PP: in park area
FS: 54–064 Kamehameha Highway, Hau'ula
 H: Kahuku Community Hospital, Hospital Road, Kahuku
SS: Kamehameha Highway, Hau'ula
WA: beachcombing; diving; snorkeling; swimming
WC: safe all year, except during very high or stormy surf; strong rip currents in channels through outer reef
PA: unlimited

Punalu'u, in this place, means "to dive for coral." The name probably refers to the way in which coral was obtained for the making of lime. Hawaiian women of fashion, in the olden days, changed the color of their hair by using a bleach of powdered lime mixed with an infusion of ti leaves. The process was described by Ludwig Choris, an artist with Captain von Kotzebue's first visit to the Hawaiian Islands in 1816. The effects of the bleaching are shown in some of his portraits of Hawaiian women. The lime was obtained by burning pieces of coral in an *umu,* or kiln. In later years, this process was used to obtain lime for preparing construction mortar, such as was needed in the building of Lanakila Church in Hau'ula and Kawaiaha'o Church in Honolulu.

One of the most famous temples in Ko'olauloa stood in Punalu'u, near the present beach park. The chief of the district at the height of the *heiau*'s importance was Kekuaokalani, who made his home in Maliko, the shoreline area between the park and Maipuna Stream. Kahonu was the priest in charge of the temple that stood just *mauka* of the chief's residence. It was said that on sacred nights the eyes of all the pigs near the boundaries of the *heiau* would turn red. For this reason it was called Kaumaka'ula'ula, "the red eyes."

Christine A. Takata

Punaluʻu Beach Park. A popular camping area, Punaluʻu Beach Park is a narrow strip of land separating Kamehameha Highway from the ocean. Over the years this park has been severely eroded by winter storms. Large boulders have been placed along certain sections of the park's shoreline to stay the loss of land to the ocean.

At the western end of Punaluʻu Beach Park, Waiono Stream empties into the ocean. It was a deep, fast-flowing river before its waters were diverted in the valley above. The bridge crossing the river was a favorite diving platform for children in Punaluʻu. The ocean was very turbulent where the fresh and salt water met. Waiono was an excellent grounds for ʻoʻopu, the gobie fish, the most abundant varieties being the kaniʻoniʻo, nākea, ʻōkuhekuhe, and the nāpili.

In early days the deep channel in the ocean bottom cut by the swift-flowing waters of Waiono made the off-shore bay a favored stopping place for the coastal schooners and steamers that journeyed around Oʻahu.

A long pier was built near the mouth of the stream, one very similar to the former pier at Pounders Beach in Lāʻie-maloʻo. The ships came inshore here to deliver supplies and to pick up the locally grown rice, which was milled in Honolulu. Today Waiono is little more than a shallow, muddy stream. Nothing remains of the pier.

During World War II, the U.S. Army established many training areas for jungle warfare on the windward side of Oʻahu. In the village of Kaʻaʻawa, a few miles away, the Army set up a barracks camp and head-quarters in the present Swanzy Beach Park. In true military fashion, the two primary training valleys were identified by a color code: Kahana was called "Blue Valley" and Punalu'u, "Green Valley." From that time on, Punalu'u has been known to many islanders as "Green Valley," especially to O'ahu's teenagers who have hiked into it to ride back down to the lowlands in the irrigation flumes.

Punalu'u Beach Park is a narrow three-acre park lying between Kamehameha Highway and the sea. Its shoreline has experienced very severe erosion. In an effort to prevent further loss of sand, large boulders were placed at the Hau'ula end of the park, where the damage was the most serious. This section of shoreline was a former canoe landing called Makaīwa.

The beach is relatively narrow and straight and provides excellent swimming grounds. The inshore waters are shallow, with patches of coral and sand, and are well protected by the offshore fringing reef. The only dangerous currents in Mamalu Bay are found outside Waiono Stream where Punalu'u Channel crosses the outside reef. When the ocean is rough or the surf is big, some very strong rip currents run seaward through the channel.

Just offshore from the beach park is another small tributary channel that extends eastward toward Kahana Bay. It is commonly called "Shingle Channel," after the prominent island family who had a beach home in Maliko for many years. It is a popular fishing grounds.

The rest of the shoreline in the Punalu'u district runs from the beach park to Kahana Bay. This section of coast passes through Maliko, around Makali'i Point, and through Kula 'Āhulili. The beach is very similar to the area fronting the park, and is just as safe for swimming. The Kula 'Āhulili section has experienced very severe erosion and is completely underwater at high tide.

There is no convenient public access to this part of Punalu'u's shoreline.

Kahana Bay Beach Park

52-222 Kamehameha Highway, Kahana

F: 1 comfort station; 2 lifeguard towers; cooking stands and picnic tables; 1 boat ramp; 26 parking stalls

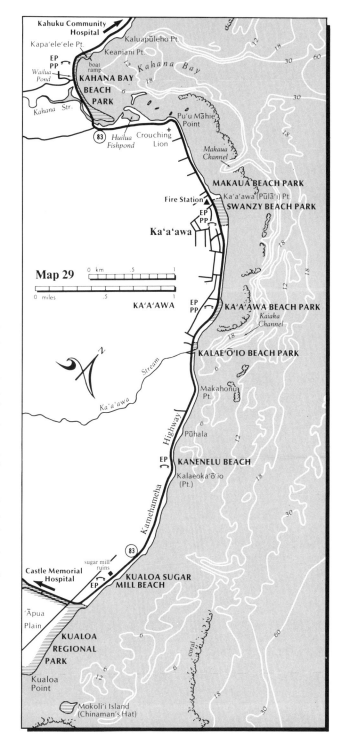

153

Among fishermen in the islands, Kahana Bay is known for the immense schools of *akule*, or big-eyed scad, that used to visit its waters every year. The coming of the *akule* was a very important and exciting time for the large Hawaiian community that formerly lived in the valley. A spotter posted high on a bluff overlooking the sea would cry loudly to the villagers onshore as soon as he saw the first schools approaching. As the fishermen moved out into the bay in their canoes laden with nets, the spotter directed their movements, signaling either with his arms or with a flag. Kahana was an ideal place for this method of fishing with surround nets, because the waters there are comparatively calm and protected. *Akule* were caught at other places in Ko'olauloa, such as Hau'ula and Lā'ie-malo'o, but fishing in those waters was more difficult because of the stronger currents.

The *akule* schools that entered Kahana often were so immense that a large enclosure made of double nets hung from supporting fence poles was erected to confine the surplus fish in the bay. In later years when the fish were hauled to the markets of Honolulu rather than

Christine A. Takata

Kahana Bay Beach Park. Fishermen and swimmers congregate around Kapa'ele'ele Boat Ramp in Kahana Bay, the only public launching site for many miles in either direction up or down the coast. The facility was blessed and named by Peter Kau, a long-time resident of Kahana Valley, after a fishing shrine of the same name that was located on a bluff overlooking the ramp.

kept for the use of the people alone, often several days were needed to empty the underwater corral. Traditionally, everyone in the valley participated in helping with the nets, and they were given a share of the catch in thanks for their efforts. *Akule* were given also to all older people who could no longer help draw in the nets or fish for themselves. By their sharing with the entire community, the fishermen insured their continued success and good fortune. Everyone who took fish home remembered those generous men in prayers to the gods and asked that the luck of the fishermen be ever good. Fishermen who in their greed violated the traditional sharing of the catch soon found their success in fishing slowly waning, never to return.

Kahana Bay curves between the two points of Kaluapūleho on the west of Pu'u Mahie on the east. Kaluapūleho means "the hole of the cowrey shell," and refers to a legend about a huge *pūleho,* who lived in the area. Guarded by a large eel, he appeared only at certain times of the year, much as *mo'o* did in other parts of O'ahu. The next small point shoreward of Kaluapūleho was called Keaniani, "the softly blowing breeze." The last point on the western side of the bay was called Kapa'ele'ele, "black tapa," which took its name from a fishing shrine for *akule* that once stood on the bluff above. Kapa'ele'ele is also the formal name of the public boat ramp located on this point. The ramp was blessed and christened by Peter Kau, a much beloved long-time resident of Kahana Bay.

The sand beach in Kahana lies between two former fishponds, one natural and one man-made. In former times the *muliwai* of Wailua at the western end of the beach was a natural fishpond formed by a small mountain stream meeting the waters of the bay. Wailua, however, was much overshadowed by its sister pond, Huilua, at the opposite end of the beach. Huilua, its shape still intact, can be seen near the mouth of Kahana Stream. The pond has not been used for many years. Beyond Huilua the shoreline is primarily a rocky cliff ending at the point of Pu'u Mahie, "pleasant hill."

Although the entire valley of Kahana is now owned by the State, the City and County maintains the eight-acre beach park along the bay's sandy shoreline. The shore itself is a long barrier beach that is fairly wide and flat almost all year long. The sandy ocean bottom has a very gentle slope toward the deeper offshore waters, making it a very safe and popular swimming area. A small easy shorebreak rolls in almost continually, providing ideal bodysurfing conditions for young or novice bodysurfers. When a big swell is running across the offshore reefs at the mouth of the bay, occasionally waves suitable for beginning board surfers form outside the shorebreak. The wide sand-bottom channel that runs out to the middle of Kahana Bay is one of the largest on O'ahu. The channel provides good entry and exit for Kapa'ele'ele Boat Ramp.

Makaua Beach Park

51–541 Kamehameha Highway, Makaua (Pūlā'ī Point)

  F: none; roadside parking along Kamehameha Highway
LG: none
EP: Swanzy Beach Park, Ka'a'awa
PP: Swanzy Beach Park, Ka'a'awa
FS: 51–518 Kamehameha Highway, Ka'a'awa
  H: Kahuku Community Hospital, Hospital Road, Kahuku
SS: Kamehameha Highway, Hau'ula
WA: diving; pole fishing; swimming
WC: ocean bottom very shallow and rocky; rocks exposed at low tide; abrupt drop from shallow area into Makaua Channel; strong rip currents in channel, especially when surf is high or stormy
PA: unlimited

Makaua, "eye of the rain," is a small district that often is included as part of its better-known neighbor, Ka'a'awa. On the shoreline, Makaua stretches from Pu'u Mahie Point to Pūlā'ī Point, more commonly called Ka'a'awa Point. Makaua is best known as the place of the rock formation resembling a crouching lion. The Crouching Lion Inn, a public restaurant located below the ridge bearing that distinctive formation, is a former private residence that has been converted into a public lodge, dining room, and gift shop.

The first owner of the home was George F. Larsen, Sr., who came to Hawai'i in 1912 and entered the construction business in Honolulu. Some years after his arrival, the land below the Crouching Lion was offered for sale. In 1925, Larsen and Robert Chase, another contractor, purchased two adjoining parcels of land. Chase

155

built the house that still stands at the bend in the highway leading into Kahana Bay. He also constructed a boat landing and a small pier, the location of which is marked now only by a few pilings. The pier was destroyed during a tsunami.

Larsen built the large structure that is now the Crouching Lion Inn. The house was designed by his wife, whose ideas were put into building plans by architect Lou Davis. Construction began in 1926 and was completed in 1928. All of the lumber was milled in the Pacific Northwest and was purchased locally from Lewers and Cooke Co., Ltd. Very little paint was used; most of the wood for the interior was rough-hewn, burned slightly with a blow torch to give it a hand-cut and aged effect, and then oiled. Much of the blue rock that was excavated for the building's foundation was used in constructing the massive exterior walls.

The furniture was of rough, hand-hewn wood and many of the decorative furnishings, such as rugs, paintings, and pottery, were imported from Norway. The wrought iron hinges and other metal fixtures made to order by Honolulu Iron Works are still in evidence on the main doors. The emblem of the hod carrier, a man shouldering a wooden tray for carrying mortar and bricks, was placed on the front door in Scandinavian tradition to signify Larsen's trade as a plastering, lathing, and bricklaying contractor.

The house originally had no electricity, for in 1928 the power lines had not yet reached Makaua. Larsen, however, had his entire home wired. Eventually when electric lines were extended, the house was simply connected to the public source.

The Larsen family lived in "Hale Liona," House of the Lion, as they referred to their home, until 1931, when they moved to Honolulu. In 1937 the estate was sold to Reginald Faithful, then president of Honolulu Dairymen's Association. In July 1951, Hale Liona was opened as a lodge and dining room and renamed the Crouching Lion Inn. It has remained open to the public since that time and today is one of the most popular tourist attractions on this side of O'ahu.

Makaua Beach Park, just down the road toward Ka'a'awa from the Crouching Lion Inn, is small and undeveloped. The sand beach in Makaua is very narrow and in the park area disappears completely at high tide.

There are no good swimming spots; the ocean bottom is shallow and primarily of coral reef. Just offshore from the beach park, a large sand-bottom channel cuts through the reef. This channel is a favorite fishing ground for both divers and pole fishermen. It also accommodates small craft that anchor off Pūlā'ī Point.

The channel often has very strong rip currents in its outer regions that preclude recreational swimming.

Swanzy Beach Park
51–392 Kamehameha Highway, Ka'a'awa

F: 1 comfort station; 1 combination basketball/volleyball court; 1 softball field; children's play apparatus; cooking stands and picnic tables; 1 lifeguard tower; 32 parking stalls
LG: none
EP: in park area
PP: in park area
FS: 51–518 Kamehameha Highway, Ka'a'awa
H: Kahuku Community Hospital, Hospital Road, Kahuku
SS: Kamehameha Highway, Hau'ula
WA: diving; snorkeling; swimming
WC: safe all year, except during high or stormy surf; strong rip currents in channels through outer reef; inshore areas shallow and rocky
PA: unlimited

During the 1920s the City and County of Honolulu was seriously considering opening a public beach park in Kualoa, near Chinaman's Hat. Mrs. Julie Judd Swanzy, a prominent island resident who lived about a mile from the proposed site, (and who had inherited Kualoa and Ka'a'awa from her father, Dr. Gerrit P. Judd I), became very disturbed at the prospect of having a public park so close to her country home. To protect her privacy she thought of an alternative. She asked Mayor John H. Wilson to accompany her on a drive to Ka'a'awa. During the course of the ride she offered to give the City and County five acres of beach land in Ka'a'awa if the plans to develop the park near her home at Kualoa were abandoned. Mayor Wilson accepted her offer on condition that Mrs. Swanzy add another narrow strip of land about a mile down the beach for use as a park, and an additional acre inland from that for an elementary school. The entire transaction was conclud-

Swanzy Beach Park. At high tide this narrow sand and rubble beach fronting the beach park is often completely under water. The ocean bottom between the retaining wall and the offshore reef is relatively shallow and is a good octopus ground.

Fishermen can often be seen wading through the area with spears and glass-bottomed boxes searching for octopus, or "squid" as these animals are commonly, but incorrectly, called in Hawaii.

ed for the token price of one dollar. The larger gift of land was designated Ka'a'awa-nui Park and the smaller one Ka'a'awa-iki Park. In 1950 Ka'a'awa-nui Park was officially renamed Julie Judd Swanzy Park in honor of the donor of the land, and in recognition of her work with Honolulu's Public Playground and Recreation Commission, of which she had been president for many years. After Ka'a'awa-nui Park was renamed for Mrs. Swanzy, its smaller companion opposite the school was called simply Ka'a'awa Park.

During World War II, the larger park was used as a headquarters for the U.S. Army's extensive jungle warfare training program in Kahana Valley. The temporary buildings left in the park by the Army when the war ended were entirely demolished by the tsunami that struck

the islands on April 1, 1946. The park's present facilities were opened to the public in August 1957.

The entire *makai* edge of Swanzy Beach Park is defined by a high masonry seawall. The beach in front of the wall consists almost entirely of rocks and small boulders, with patches of sand interspersed. The winter storms of 1968/69 severely damaged the beach and undermined the seawall. The usual and expected accretion of sand did not occur in the summer of 1969 to repair the damage of the previous winter, and succeeding years have not corrected the situation.

Recreational swimming is safe in the area, but not appealing because of the lack of a good sand beach. The shallow offshore waters are frequented by fishermen.

The only major water hazard in the area is not in the

immediate vicinity but in a small channel well offshore in the fringing reef, beyond the houses on the Kāne'ohe side of the park. This rather inconspicuous break in the reef often has a very powerful rip current running seaward through it. When military units were stationed in Ka'a'awa during World War II, the channel currents caught many unsuspecting servicemen who ventured out into deeper waters. The channel is still dangerous and is well known among divers who frequent the area.

Ka'a'awa Beach Park
51–369 Kamehameha Highway, Ka'a'awa

F: 1 comfort station; 1 lifeguard tower; cooking stands and picnic tables; 8 parking stalls

LG: daily service provided by City and County from June through August
EP: Swanzy Beach Park
PP: in park area
FS: 51–518 Kamehameha Highway, Ka'a'awa
 H: Kahuku Community Hospital, Hospital Road, Kahuku
SS: Kamehameha Highway, Hau'ula
WA: diving; snorkeling; swimming
WC: safe all year, except during high or stormy surf; inshore areas are shallow pockets of sand and coral; strong rip current in Kaiaka Channel to right of beach park at edge of reef
PA: unlimited

Ka'a'awa means "the 'a'awa," the Hawaiian name for the yellow wrasse. Still fairly common, in olden times these reef dwellers were found in abundance in the district's offshore waters, along with e'a, another species of wrasse differentiated by its dark purple color. Pole fish-

Christine A. Takata

Ka'a'awa Beach Park. Looking across Kaiaka Bay to Makahonu Point. Although this park is but a very narrow strip of land bordering Kamehameha Highway, it is a very popular camping area, especially during the summer months when tents often fill its entire length. Mōkapu Peninsula, barely visible in the distance, can be easily imagined to resemble a turtle from this particular vantage point.

ermen often hooked tubs full of *'a'awa* in Makaua Channel off Pūlā'ī Point.

Ka'a'awa Beach Park is a narrow two-acre strip bordered by Kamehameha Highway. Erosions, which have been frequent to this beach, have increased in severity since 1962. In December 1968 the City and County set a barrier of rocks around many coconut trees, the comfort station, and along a portion of the beach. This emergency protective measure was an attempt to retard the severe erosion begun during the damaging storms that struck O'ahu's windward shore in that year.

Although the present beach is very much smaller than it was in former years, it is still a pleasant and safe place. The waters fronting the entire park area are shallow and well protected by an offshore coral reef. During the summer the park is filled with campers.

Kalae'ō'io Beach Park

51–237 Kamehameha Highway, Ka'a'awa (Kaiaka Bay)

F: picnic tables; roadside parking along Kamehameha Highway
LG: none
EP: Swanzy Beach Park

Christine A. Takata

Kalae'ō'io Beach Park. Located on the shoreline of Kaiaka Bay in Ka'a'awa, this tiny beach park is not easily differentiated from the private property along the same stretch. The park was named after Ka Lae o ka 'Ō'io, the point of the *'ō'io* (fish), a popular fishing and surfing area nearby. The mountain ridge so prominent in the picture is Kānehoalani, which divides the districts of Ka'a'awa and Kualoa.

159

PP: Ka'a'awa Beach Park
FS: 51–518 Kamehameha Highway, Ka'a'awa
 H: Kahuku Community Hospital, Hospital Road, Kahuku
SS: Kamehameha Highway, Hau'ula
WA: beachcombing; diving; snorkeling; swimming
WC: safe all year in inshore areas, except during high or stormy surf; strong rip currents in Kaiaka Channel offshore from park
PA: unlimited

LG: none
EP: in beach area
PP: Ka'a'awa Beach Park
FS: 51–518 Kamehameha Highway, Ka'a'awa
 H: Kahuku Community Hospital, Hospital Road, Kahuku
SS: Kamehameha Highway, Hau'ula
WA: beachcombing; diving; shore casting; board surfing; swimming
WC: safe all year; strong currents along shore during high or stormy surf; novice surfing break offshore
PA: unlimited
AI: popular fishing and surfing area

Kalae'ō'io Beach Park is a small one-acre strip located at 51–237 Kamehameha Highway. It takes its name from Kalaeoka'ō'io, "the point of the 'o'io," or bonefish, that separates the districts of Kualoa and Ka'a'awa. This point lies about a mile to the east of the park, on the way toward Kāne'ohe. The point also has been called Kalaeoka'oi'o, "the point of the night marchers." This alternate definition is derived from a different pronunciation of the last word in the name, and is attributed to the fact that the legendary Pohukaina Cave, said to have had its entrance in the foot of the nearest mountain, was believed to be one of the entrances by which the spirits of the dead went down into the Land of Milu.

The park is situated on a small bay that was formerly known as Kaiaka, "shadowy sea." The inshore waters of Kaiaka are shallow, sandy, and safe for swimming, but occasionally, when the ocean is rough or the tides are changing, a strong rip current runs out through Kaiaka Channel. Lifeguards stationed at nearby Ka'a'awa Beach Park have had to rescue several unwary swimmers being carried seaward by this current.

The bay of Kaiaka curves around to Makahonu Point, the reef and small point marked by a small grove of ironwood trees on the *makai* side of the highway. Makahonu means "eye of the turtle," and refers to times when Kaiaka was a feeding and nesting ground for these creatures.

Kanenelu Beach

(also Kalaeoka'ō'io or 'Ō'io Point and Kuloa Point)
50–000 area of Kamehameha Highway (at boundary between Ka'a'awa and Kualoa)

F: none; roadside parking along Kamehameha Highway

Kanenelu means "the marsh," and refers to a time when most of the shoreside of this part of Ka'a'awa valley was a swamp. Then there were many banana patches in Kanenelu. The taro patches of Ka'a'awa were situated farther north, in the marsh lands across from the present Ka'a'awa Beach Park. Kanenelu Beach stretches from the place called Pūhala to Kalaeoka'ō'io, the point separating not only Kualoa from Ka'a'awa but also Ko'olauloa from Ko'olaupoko. Pūhala, or "pandanus tree," was the name of a cottage owned by Mrs. F. M. Swanzy that is located midway between Kalaeoka'ō'io and Makahonu. The beach opposite the house is marked by one lone *hala* tree, although now the cottage itself is almost hidden behind a stand of *pūhala*. In the old days the people of Ka'a'awa made *lei* from the orange *hala* fruits because flowers were scarce and *hala* trees grew in plenty at the northern side of the valley, near the present schoolhouse.

Kanenelu is a favorite stopping place for many people who are driving around the island. It is the first good swimming beach bordering Kamehameha Highway after the long drive around Kāne'ohe Bay. Kanenelu is also a popular surfing area, the small offshore waves attracting many resident and visiting surfers. Wherever they come from, surfers usually refer to the break, quite incorrectly as "Kūloa Point." In doing so, they both mispronounce the name and misplace the neighboring district of Kualoa. Probably the beach is most heavily used by shorecasters, fishing for *moi, 'ō'io,* and *pāpio.*

Kanenelu is a rather narrow, moderately steep sand beach. The ocean bottom is shallow, consisting of sections of coral reef and pockets of sand. Generally it is safe for recreational swimming, being affected only occasionally by strong alongshore currents.

The Beaches of Koʻolaupoko District

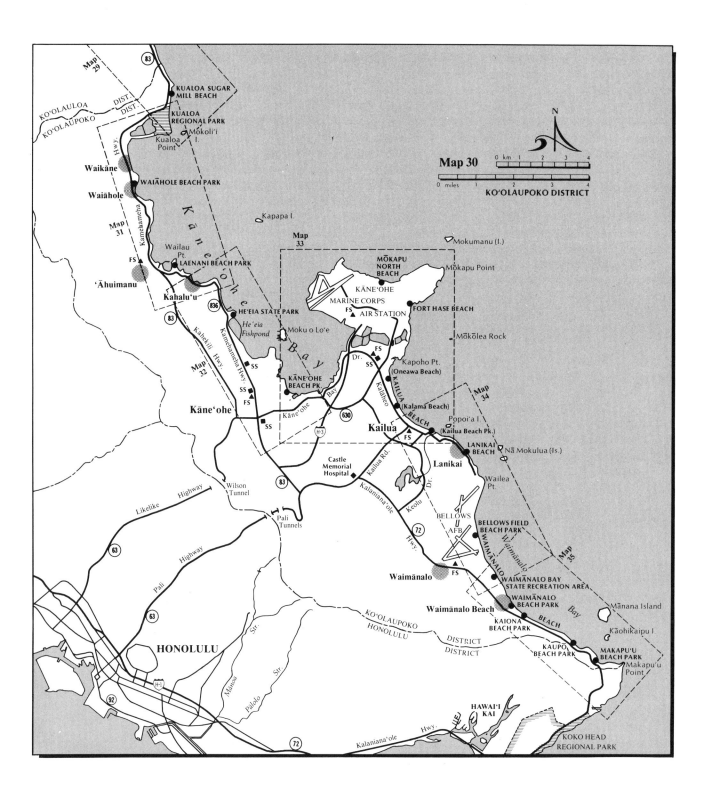

Map 30

N

0 km 1 2 3 4

0 miles 1 2 3 4

KO'OLAUPOKO DISTRICT

Map 29

KO'OLAULOA DIST.
KO'OLAUPOKO DIST.

KUALOA SUGAR MILL BEACH

KUALOA REGIONAL PARK

Mōkoli'i I.

Kualoa Point

Waikāne

WAIĀHOLE BEACH PARK

Waiāhole

Map 31

Wailau Pt.

LAENANI BEACH PARK

FS

'Āhuimanu

Kahalu'u

Kāne'ohe

Kapapa I.

Mokumanu (I.)

Map 33

MŌKAPU NORTH BEACH

Mōkapu Point

KĀNE'OHE MARINE CORPS AIR STATION

FS

FORT HASE BEACH

HE'EIA STATE PARK

He'eia Fishpond

Moku o Lo'e

Bay

Mōkōlea Rock

SS

Dr.

SS

FS

Kapoho Pt. (Oneawa Beach)

Kahekili Hwy.

Kamehameha Hwy.

SS

FS

KĀNE'OHE BEACH PK.

Kāne'ohe

Bay

630

SS

H-3

KAILUA BEACH

(Kalama Beach)

Kalāheo

Map 32

Kāne'ohe

Kailua

FS

(Kailua Beach Pk.)

Popoi'a I.

Map 34

LANIKAI BEACH

Nā Mokulua (Is.)

Castle Memorial Hospital

Kailua Rd.

Keolu Dr.

Lanikai

Wailea Pt.

Wilson Tunnel

Likelike Highway

Kalaniana'ole

83

BELLOWS AFB

BELLOWS FIELD BEACH PARK

Pali Tunnels

Pali Highway

72

63

FS

Waimānalo

Waimānalo

Waimānalo

WAIMĀNALO BAY STATE RECREATION AREA

Map 35

WAIMĀNALO BEACH PARK

KO'OLAUPOKO HONOLULU DISTRICT DISTRICT

Waimānalo Beach

BEACH

Bay

Mānana Island

KAIONA BEACH PARK

Kāohikaipu I.

KAUPŌ BEACH PARK

HONOLULU

Mānoa Str.

Pālolo Str.

92

H-1

MAKAPU'U BEACH PARK

Makapu'u Point

63

HAWAI'I KAI

72

Kalaniana'ole Hwy.

KOKO HEAD REGIONAL PARK

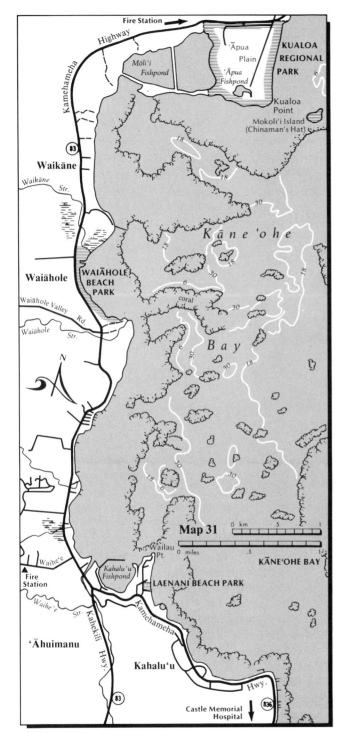

Kualoa Sugar Mill Beach

49–500 area of Kamehameha Highway, Kualoa

  F: none; roadside parking along Kamehameha Highway
LG: none
EP: in beach area
PP: Ka'a'awa Beach Park
FS: 51–518 Kamehameha Highway, Ka'a'awa
  H: Castle Memorial Hospital, 640 'Ulukahiki Street (Kalaniana'ole Highway at Kailua Road), Kailua
SS: Kamehameha Highway, Waikane or Kahalu'u
WA: diving; snorkeling; swimming
WC: safe all year; two narrow sections of roadside beach between residential housing; ocean bottom is shallow and rocky
PA: unlimited

When Captain Cook discovered the Hawaiian Islands in 1778, many varieties of sugarcane were being grown here. In later years, after foreigners came to live in the islands, the value of sugarcane as a source of sugar was realized, and many attempts were made to grow it on a commercial scale. During the twenty-year period between 1860 and 1880, five sugar plantations were started in the district of Ko'olaupoko alone, at Kāne'ohe, He'eia, Kea'ahala, Ka'alaea, and Kualoa. All of these plantations were eventually abandoned, principally because profits were too low to sustain the costs of growing the sugarcane. Methods of irrigation and fertilization were practically unknown then, and the machinery for processing the harvested cane was very inefficient. Today only the endangered masonry of Dr. G. P. Judd's sugar mill at Kualoa still stands, although the mill itself was closed in 1871.

The two sections of public beach near ''the Old Sugar Mill'' are very narrow and undeveloped. The ocean bottom is shallow and completely rocky. Only a few sand pockets in the reef are suitable for swimming and these are usable only at high tide. The area is frequented primarily by fishermen who search the shallows for octopus.

Kualoa Regional Park

49–600 area of Kamehameha Highway, Kualoa (across from Mokoli'i Island)

- F: 2 comfort stations, picnic and camping facilities, group activity facilities
- LG: daily service provided by City and County from June to August and on all weekends throughout the year
- EP: on Kamehameha Highway near park entrance
- PP: none
- FS: 51–518 Kamehameha Highway, Ka'a'awa
- H: Castle Memorial Hospital, 640 'Ulukahiki Street (Kalaniana'ole Highway at Kailua Road), Kailua
- SS: Kamehameha Highway, Waikane or Kahalu'u
- WA: diving; swimming
- WC: safe all year; occasionally strong currents along shore; long, narrow sandy beach; shallow inshore ocean bottom made of pockets of sand and reef
- PA: open 7:00 A.M.–7:00 P.M.; camping permits required
- AI: Mokoli'i Island (Chinaman's Hat, Poi Pounder Island) is part of beach park

This park is listed in the National Register of Historical Places because of its great importance in the life of native Hawaiian people.

Kualoa means "long back," but can be translated symbolically as "long ancestral background." The name probably refers to the times when the entire dis-

Christine A. Takata

Kualoa Regional Park. Blessed with an unobstructed view of not only the surrounding mountains, but Kāne'ohe Bay as well, Kualoa Regional Park is undoubtedly one of the most beautiful picnic and camping areas on O'ahu.

trict was one of the most sacred places on Oʻahu. Generations of Oʻahu's chiefs brought their infant children to this region to be raised by foster parents. Here the youths who would be rulers in the future were trained in the arts of war and the traditions of their heritage. Here also stood the temples housing the two sacred drums of Kapahuʻula and Kahauʻulapunawai. In deference to the sacredness of Kualoa, all canoes traveling past the area had to lower their sails from Waikāne to Kaʻaʻawa.

The plains of Kualoa that make up the present beach park were called ʻĀpua. This also is the name of a small fishpond in the area.

One of the most famous stories about Kualoa is told of Hiʻiaka, a sister of Pele, the goddess of the volcano. When Pele finally made her home on the Big Island, she wandered still in her dreams as a spirit. During one of these travels, she met and loved a handsome prince of Kauaʻi, but she was not content with only a spiritual intercourse. Pele wanted Lohiʻau present in body as well. She begged each of her sisters in turn to journey to Kauaʻi and bring back her lover. They all refused, forseeing the perils awaiting them in such a venture. Finally the youngest of the girls, Hiʻiaka, accepted the undertaking. As Hiʻiaka was following the shoreline trail around Kāneʻohe Bay, she was confronted by a *moʻo,* a large dragonlike creature. The *moʻo* who challenged her passing was killed by the young goddess. Hiʻiaka cut off his tail and threw it into the ocean, where it became an island. It is there still, offshore from the plains of ʻĀpua, and is called Mokoliʻi, "little dragon" (*moko* being an archaic form of *moʻo*). The island is also variously known as Chinaman's Hat, Pāpale Pake, and Poi Pounder Island.

An interesting aspect of the numerous legends about *moʻo* told throughout these islands is that there are no true land reptiles in the Hawaiian Archipelago other than a few species of small lizards, the gekkos and the skinks. It is doubtful that these lizards inspired in Hawaiians the fear, the respect, and the tales of great feats of battle between the gods and the *moʻo*. These legends suggest that during some earlier period in the migrations of the Polynesians the people may have encountered huge lizards such as those found on Komodo Island in Indonesia. The giant Komodo lizards are believed also to have inspired the dragons of Chinese mythology. At any rate, the origins and frequent mention of *moʻo* in Hawaiian legends make for interesting speculation.

Kualoa Regional Park, on the plains of ʻĀpua, is being developed by the City and County of Honolulu. When the eleven planned phases of development are completed, it will undoubtedly be one of the most beautiful parks on Oʻahu, offering as it does a spectacular view not only of the magnificent Koʻolau mountains but of the expanse of Kāneʻohe Bay and the islands beyond as well. The sand beach fronting the huge park is very long and narrow, having been eroded for most of its length back to the shoreline vegetation. The offshore waters are shallow and experience strong alongshore currents only infrequently. The bottom is a mixture of patches of coral reef and sand-filled pockets. The entire area is safe for swimming.

Mokoliʻi Island is also a part of the park. It is the only offshore island around Oʻahu, besides Coconut Island, that is not a State-owned bird refuge or sanctuary. The distance from Kualoa Point to the island is 500 yards.

Kāneʻohe Bay

Kāneʻohe means "bamboo man," or "bamboo husband." According to one legendary account, a woman compared her husband's cruelty to the cutting edge of a bamboo knife. Thereupon the place where they lived was called Kāneʻohe.

Although Kāneʻohe proper is only one of several districts of Koʻolaupoko, the huge sweep of sea extending from Kualoa Point to the Heʻeia section of Mōkapu is called Kāneʻohe Bay. Formerly it was known as Koʻolau Bay, but the name Kāneʻohe became prevalent in the 1840s with the coming of the first Protestant missionaries to live in Koʻolaupoko. The Kāneʻohe Mission was established by Benjamin W. Parker in 1835. Because the mission became a focal point for the entire area, soon the bay itself was referred to as Kāneʻohe.

Much of the eight-mile shoreline of Kāneʻohe Bay has been made artificially, the result of dredging, filling, and construction of retaining walls and other structures, including open piers for recreational craft. Because the bay includes a deep lagoon between the outer reef and the shore, the reef is considered by some geologists to be a true barrier reef, the only example of such a one in

Hawai'i. The few beach areas along the shoreline are composed almost entirely of silt and mud flats because the low amount of wave energy within the bay is unable to redistribute the large quantities of material washed down from the land.

In recent years the amount of topsoil carried into Kāne'ohe Bay by its ten tributary streams has become a critical problem. The effect on the bay itself has been dramatic. The abundance and distribution of corals have been considerably reduced because of sedimentation and exposure to diluted seawater caused by flooding with freshwater. Because the bay watershed has been scarred by development, and many acres of earth have been exposed in clearing land for housing and highway construction, runoff of both soil and water after heavy rains has been tremendous.

In addition to the effect of the runoff on the coral and fish life in the bay, shoreline recreational swimming too has been made almost impossible. There is not one good beach along the entire length of Kāne'ohe Bay. The three public beach parks, at Kāne'ohe, Laenani, and Waiāhole, are frequented primarily by picnickers and fishermen. A fourth park, overlooking He'eia fishpond, is presently being planned. Their inshore waters are safe and relatively hazard free, but the numerous shallow (and odorous) mud flats preclude almost all swimming except by the most nondiscriminatory.

Waiāhole Beach Park

48–181 Kamehameha Highway, Waiāhole

F: none; roadside parking along Kamehameha Highway
LG: none
EP: Kamehameha Highway, near entrance to Kualoa Regional Park
PP: none
FS: 47–304 Waihe'e Road, Kahalu'u
H: Castle Memorial Hospital, 640 'Ulukahiki Street (Kalaniana'ole Highway at Kailua Road), Kailua
SS: Kamehameha Highway, Waikane or Kahalu'u
WA: beachcombing; pole fishing
WC: safe all year; entire shoreline is fronted by shallow coral reef and mud flats; water very murky
PA: unlimited

Waiāhole means "mature āhole (fish) water." This fish is commonly known to local fishermen today as āholehole, a term the Hawaiians reserved for the growing stage of the fish. Although the āhole is primarily a saltwater inhabitant, it is also found in freshwater, often in stream mouths, which is why the name has *wai,* "freshwater," in it as opposed to *kai,* "salt water." Āhole are excellent eating and are sought after by pole and throw-net fishermen as well as by divers.

Waiāhole Valley was probably most famous for its taro, the high quality of which was known throughout the islands. The Waiāhole Poi Factory, located at the intersection of Waiāhole Valley Road and Kamehameha Highway, was operational from 1904 until May of 1971. It was one of the largest *poi* factories on O'ahu. The old building is now a Hawaiian artifact and art center.

Waiāhole is also known as the site of the Waiāhole Tunnel, actually a network of tunnels, drilled through the Ko'olau Mountain Range to collect and channel water from windward O'ahu to irrigate leeward O'ahu. The project was started in 1913 and completed in 1916.

Waiāhole Beach Park is undeveloped and fronted by shallow mud flats. It is frequented primarily by fishermen and beachcombers.

Laenani Beach Park

47–053 Laenani Drive, He'eia (off Kamehameha Highway)

F: 1 comfort station; 1 basketball court; 1 volleyball court; 1 softball field; children's play apparatus; 9 parking stalls
LG: none
EP: none
PP: none
FS: 47–034 Waihe'e Road, Kahalu'u
H: Castle Memorial Hospital, 640 'Ulukahiki Street (Kalaniana'ole Highway at Kailua Road), Kailua
SS: Kamehameha Highway, Kahalu'u or Kāne'ohe
WA: pole fishing; swimming
WC: safe all year; no beach; park edged by retaining wall; shallow and rocky ocean bottom
PA: unlimited
AI: Laenani means "beautiful point of land"

Laenani means "beautiful point of land." Laenani Beach Park is located on Wailau Point in the district of Kahalu'u. This point was formerly known as Libbyville and was once the center of a major pineapple-growing and -canning operation in Kahalu'u.

During the late 1800s, before pineapple was introduced to Ko'olaupoko, rice was produced commercially here on a large scale. By the early 1900s, however, Hawai'i's rice production had suffered a major decline because local growers could no longer compete successfully with those on the mainland. In 1909 a cannery was opened on Wailau Point to process the pineapple that had been introduced as the successor to the rice. The village that grew up around the cannery was called Libbyville after Libby, McNeill, and Libby, the company that owned and headed the pineapple operations. The Libbyville cannery was eventually closed in 1926 when plant diseases halted all pineapple production in this area of O'ahu. St. John's-by-the-Sea Church now occupies the former cannery site. Laenani Beach Park is a small, flat park on the Kailua side of Wailau Point. Its ocean border is a low sea wall with no beach. The inshore bottom is rocky with shallow mud flats, so recreation swimming is poor.

He'eia State Park

46–465 Kamehameha Highway

   F: none
  LG: none
  EP: none
  PP: Kāne'ohe Bay Shopping Center, Kamehameha Highway
  FS: 45–910 Kamehameha Highway, Kāne'ohe
   H: Castle Memorial Hospital, 640 'Ulukahiki Street (Kalaniana'ole Highway at Kailua Road), Kailua
  SS: Kamehameha Highway in Kāne'ohe
  WA: fishing
  WC: shallow and rocky ocean bottom
  PA: unlimited
  AI: to be developed as a scenic park overlooking historic He'eia fishpond, one of the few old Hawaiian fishponds remaining in Kāne'ohe Bay

When the goddess Haumea moved to the Kualoa area at the northern end of Kāne'ohe Bay, she brought the

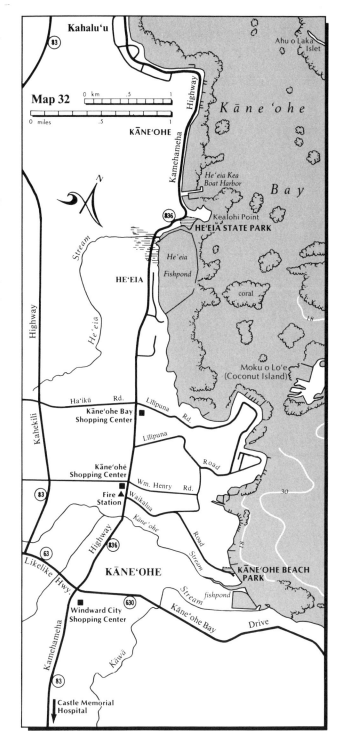

grandson of ʻOlopana with her to her new home. She named her foster child Heʻeia and the place near Kāneʻohe called Heʻeia was named in his honor.

Heʻeia is probably best known as the site of the Heʻeia fishpond, one of the few ancient fishponds on Oʻahu still fully intact. Kealohi, the name of the high point that the pond adjoins, is thought by some historians to also be the name of the pond, but many others do not agree with this. When the pond was maintained, it was famous for its excellent mullet.

Heʻeia State Park is presently an undeveloped parcel of land on Kealohi Point overlooking the old fishpond and Kāneʻohe Bay. There is no beach around the point and access is difficult, so there is very little recreational water activity in the area.

Kāneʻohe Beach Park
end of Waikalua Road, Kāneʻohe

F: 1 comfort station; picnic tables; children's play apparatus; 7 parking stalls
LG: none
EP: none
PP: none
FS: 45–910 Kamehameha Highway, Kāneʻohe
H: Castle Memorial Hospital, 640 ʻUlukahiki Street (Kalanianaʻole Highway at Kailua Road), Kailua
SS: Kamehameha Highway, Kāneʻohe
WA: clamming (during season); pole fishing
WC: safe all year; entire shoreline is fronted by shallow coral and mud flats; water very murky
PA: unlimited

North Beach, Mōkapu
(formerly Heleloa Beach: includes Pyramid Rock and Fourteenth Hole)
Kāneʻohe Marine Corps Air Station (fronting golf course)

F: none; roadside parking on nearby streets
LG: service provided by military personnel
EP: none

PP: on base
FS: Military: First Street and E Avenue; Civilian: 45 Kāneʻohe Bay Drive, ʻAikahi
H: Military: Tripler Army Medical Center, Jarrett White Road (off Moanalua Road); Civilian: Castle Memorial Hospital, 640 ʻUlukahiki Street (Kalanianaʻole Highway at Kailua Road), Kailua
SS: Military: on base; Civilian: ʻAikahi Shopping Center or Kailua town
WA: beachcombing; diving; board surfing; bodysurfing; swimming
WC: strong currents with high or stormy surf; long stretch of sand beach and dunes; many sections of beachrock and reef at water's edge; several good board surfing and bodysurfing areas
PA: limited to military personnel

Mōkapu is the large, wide peninsula that separates the two bays of Kāneʻohe and Kailua. In ancient times, before their attention shifted to Waikīkī, Mōkapu was a favorite resort and fishing area for the Hawaiian *aliʻi*. Kamehameha the Great used the peninsula as a meeting place for his chiefs, and it was from such gatherings of the Hawaiian nobility that the area was named: *mo* is a contracted form of *moku,* or district, and therefore Mōkapu means "sacred district."

Today the entire Mōkapu Peninsula is occupied by a United States Marine Corps air station. The first military installation there, a naval air station, was intended only as a small seaplane base when work began in the late 1930s. Intelligence specialists liked the isolated location. With only one road leading to the base, maximum security could be maintained. The flat plain of Heʻeia also appealed to the naval planners and engineers: the main flight paths to and from the seaplane base would be over unpopulated areas and into the prevailing trade winds.

Civilian contractors started dredging and filling operations in 1939. By late 1941 the major part of the planned construction had been completed. Then came December 7, 1941, during which the air station recorded three historic firsts. It was the first place to be attacked, even before Pearl Harbor; the first plane of Japanese origin was shot down here; and the first Medal of Honor awarded in World War II was given to a navy chief petty officer at the station, John Finn. Nineteen sailors and one Japanese pilot killed in the attack were buried in the

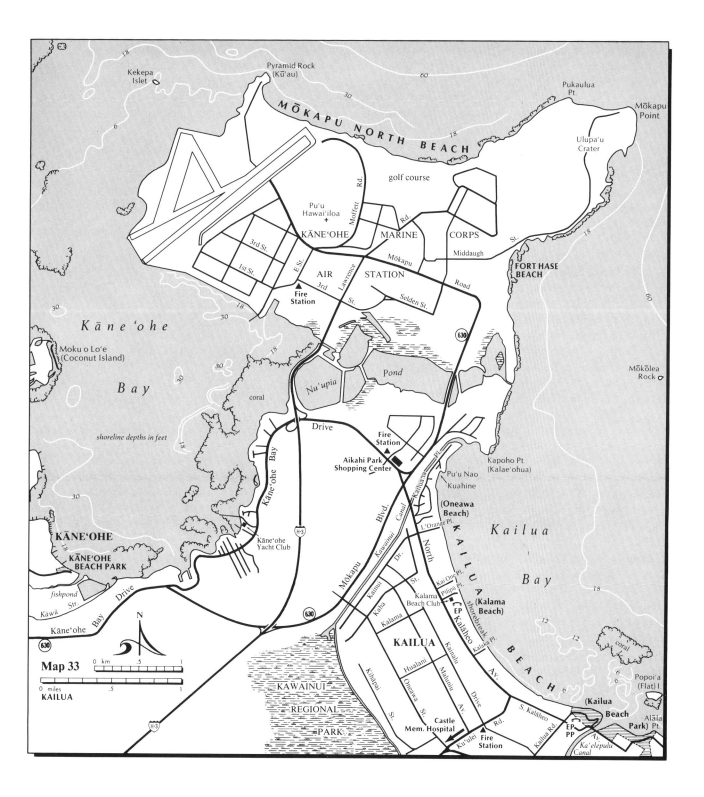

Kekepa
Islet

Pyramid Rock
(Kūʻau)

Pukaulua
Pt.

Mōkapu
Point

M O K A P U   N O R T H   B E A C H

golf course

Ulupaʻu
Crater

30

60

18

18

60

Puʻu
Hawaiʻiloa

KĀNEʻOHE   MARINE   CORPS

Moffett Rd.

Rd.

St.

Middaugh

FORT HASE
BEACH

3rd St.

1st St.

E St.

AIR   STATION

Mōkapu

Lawrence   St.

Road

Mōkōlea
Rock

Fire
Station

3rd St.

Selden St.

630

Kāneʻohe

Moku o Loʻe
(Coconut Island)

30

30

18

18

18

30

Nuʻupia   Pond

Bay

coral

shoreline depths in feet

30

Drive

Kapoho Pt.
(Kalaeʻohua)

Fire
Station

Kaʻthana Pl.

Puʻu Nao
Kuahine

Aikahi Park
Shopping Center

Kailua

Kāneʻohe   Bay

H-3

Kāneʻohe
Yacht Club

(Oneawa
Beach)

LʻOrange Pl.

Bay

KĀNEʻOHE

KĀNEʻOHE
BEACH PARK

18

Blvd.

Kawainui   Canal

North

KAILUA

18

fishpond

Kāwā   Str.

Kāneʻohe   Bay   Drive

630

Mōkapu

Kainui   Dr.

St.

Kai One Pl.

Pilipū Pl.

Kalama
Beach Club

EP

(Kalama
Beach)

Kalana Pt.

12

12

coral

Popoiʻa
(Flat) I.

Kaha

Kalama

Kainalu

Kaʻlaheo

6

6

6

N

Map 33

0 km   .5   1

0 miles   .5   1

KAILUA

H-3

KAWAINUI

REGIONAL

PARK

Kīhāpai   St.

Hualani

Oneawa   St.

Maluniu   Av.

Kainalu   Drive

Castle
Mem. Hospital

Kuʻulei   Rd.

Fire
Station

S. Kalāheo   Av.

Kailua Rd.

EP
PP

(Kailua
Beach)

Alāla Pt.

Kaʻelepulu
Canal

Park) Pt.

KAILUA   BEACH

sands of Heleloa on Mōkapu. The outbreak of World War II turned the air station into one of the major air bases in the Pacific. With the ending of the war in 1945, activity at the air station declined. One of the last traces of wartime to disappear from Mōkapu was the temporary cemetery where the dead of December 7 had been buried. In June 1946 the bodies of the Americans were removed and sent to the mainland for final interment. The remains of Lieutenant Iida, the Imperial Japanese Navy pilot, were returned to his homeland in 1948, at the request of Japanese authorities. In 1949 the Kāne-'ohc Naval Air Station was decommissioned.

Except for a small security detail, the station remained idle until 1952, when the United States Marine Corps reopened the base as a permanent training area. In 1956 the First Marine Brigade was re-established at the station and it continues today as the sole unit occupying Mōkapu Peninsula.

The He'eia shoreline of Mōkapu once offered islanders an excellent swimming beach. During the 1930s this became a fashionable place in which to own a country home. This section of shoreline, however, was drastically altered by the construction of an airfield extension and a revetment. By 1943 dredging and filling operations had added 280 acres of new land to the original ocean frontage, totally eradicating the former beach. During the 1930s the nearby Ku'au, or Pyramid Rock, area was a popular bodysurfing site, considered by many water enthusiasts to have the finest bodysurfing waves on O'ahu. Pyramid Rock Beach remains one of the most frequented swimming areas on the base.

Probably the most popular stretch of shoreline on Mōkapu is North Beach, the long reach of sand fronting the golf course. Formerly known as Heleloa, North Beach is a steep sandy shore bordered almost entirely at the water's edge by sections of beach rock and raised coral reef. Its waters are frequented primarily by board surfers and bodysurfers, occasionally by swimmers and beachcombers. The inshore areas are relatively shallow and rocky, with scattered pockets of sand. The alongshore currents often are strong, especially when the surf is big. North Beach is open only to military personnel, their dependents, and guests. One section of the beach is also known as ''Fourteenth Hole'' because of its proximity to this part of the golf course.

Fort Hase Beach

Kāne'ohe Marine Corps Air Station (fronting Fort Hase housing area)

F: 1 lifeguard tower; roadside parking along beach
LG: service provided by military personnel
EP: none
PP: on base
FS: Military: First Street and E Avenue; Civilian: 45 Kāne'ohe Bay Drive, 'Aikahi
H: Military: Tripler Army Medical Center, Jarrett White Road (off Moanalua Road); Civilian: Castle Memorial Hospital, 640 'Ulukahiki Street (Kalaniana'ole Highway at Kailua Road), Kailua
SS: Military: on base; Civilian: 'Aikahi Shopping Center or Kailua town
WA: diving; shorecasting; board surfing; swimming
WC: strong currents when surf is big or stormy; almost entire shoreline is fronted by beachrock and raised reef; several surfing breaks offshore
PA: limited to military personnel

In 1918, the land called Kuwa'a'ohe on Mōkapu was established as an Army reservation by presidential Executive Order. Appropriately enough, it was named Kuwa'a'ohe Military Reservation. In 1941, the adjoining land of Ulupa'u was added to the reservation, which was then renamed Camp Ulupa'u. With the outbreak of World War II, the camp was designated as Fort Hase. It was the only section of Mōkapu Peninsula that was not acquired by the Navy. In 1952, however, the Fort Hase acreage was acquired by the Marines, thus placing the entire peninsula under one command.

The only reminder today of the former Fort Hase is the beach of the same name on the Kailua side of Ulupa'u Crater. Fort Hase Beach is a narrow strip of alternating sections of sand and coral. The primary swimming area is shallow and well protected by a small coral reef offshore. Although the beach is safe for swimming, it is not particularly attractive to most adults because of the predominantly rocky shoreline. Farther down the coast toward Kailua, the offshore surf attracts many board surfers, but other than these, and occasional fishermen, few people frequent the beach.

Kailua Beach

Kailua Beach is a beautiful two-mile stretch of sandy shoreline between the rocky points of Kapoho and

Alāla. Bordering the entire length of Kailua Bay, this region of prime beachfront property is divided roughly into three sections: Oneawa, Kalama, and Kailua Beach Park. Because of their respective lengths and histories, each section will be described here individually. Kailua, the general name for the whole beach and for the district, usually is translated as "two currents in the sea," although alternate readings have been made. One of these proposes that Kailua is an abbreviated form of Kai-ulua, "sea of the *ulua*," just as Mōkapu is an abbreviation of Moku Kapu.

Oneawa Beach

(also Castle's Beach; formerly Pu'u Nao and Kuahine beaches)
shoreline areas on either side of mouth of Kawainui Canal, Kailua

  F: none; roadside parking on North Kalāheo Avenue
 LG: none
  EP: beach end of public right-of-way between Kailuana Place and L'Orange Place
  PP: 'Aikahi Shopping Center
  FS: 45 Kāne'ohe Bay Drive, 'Aikahi
  H: Castle Memorial Hospital, 640 'Ulukahiki Street (Kalaniana'ole Highway at Kailua Road), Kailua
 SS: 'Aikahi Shopping Center or Kailua town
 WA: diving; board surfing (novice); swimming
 WC: safe all year; small shorebreak surf; water occasionally murky from runoff from Kawainui Canal; shallow, sandy bottom slopes gently to deeper offshore waters
  PA: unlimited; four public rights-of-way from North Kalāheo Avenue

The shoreline boundaries of Oneawa lie roughly between the point called Kalae'ohua and the street now called Kaione. Oneawa, "sands of the milk fish," was a famous fishing grounds, especially for *'ō'io*. Kalae-'ohua, the western end of Oneawa and of Kailua Bay, today is more commonly called Kapoho Point. Kapoho was the name of a pond not far from the point, the water from which was used to fill the shallow salt pans nearby in which salt was made by the evaporation process. Kapoho has long since been filled, but the name, extended to include the nearby point, has remained to

this day. The older name of Kapoho Point, Kalae'ohua, means "the point of the *'ohua*," the young forms of such reef fish as *hinalea, kala, manini, pualu,* and *uhu*. The shallow reef shelf inside of Kalae'ohua once abounded with these fry, besides being an excellent octopus ground.

The next well-known beach area in Oneawa is an elevated rocky ledge that was called Pu'u Nao, "grooved hill." The constant force of the ocean pounding against this beach rock has made shallow, cavelike indentations and crevices along its entire base. The rocky ledge is located just to the east of the mouth of Kawainui Canal.

The beach adjoining Pu'u Nao was known as Kuahine, or "sister." This was a place of drifting seaweed, the most prized being the *limu lipoa,* one of the tastiest of edible seaweeds. Although the Hawaiian name has long since been forgotten, Kuahine still remains the most popular place for limu-gathering in Kailua. Pu'u Nao forms a natural barricade on the shore, keeping the seaweed from washing farther along the beach.

During the more recent history of Kailua, the entire section of Oneawa, including Kalae'ohua, Pu'u Nao, and Kuahine, was acquired by the W. H. Castle family. To the majority of the surfers and fishermen who frequent the area, Oneawa is simply known as "Castle Beach" or "Castle's."

The shoreline of Oneawa is sandy and safe for swimming. The bottom slopes very gently to the deeper offshore waters, making an ideal wading area. The predominant trade winds create an almost continuous shorebreak that accommodates many young board surfers and bodysurfers. Occasionally, the alongshore currents are strong, but usually they are so only when the ocean is rough. The only real danger here is the Kawainui Canal, a long drainage ditch emptying into the sea in the middle of Oneawa Beach. It is deep and wide, and is a potential hazard for wandering children.

The single island offshore from Oneawa is called Mōkōlea, "plover island." Before Kailua was developed after the turn of the century, Kula o 'Ālele, the Coconut Grove area of the little town, was often visited by large flocks of golden plovers. In the evening the birds flew to Mōkōlea to pass the night, thus giving the island its name. Plovers were a favorite food of Hawaiians, and hunters often went to Mōkōlea by canoe or boat to catch them. Mōkōlea is known also as Black Rock and Kukaʻe Manu Island, "bird feces," because of the guano deposits that cover it. Mōkōlea is a state bird refuge with no restrictions against people landing, although the birds must not be molested.

Kalama Beach
300 area of North Kalāheo Avenue, Kailua

F: none; roadside parking on North Kalāheo Avenue and on adjoining public streets
LG: none
EP: public rights-of-way at Pilipu Place and next to Kalama Beach Club
PP: none
FS: 211 Kuʻulei Road, Kailua
H: Castle Memorial Hospital, 640 ʻUlukahiki Street (Kalanianaʻole Highway at Kailua Road), Kailua
SS: Kailua town
WA: board surfing; bodysurfing; swimming
WC: safe all year; occasional strong currents; generally considered as roughest shorebreak section of Kailua Bay; shallow, sandy bottom slopes gently to deeper offshore waters
PA: unlimited; four public rights-of-way from North Kalāheo Avenue
AI: two areas of Kalama Beach are off limits by state regulation to all surfriding devices: Area A: between Kaione Place and Pilipu Place; and Area B: between Kalaka Place and the Kalama Beach Club, 280 North Kalāheo Avenue

In November 1925 the Hawaiian Trust Company opened the first formal housing project in Kailua. The tract was named Kalama in honor of the wife of King Kamehameha III, a former owner of the district of Kailua. When Kamehameha III died, his will provided for the payment of his debts and for the allotment of certain lands to his queen, in lieu of her dower right in the whole. Among other lands, the queen was given the three *ahupuaʻa* of Hakipuʻu, Kāneʻohe, and Kailua. In retirement after the death of her husband, Queen Kalama took considerable interest in the development of a sugar plantation on her windward lands. Unfortunately, as with many other such ventures in Koʻolaupoko at this time, her plantation was not successful.

Soon after the turn of the century, another business venture was launched on the windward side. In 1908 a small group of businessmen organized the Hawaiian Copra Company. With a capital of $30,000, the company set out to plant coconut trees of choice quality in Kailua. The initial 10,000 trees were planted in a 200-acre tract on the plains known as Kula o ʻĀlele. The original coconut grove (using today's landmarks) was located approximately between the main crossroads in Kailua town and Kaha Street and *mauka* of Maluniu Street. Arthur Rice, often acknowledged as the founder of the Hawaiian Copra Company, was not involved initially in the venture. However, he joined the plantation group when they requested the use of seventy-six acres of land he owned *mauka* of the present Oneawa Street. The copra venture, the first large-scale business development undertaken in Kailua, failed. Eventually the land was subdivided and sold for home sites.

In November 1925, Harold Kainalu Long Castle opened the first housing tract in Kailua, just *makai* of the former coconut plantation. (This tract, as has been indicated, was named Kalama in honor of the queen who had owned the entire district of Kailua.) A beach frontage was set aside for the exclusive use of the tract's residents. A clubhouse and pavilion were proposed, to be owned and governed by residents of the subdivision. The beachside facilities, located at 280 North Kalāheo Avenue, were completed in the summer of 1928 and the formal opening was held on July 29 of that year. Primarily because of the presence of the Kalama Clubhouse the center section of Kailua Beach is called Kalama. The facility is still privately owned, and its use is regulated by members.

Kalama Beach probably is the most frequented of the non-park areas of Kailua Beach. The shorebreak usually is bigger at this portion of the beach than anywhere else on the long shoreline. Many board surfers and bodysurfers crowd the shallow breaks when the waves are good. They call the surf between the Kalama Beach Club and Oneawa Beach "Shorebreak." This congested situation once created a serious conflict between the surfing and swimming people, until the trouble was partly resolved in December 1968. The State Department of Transportation placed two sections of Kalama totally off limits to all surfriding devices. Area A is between Kaione and Pilipu streets; Area B is between Kalaka Place and the public right-of-way bordering the Kalama Beach Club property. These restricted areas have helped to ease the tensions created by runaway surfboards and paipo boards that were menacing to swimmers.

The shoreline in the Kalama area generally is steeper and narrower than in any other part of Kailua Beach because here the shorebreak waves are bigger and stronger and therefore more erosive. The alongshore currents are occasionally swift, especially during rough surf, but otherwise there are no water dangers out of the ordinary. The ocean bottom is sandy and slopes gently to the deeper offshore area.

Kailua Beach Park

450 Kawailoa Road

F: 2 comfort stations; 1 pavilion; 1 food and beverage concession; 1 volleyball court; picnic tables; 1 boat ramp; 3 lifeguard towers; 191 parking stalls
LG: daily service provided by City and County
EP: in park area
PP: in park area
FS: 211 Ku'ulei Road, Kailua
H: Castle Memorial Hospital, 640 'Ulukahiki Street (Kalaniana'ole Highway at Kailua Road), Kailua
SS: Kailua town
WA: boating; diving; sailing; snorkeling; board surfing; swimming
WC: safe all year; ocean bottom sandy, sloping gently to deeper offshore waters; beach park divided by Ka'elepulu Canal; channels and holes in canal bottom are dangerous for little children; surfing and diving next to Popoi'a Island (Flat Island) offshore
PA: unlimited

Kailua Beach Park is a thirty-acre public park located at the eastern end of Kailua Bay. Besides its grassy spaces and picnic facilities, the beach park has three lifeguard towers, one of which is manned daily all year long, and a public boat ramp at Alāla Point, the only one in Kailua. The beach is always sandy and wide, narrowing only in the boat ramp area. The ocean bottom slopes gently to the deeper offshore waters, providing an ex-

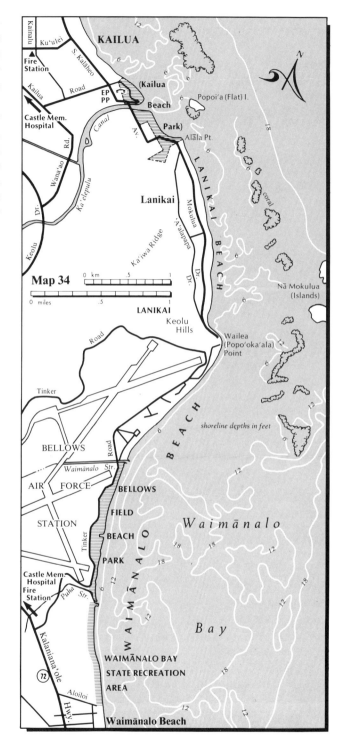

Kailua Beach Park. Sunbathers enjoy a sunny day in Kailua. The *makai* end of Ka'elepulu Canal, which divides the beach park, is sealed off from the ocean by a wide sandbar, creating a shallow pond of brackish water, seen to the left of the pic- ture. This pond, or *muliwai,* is a hazard to unsupervised children because of the deep holes that the canal waters sometimes erode in the pond's sandy bottom.

cellent swimming area. There are no hazardous water conditions.

The major problem in Kailua Beach Park is the *muliwai,* the pond of brackish water in the middle of the park, where Ka'elepulu Canal meets the shoreline. The stream water is almost always separated from the ocean by a wide sand bar. The resulting pond attracts almost every little child on the beach and has been the scene of many near drownings. There are many small holes and channels in the *muliwai* in addition to the deeper water under the nearby bridge. Danger signs posted on the banks of the stream usually go unheeded. Little children should not be allowed to play or swim unsupervised in this area. The only other danger in the park is the occasionally large number of sailing craft arriving and departing from the boat ramp area.

The Kāne'ohe half of Kailua Beach Park formerly was known as Kalapawai, "the water rascal." In ancient times Kalapawai was said to have been an excellent surfing area. The god Lono, among others, is mentioned in legend as having ridden the waves here. During the early 1900s, a piece of land in Kalapawai, along the present Lihiwai and Kailua roads, was purchased by Solomon Mahoe, Sr. Mr. Mahoe placed a sign at the entrance to his property stating the name of the area. When a portion of his land at the corner of Kalaheo and Kailua streets was leased to a storekeeper, the man adopted the name Kalapawai for his establishment. Kalapawai Store remains to this day, the only evidence of the former place name.

On the Waimānalo side of Ka'elepulu Canal the park formed the shoreline edge of the lands once known as

Kawailoa, "the long water." Now the only evidence of this old place name is Kawailoa Road, the single access from Kailua to Lanikai.

Just offshore from Kailua Beach is Popoiʻa Island. Popoiʻa means "rotten fish," and probably refers to the numerous offerings once left at an old fishing shrine in the middle of the island. This *koʻa* was obliterated in the tidal wave of 1946. Popoiʻa is now commonly known in Kailua as "Flat Island." Little imagination is needed to see the reason for its English nickname. Popoiʻa is a designated State Bird Refuge on which people are permitted to land. The island and its seabirds are protected by law and may not be disturbed.

Lanikai Beach

(formerly Kaʻōhao Beach)
(entire length of Mokulua Drive, Lanikai)

 F: none; roadside parking along Mokulua Drive and on adjoining public streets
LG: none
EP: Kailua Beach Park
PP: Kailua Beach Park
FS: 211 Kuʻulei Road, Kailua
 H: Castle Memorial Hospital, 640 ʻUlukahiki Street (Kalanianaʻole Highway at Kailua Road), Kailua
SS: Kailua town
WA: diving; snorkeling; board surfing (occasional); swimming
WC: safe all year; long sandy beach; bottom slopes gently to deeper offshore waters
PA: unlimited; three public rights-of-way from Mokulua Drive

Lanikai is the name of the residential community situated in the headlands between Kailua Bay and Waimānalo Bay. Lanikai is not a proper Hawaiian word, but was devised by this community's promoters. The name probably was intended to mean "royal sea" or perhaps "heavenly sea," which in proper Hawaiian, would have been Kailani, but the words were transposed and joined as they would be in English, rather than in Hawaiian.

The land that comprised the original Lanikai tract was called Kaʻōhao, "the tying." One story about the naming of Kaʻōhao concerns a chief who played a game of *kōnane* with two women. The women wagered themselves against the chief's double canoes, their contents, and the crews. The unscrupulous chief cheated and won and then led the women, tied together, to the place where his canoes were beached. Thereafter the landing was called Kaʻōhao, "the tying," because of this incident. Kaʻōhao also means a swelling, as from the accumulation of fluids in a body during sickness. Other stories are told of people from this area who suffered from such a dropsical condition, again accounting for the name Kaʻōhao.

Kaʻōhao extended from Alāla Point to the hill sloping down from Kaʻiwa Ridge, just about opposite the present Onekea Street. In the ocean fronting Kaʻōhao was a flat reef covered with seaweeds that was known as ʻAʻalapapa, the "fragrant shelf." The *papa* was noted especially for its *limu lipeʻepeʻe,* which is one of the fragrant seaweeds.

The region between Kaʻōhao and Popoʻokaʻala was called Mokulua because of Nā Mokulua, the two islands, just offshore. In former times, a single stream ran through this region of Mokulua that was called Wailea, "pleasing water." The *muliwai* where Wailea met the ocean was often filled with fish. In later years the name Wailea was extended to the nearby point, once known as Popoʻokaʻala. Popoʻo, as it was more commonly called was, like Alāla, important as the site of a fishing shrine. Both points were used by fishermen as landmarks for locating offshore fishing areas. Besides being called Wailea Point, Popoʻo is also known as "Smith's Point," for Helen and Alvin Smith who purchased 1.6 acres there in 1936.

Late in the year 1925, Charles R. Frazier bought the land called Kaʻōhao, 111 acres of the beach portion of Maunawili Ranch, and developed the subdivision that he named Lanikai. He also erected the tall monument that still stands beside the road at Alāla Point. It was constructed to resemble a New England lighthouse. The Trent Trust Company, organized in 1907 by Richard H. Trent, was in charge of selling the lots; Trent and Frazier were good friends. In January 1926, the Trent Trust Company announced that thirty-two lots in the subdivision were on the market. Water was available from a spring on Maunawili Ranch. Later in 1926 the Mokulua Tract, 200 acres adjacent to the first portion, was purchased from Maunawili Ranch to complete the entire Lanikai area as it is today. The watermelon plan-

Christine A. Takata

Lanikai Beach. Various kinds of sailing craft decorate the front yards of the private beachside residences in Lanikai. The prevailing tradewinds that blow almost continuously on this side of Oʻahu make the waters off Lanikai and Kailua an idea place for sailors and wind surfers.

tations and gardens that had been established in Ka-ʻōhao and Mokulua before their purchase by Frazier fell victims to progress. By 1934 Lanikai was described as "a second Kāhala," with up-to-date houses and a garage on every lot. It was and still is an excellent, close-knit residential community. The only home and garage still existing (in 1977) from the original subdivision are located at 1064 Mokulua Drive.

Lanikai Beach is a nearly straight sandy stretch more than a mile long, varying between 20 and 100 feet in width. Many of the beachfront lots are bordered by seawalls to prevent further erosive action of the ocean. Ironically, such protective construction has been a primary cause of the loss of the sand beach in several sections. Swimming is safe along the entire beach. The sandy ocean bottom is shallow, and the inshore waters are well protected by the offshore reef, which dissipates most of the ordinary wave energy. There are no particularly hazardous areas anywhere along Lanikai Beach. Three rights-of-way for the general public are provided along its length.

Offshore are Nā Mokulua, "the two islands," more

commonly known as "Twin Islands." The former Hawaiian community in Kailua referred to the bigger island as Moku Nui and to the smaller as Moku Iki. Today both are State bird sanctuaries, and landing is prohibited without permit from the Division of Fish and Game. However, because of the popularity of its beach as a picnicking area and as a landing for small sailing craft, recreational permits for Moku Nui are always granted free of charge. Access to the rest of the island and all of Moku Iki are still restricted.

Waimānalo Beach

Waimānalo Beach is the longest continuous sand beach on Oʻahu, curving around the shore of Waimānalo Bay for 3½ miles. Beginning at Popoʻokaʻala Point (also called Wailea Point), the Waimānalo shoreline includes Bellows Field, Sherwood Forest, Waimānalo Beach Park, and finally Kaiona Beach Park. During the last decades of the Hawaiian monarchy, much glamour was attached to this region. It was the site of the estate of John M. Cummins, a wealthy half-Hawaiian nobleman, who was the founder and first owner of the Waimānalo Sugar Plantation. The plantation was organized in 1878 and was liquidated in 1947. Waimānalo means "drinkable water," but the reason for giving the name to this region is unknown.

Bellows Field Beach Park

(between Waimānalo and Puha streams, Bellows Field, Kalanianaʻole Highway, Waimānalo)

F: 2 comfort stations; cooking stands and picnic tables; 2 lifeguard towers; unmarked parking area available near beach
LG: service provided by City and County on weekends and national holidays
EP: none
PP: none
FS: Military: Whiteman Road, Bellows Field; Civilian: 1301 Kalanianaʻole Highway, Waimānalo
H: Castle Memorial Hospital, 640 ʻUlukahiki Street (Kalanianaʻole Highway at Kailua Road), Kailua

SS: Kalanianaʻole Highway, Waimānalo
WA: beachcombing; pole fishing; board surfing; bodysurfing; swimming
WC: safe all year; occasionally strong currents along shore; small shorebreak surf almost all year; ocean bottom is sandy, sloping gently to deeper offshore waters; waves occasionally create channels and holes in sand bottom that are hazardous for little children
PA: limited from 12:00 noon on Friday to midnight on Sunday and from dawn to midnight on holidays; take turnoff into Bellows Field
AI: Bellows Recreation Center (from Popoʻokaʻala Point to Waimānalo Stream) is limited to military personnel

In 1917 the Waimānalo Military Reservation, 1,496 acres of sand dunes and sugarcane land, was established by presidential Executive Order. In 1933 the reservation was renamed for 2nd Lieutenant F. B. Bellows, who had been killed in an airplane accident. Before World War II, Bellows Field was administered as an annex of the Army Air Corps' Wheeler Field in Wahiawā. The Bellows Field complex included a firing range and gunnery training site as well as recreation areas.

On December 7, 1941, Bellows Field, along with Pearl Harbor and Kāneʻohe Air Station, was attacked by war planes of the Imperial Japanese Navy. At Bellows Field, two Americans were killed. The following morning a Japanese prisoner, believed to be the first one captured in World War II, was taken on the beach. He was a naval officer who had swum ashore after his two-man submarine had gone aground on the reef in Waimānalo Bay. Later, the body of the sub's other crew member, an enlisted man, was washed ashore. Still later, the submarine itself was salvaged by the U.S. Navy. During World War II, Bellows was expanded extensively, and played an important role in training U.S. Air Force personnel for combat in the Pacific Theater.

On July 4, 1964, forty-six acres of shoreline property within the present military reservation were turned over to the State for use by the public on weekends and national holidays. Today this section is known as Bellows Field Beach Park and is maintained by the City and County.

The park is situated between Waimānalo Stream at the west end and Puha Stream at the east end. It is open to the public from noon on Fridays until midnight on Sundays, and from dawn until midnight on all national

Christine A. Takata

Bellows Field Beach Park. One of the island's most popular sites for novice board surfing and bodysurfing, and for camping as well. Residents come here from all over O'ahu to relax and swim. The beach park, however, is located within a military reservation and is open to the public only during specific hours, generally on the weekends and national holidays.

holidays. Camping permits are issued by the City and County for weekends and national holidays. During the week the park is available to military personnel, to whom permits are issued by the Air Force. The remaining shoreline area of the reservation, extending from Waimānalo Stream to Popo'oka'ala Point, comprises the Bellows Recreation Center, which is reserved for military personnel.

Bellows Field Beach Park, the forty-six-acre section available to the public, is one of the most popular beach recreation areas on O'ahu. During the summer the park is almost invariably crowded from stream to stream with campers, picnic groups, board surfers, swimmers, and bodysurfers. The popularity of the area is attributed to the extensively wooded and relatively undevel-

oped park, coupled with its long, wide, sand beach that is ideal for campers and picnickers. The shallow waters and the small, consistent shorebreak provide excellent and comparatively gentle surfing waves for beginners. To prevent conflicts between surfers and swimmers, the City and County lifeguards prohibit board surfing in the section lying between the two lifeguard towers.

When the surf is good, the sea sometimes cuts small channels throughout the shallow sand bottom. These little channels are dangerous to young children. The shorebreak as well as the incoming tide form currents along the shore that can catch youngsters offguard. Except for the surfboard traffic, Bellows is a safe, enjoyable beach that presents problems only for the very young. The only other problem areas are the two streams, Waimānalo and Puha, at either end of the public park. They are potentially dangerous to wandering children.

For people interested in marine life, a variety of sea creatures can be found on shore and in the water at Bellows Beach. When the prevailing trade winds blow steadily, the *pa'i malau,* or Portugese man o'war, comes ashore in abundance. Resembling a small, floating bubble, the *pa'i* can inflict painful stings upon unwary swimmers. The *pa'i* frequently are accompanied by an interesting kind of snail, the *pūpū pani,* or "cork shell." These sea snails are among the most fragile and delicate of all marine mollusks. Their thin shells, purple or lavender in color, are somewhat transparent and have a spiral shape. The *pūpū pani* are pelagic and drift freely in the open ocean. The animals produce a bluish or purplish fluid which they discharge when disturbed. This is always an amusing reaction to inquisitive children. The *pūpū pani* are reported to feed upon the *pa'i malau,* so the two are often found together on the beach.

When the trade winds are exceptionally strong, the *'ua'u kani,* or wedge-tailed shearwaters, can be found at Bellows Beach as well as throughout the rest of the Waimānalo area. These sea birds nest on nearby Rabbit Island. Frequently they are blown ashore, often far inland, by strong storm winds that prevent the birds from returning to their nesting grounds. The *'ua'u kani* are extremely determined birds, however, and will fight against the wind until they collapse from sheer exhastion. Eventually they are washed up on the beach, where they rest and wait for the wind to subside.

Another interesting creature found at Bellows is the *'ala 'eke,* the Pacific mole crab. More commonly known as "sand turtles," these little crabs live at the water's edge. They ride up and down the beach with incoming and receding waves in search of food. If these crabs should miss an outgoing wave, they immediately burrow out of sight in the wet sand, showing why they are called mole crabs. Usually not more than an inch long, the *'ala 'eke* have a rounded shell very similiar to that of a tiny turtle. This feature gave rise to their popular local name, "sand turtles." They are found on many other beaches besides Bellows. These speedy little crabs can provide many hours of entertainment for children trying to catch them.

Waimānalo Bay State Recreation Area
(commonly known as Sherwood Forest)
(Kalaniana'ole Highway between Bellows Field and Aloiloi Street, Waimānalo)

F: to be developed; unmarked parking area available near beach
LG: none
EP: public right-of-way between 41–915 and 41–921 Laumilo Street, Waimānalo
PP: none
FS: 1301 Kalaniana'ole Highway, Bellows
H: Castle Memorial Hospital, 640 'Ulukahiki Street (Kalaniana'ole Highway at Kailua Road), Kailua
SS: Kalaniana'ole Highway, Waimānalo
WA: board surfing; bodysurfing; swimming
WC: occasional strong currents along shore; generally considered roughest shorebreak area of Waimānalo Bay; waves occasionally create channels and holes in sand bottom that are hazardous for little children; sandy bottom slopes gently to deeper offshore waters
PA: unlimited; from Aloiloi Street

In July 1966, seventy-six acres of Bellows Field were transferred to the State from military control. This acreage included approximately half a mile of sea shore, all of which is scheduled for development as a State beach park. During World War II, this area was called "Bagley Beach," for Vice-Admiral David W. Bagley, commandant of the Fourteenth Naval District. In the 1950s, this end of Bellows Field was abandoned as a military recreational area, in favor of the Kailua end of the reservation. During the early 1960s, this area, which is heavily wooded with ironwood trees, became a popular spot for stripping cars, sex offenses, and other clandestine operations. The activities of the gang that used the area were compared with those of Robin Hood and his Merry Men in England, so naturally this section of shoreline was called "Sherwood Forest." Officially, the park is named the Waimānalo Bay State Recreation Area, but among islanders it is most commonly referred to as Sherwood Forest.

The beach at Sherwood Forest is a long, wide sandy stretch situated between Puha Stream and Aloiloi Street in Waimānalo. It is similiar to Bellows Beach except that the foreshore is steeper and the shallow inshore bottom drops off more abruptly toward the deeper waters. Because of this difference the waves here often are bigger and break harder than they do at Bellows. The

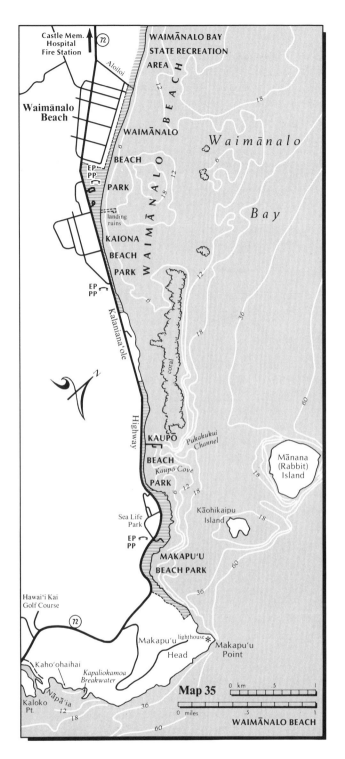

WAIMĀNALO BEACH

Map 35

alongshore currents frequently are strong, especially during the winter, and move down the beach at a fast rate. These currents usually are of negligible danger to adults, but can be a hazard to little children. Sherwood Forest beach is visited primarily by board surfers and bodysurfers. The main entrance to this park is from Aloiloi Street.

Waimānalo Beach Park

41–741 Kalaniana'ole Highway, Waimānalo

F: 1 recreation building/pavilion; 1 comfort station; 2 basketball courts; 1 baseball field; 2 softball fields; cooking stands and picnic tables; 23 marked camping sites with parking; 1 lifeguard tower; 112 parking stalls

LG: none

EP: in park area

PP: in park area

FS: 1301 Kalaniana'ole Highway, Waimānalo

H: Castle Memorial Hospital, 640 'Ulukahiki Street (Kalaniana'ole Highway at Kailua Road), Kailua

SS: Kalaniana'ole Highway, Waimānalo

WA: snorkeling; swimming

WC: safe all year; occasional strong currents along shore when ocean is stormy; sand bottom slopes gently to deeper offshore waters

PA: unlimited

Waimānalo Beach Park is a spacious area of thirty-eight acres located at 41–741 Kalaniana'ole Highway. This tract of land was set aside for public use by presidential Executive Order in April 1921. The place had been the site of the old Waimānalo Landing, which extended into the ocean across from the present intersection of Huli Street and Kalaniana'ole Highway. The landing was used by interisland steamers and other vessels that visited the different sugar plantations and towns on O'ahu's coasts. Other similar landings were built in Lā'ie-malo'o, Punalu'u, and Waikāne. The landing at Waimānalo served both the sugar plantation, which was established in 1878, and the community that grew up around it.

The beach fronting the park is wide and sandy. It is an excellent sunbathing and swimming area, posing no particular water hazards. Occasionally, a small shorebreak forms at the water's edge, but the alongshore currents are usually gentle, becoming stronger only when the ocean is rough.

Kaiona Beach Park

(formerly Pāhonu; also Shriner's Beach)
41–575 Kalaniana'ole Highway, Waimānalo

 F: 1 comfort station; cooking stands and picnic tables; 21 parking stalls
LG: none
EP: in park area
PP: in park area
FS: 1301 Kalaniana'ole Highway, Waimānalo
 H: Castle Memorial Hospital, 640 'Ulukahiki Street (Kalaniana'ole Highway at Kailua Road), Kailua

SS: Kalaniana'ole Highway, Waimānalo
WA: diving; snorkeling; swimming
WC: safe all year; ocean bottom is shallow, with pockets of sand and coral
PA: unlimited

Kaiona Beach Park is small, consisting of four acres located at 41–575 Kalaniana'ole Highway at the eastern end of Waimānalo Bay. The name Kaiona means "attractive sea," undoubtedly referring to the beautiful ocean and the offshore reefs. The sand beach fronting the park, narrow in comparison with other sections of Waimānalo Beach, still provides a good sunbathing area. The inshore ocean bottom is shallow, consisting of a mixture of sand pockets and patches of coral reef. Swimming is safe. The outer reefs protect the shoreline from strong currents.

Adjoining Kaiona Beach Park are several large pri-

Christine A. Takata

Kaiona Beach Park. The rock wall pictured is said to have once enclosed a turtle pond called Pahonu. Rabbit (Mānana) Island offshore still harbors rabbits within the recesses of its crater. Both the pond and the island can be seen from Kaiona Beach Park.

vate estates. The entire area, including the park and the large lots, formerly was known as Pāhonu, "turtle fence." On the shoreline in front of the Shriners' Club and the old E. O. Hall estate are the remnants of what appears to be an old fish pond. At one time, people say, its walls were five hundred feet long, extending into the present park's shoreline. The legend about this pond centers around a former chief of the district: he was so fond of turtle meat that he ordered the sea wall built to maintain a constant supply of live turtles. Every turtle caught by a fisherman in Waimānalo had to be put into the enclosure, and no one but the chief was allowed to eat turtle meat under penalty of death. From that time on the area was called Pāhonu.

An alternate reason for the naming of Pāhonu was offered in September 1906, when the S.S. *Manchuria,* a large passenger ship, ran aground on the reef offshore from the present beach park. News releases of the day said that the *Manchuria,* approaching O'ahu in a drizzling rain, had struck Pāhonu Ledge just before twilight.

As part of his story, one writer offered a translation of the name of the ledge between Rabbit Island and the Waimānalo Landing. He stated that the reef had been named for a beach inshore that had been a nesting place for turtles. When the turtles laid their eggs in the sand, they apparently deposited them in long rows, like stones in a wall. For this peculiarity, he said, the beach had been named Pāhonu, "turtle wall." The Pāhonu area is also known as "Shriners' Beach," because of the Shriners' clubhouse that was opened there on April 20, 1931.

Kaupō Beach Park

(formerly Ko'onāpou)
41–401 Kalaniana'ole Highway, Waimānalo

F: none; roadside parking along Kalaniana'ole Highway
LG: none
EP: Makapu'u Beach Park
PP: Makapu'u Beach Park
FS: 1301 Kalaniana'ole Highway, Waimānalo
H: Castle Memorial Hospital, 640 'Ulukahiki Street (Kalaniana'ole Highway at Kailua Road), Kailua

SS: Kalaniana'ole Highway, Waimānalo
WA: diving; board surfing; swimming
WC: safe all year; majority of shoreline is fronted by beachrock or reef; good swimming and surfing areas offshore
PA: unlimited

Kaupō Beach Park, a long, narrow, eight acres in extent, is located in the district of Waimānalo at 41–401 Kalaniana'ole Highway. The greater part of the park, like its neighbor Sealife Park, is situated on a fan of lava that is thought to be the most recent flow on O'ahu. In 1920, long before this rocky region was developed or even could be reached by road, an old village site here was brought to the public's attention by a Honolulu man named George Mellen. While hiking through the area, Mellen found the ruins of a stone village. Investigations revealed that a fishing village had been built there, probably during the disastrous smallpox epidemic of 1853. Hawaiians attempting to escape the disease fled from homes nearer Honolulu and settled temporarily in this region. The village was called Ko'o-nā-pou, "staff posts," referring to the timbers that held up the thatched roofs of the stone houses. Later the name was changed to Kaupō.

The beach park is used primarily by fishermen and surfers. The little cove formed by the most prominent lava point in the park often has small, easy-breaking waves, ideal for novice board surfers. When a good swell is running, the break also attracts a number of more-experienced wave riders.

Over the years the cove has been known to the surfing community by a variety of names, such as Kumu Cove, Blimp's Point, Kaupō, and The Bay. Formerly this section of the beach was called Kalapueo. An unusual object of historical interest on this beach is a large rock called Pōhaku Pa'akiki. It is a monument to an agreement reached between the Hawaiian people who lived here and the guardian shark of the offshore waters. Since the rock was put up, there have been no shark attacks in the Waimānalo area.

The long, narrow beach park is safe for swimming, but the many patches of shallow inshore reef discourage most swimmers. There are no strong alongshore currents. Besides the small offshore surf in the cove, there is another break in the eastern end of the park usually known as "Baby Makapu'u." Here, however, the shoreline is rough and rocky. Surfing or bodysurfing generally is attempted only by experienced riders.

At the Waimānalo end of Kaupō is a wide 700-foot-long pier and a small boat harbor, built and operated by Makai Range, Inc. These facilities, completed in 1969, provide a berthing, launching, and support area for undersea operations in the offshore waters. Makai Range is also an emergency refuge harbor for any boats in the vicinity that may need immediate assistance. The facilities include a submarine slip capable of handling most small research submersibles.

Just offshore from Kaupō Beach Park lies one of the best known islets on O'ahu's coastline, Rabbit Island. Before 1880 the island was called Mānana, "to stretch out or to protrude." In the late 1880s John Cummins, the first owner of Waimānalo Plantation, decided to raise rabbits as a hobby. He did not want his European hares to ruin Waimānalo's crops in case they happened to escape and multiply, so he released them on Mānana. From that time on Mānana has been known as Rabbit Island. Curiously enough, the island's profile resembles the head of a rabbit with its ears back. The rabbit's nose points toward Makapu'u lighthouse.

In 1932 the island was seriously considered as a site for a prison camp, but the idea was abandoned because of the limited water supply available then in Waimānalo. Now Rabbit Island is a State bird sanctuary. Landing is prohibited without a permit, which is usually given only for scientific reasons, to organized groups for bird watching, or to students of natural history. The Division of Fish and Game, however, considers all requests.

Rabbit Island is an old volcanic crater. The entire floor of the crater is honeycombed with the nesting burrows of the numerous seabirds that live on the island. Competition between the few wild rabbits still subsisting in the crater and the birds is not intense enough to warrant exterminating the rabbits. The rabbit population decreases in the summer, when lack of water dries up the meager vegetation, and increases during the winter, when rains replenish the growth.

The primary attraction of the island to water enthusiasts is its surfing waves. During big swells there is good surfing break off the Kailua end of the island.

Makapu'u Beach Park
41–095 Kalaniana'ole Highway, Waimānalo

F: 2 comfort stations; 1 lifeguard tower; cooking stands and picnic tables; 39 parking stalls
LG: daily service provided by City and County
EP: in park area
PP: in park area
FS: 1301 Kalaniana'ole Highway, Waimānalo
H: Castle Memorial Hospital, 640 'Ulukahiki Street (Kalaniana'ole Highway at Kailua Road), Kailua
SS: Kalaniana'ole Highway, Waimānalo
WA: diving; bodysurfing; swimming
WC: extremely dangerous currents and surf from September through April; generally calm during summer for recreational swimming; beach erodes heavily during winter, exposing many rocks and boulders in shorebreak area; sand accretes during summer
PA: unlimited
AI: board surfing is prohibited by state law; paipo boards are permitted if they are 3 feet or less in length and if they have no skeg (bottom fin); lifeguards use a flag warning system: red = dangerous; green = safe; yellow = intermediate conditions; Makapu'u is the most famous bodysurfing beach in Hawai'i

Makapu'u is the name of the easternmost point on O'ahu. Far beneath the Makapu'u lighthouse, in the very base of the steep cliffs, is a large ocean cave called Ke Ana ke Akua Pōloli, "The Cave of the Hungry God." The point on the Honolulu side of the cave was known as Moeau, while the point on the Ko'olaupoko side was called Makapu'u. A black stone with eight protrusions upon it resembling human eyes formerly stood at the Ko'olaupoko point. This stone was said to have been the *kinolau,* or physical manifestation, of a supernatural woman called Makapu'u, "bulging eyes." Although her name still remains, the *kinolau* of Makapu'u has been missing for many years.

Also gone from the point is another stone image that was known as Mālei. Mālei was embodied in a very white stone that resembled a rounded head on a torso. She was placed in the vicinity of the lighthouse by 'Ai'ai, the son of Kū'ula, the Hawaiian god of fishermen. Mālei had charge of the *uhu,* the parrot fish, from Makapu'u to Hanauma, and for many years fishermen climbed the cliffs to make offerings of *limu lipoa* to her.

Makapu'u Beach probably is the most famous place for bodysurfing in the islands. In 1933, when the coastal

Makapu'u Beach Park. Probably the most famous bodysurfing beach in all of the Hawaiian Islands; bodysurfers come from all over the island chain to ride the surf here. The photograph was taken on a relatively calm day; during the stormy winter months, Makapu'u is one of the most dangerous beaches on O'ahu.

road between Sandy Beach and Waimānalo was completed, the area began attracting swimmers from all over O'ahu. Previously the beach was frequented primarily by fishermen and bodysurfers from nearby Waimānalo. The great attraction always has been the excellent bodysurfing waves. On a good day the surf often reaches heights of twelve feet and breaks several hundred yards offshore. The waves are powerful and steep. Yet at the same time each has a comparatively slow rolling shoulder. These are ideal characteristics for bodysurfers who do not command the speed and maneuverability of the board surfer. Riders can take off on the outside peaks and, with a little skill gained from experience, can come all the way in to the shorebreak. Although the beach is bordered on both sides by rocks, there is no raised reef anywhere in the offshore waters. Bodysurfers do not have to worry about pulling out of a wave until they are well in toward shore. Makapu'u also has an excellent shorebreak. Many bodysurfers prefer the shorter and faster shorebreak rides, and visitors enjoy being tossed around in these inshore waves.

Because Makapu'u is such an immensely popular bodysurfing beach, board surfing here is prohibited by regulation of the State Department of Transportation. Paipo boards are permitted, but only if they are less than three feet long and have no skeg or bottom fin. If a person stands on the point below the park's comfort station and draws an imaginary line to Makapu'u Point below the lighthouse, the waters shoreward of this line constitute the restricted area. The regulation is strictly enforced by City and County lifeguards.

Makapu'u Beach is a curved, sandy pocket about 1,000 feet long enclosed by a high sea cliff and a point of lava rock. It experiences a great deal of seasonal variation in width. During summer months the beach is wide and the ocean is usually calm and safe. During the winter months severe erosion of the beach exposes many large rocks and boulders in the shorebreak. The often huge winter surf is very dangerous for inexperienced swimmers. These waves are the best for bodysurfing, but they are also the most hazardous for the unknowing and the unwary. When the surf is big, generally there are two very powerful rip currents that run straight out to sea. One pulls along the cliffs extending toward the lighthouse, while the other runs past "The Point," the rocks at the front of the comfort station. On a calm day the sand channels that these rip currents have formed in the ocean bottom can be seen from the road above. The locations of these rips occasionally vary, depending on the size and direction of the swell.

Heavy surf at Makapu'u also produces some very swift alongshore currents. All too often, people of all ages can be swept off their feet and dragged toward the rocks at either end of the beach. On days when the surf is big the waves break on shore with tremendous force. Inexperienced swimmers, caught up in the powerful currents and pounded by the hardhitting shorebreak, often are rendered helpless in a matter of minutes. During winter months, the lifeguards at Makapu'u make more rescues than do those at any other swimming place on O'ahu except for Sandy Beach. The two parks compare fairly closely in rescue statistics.

The many rescues at Makapu'u are made necessary because of the ignorance of so many people who have no idea how powerful, or how deadly, the ocean can be. They watch the experienced bodysurfers who know how to contend with all the adverse water conditions, and they feel that they can bodysurf just as "effortlessly." Even strong, competitive swimmers find that their strength and speed in a pool are no substitutes for experience in a turbulent ocean.

City and County lifeguards are stationed at Makapu'u every day throughout the year. Often they are assisted on especially bad days by bodysurfers who regularly frequent the beach. A flag warning system is maintained by the lifeguards: red is flown for extremely dangerous conditions, green for safe conditions, and yellow for all intermediate conditions. All swimmers at Makapu'u should be cautious at all times.

Bibliography

Allen, Gwenfread E. *Hawaii's War Years 1941–1945*. Honolulu: University of Hawaii Press, 1950.

Bird, Isabella L. *Six Months in the Sandwich Islands*. Honolulu: University of Hawaii Press, 1964.

Blickhahn, Harry M. *Uncle George of Kilauea Volcano, Hawaii:* Volcano House, Hawaii National Park, 1961.

Brennan, Joseph. *Duke of Hawaii*. New York: Ballantine Books, 1968.

Bryan, Edwin H. Jr., *Hawaiian Nature Notes*. 2nd ed. Honolulu: Honolulu Star Bulletin, 1935.

Castro, Alex H., and Yost, Harold H. *The Hawaii Almost Nobody Knows*. Honolulu: n.p., 1972.

City and County of Honolulu. *Index of Oahu's Parks and Facilities*. Honolulu: City and County of Honolulu, 1975.

Corps of Engineers, U.S. Army Engineer Division, Pacific Ocean. *Hawaii Regional Inventory of the National Shoreline Study*. Honolulu: Corps of Engineers, 1971.

Daws, Gavin. *Shoal of Time*. Honolulu: The University Press of Hawaii, 1974.

Emerson, Nathaniel B. *Unwritten Literature of Hawaii*. Rutland, Vt., and Tokyo: C. E. Tuttle, 1965.

Emerson, Olive P. *Pioneer Days in Hawaii*. Garden City, N.Y.: Doubleday, Doran, and Co., 1928.

Fiddler, Frank. *Mokapu: A Study of the Land*. Honolulu, 1956.

Gast, Ross, and Conrad, Agnes. *Don Francisco de Paula Marin*. Honolulu: The University Press of Hawaii, 1973.

Gessler, Clifford. *Tropic Landfall, the Port of Honolulu*. Garden City, N.Y.: Doubleday, Doran, and Co., 1942.

Hargreaves, Dorothy, and Hargreaves, Bob. *Tropical Trees of Hawaii*. Portland, Ore.: Hargreaves Industrial, 1964.

Hawaii Audubon Society. *Hawaii's Birds*. Honolulu: Hawaii Audubon Society, 1967.

Hawaii State, Department of Planning and Economic Development. *Hawaii's Shoreline*. Honolulu: Department of Planning and Economic Development, 1964.

Hosaka, Edward. *Sport Fishing in Hawaii*. Honolulu: Bond's, 1944.

Ii, John Papa. *Fragments of Hawaiian History,* edited by D. Barrère. Honolulu: Bishop Museum Press, 1959.

Kamakau, Samuel M. *Ka Po'e Kahiko*. Edited by Dorothy Barrère. Honolulu: Bishop Museum Press, 1964.

Kamakau, Samuel M. *Ruling Chiefs of Hawaii*. Honolulu: Kamehameha Schools, 1961.

Kelly, Marion. *Loko I'a o He'eia Fishpond*. Honolulu: Bishop Museum Press, 1975.

Kent, H. W. *Charles Reed Bishop, Man of Hawaii*. Palo Alto, Ca.: Pacific Books, 1965.

Lahaina Restoration Foundation. *Story of Lahaina*. Lahaina, Maui, Hawaii: The Lahaina Restoration Foundation, 1972.

McAllister, J. Gilbert. *Archaeology of Oahu*. Honolulu: Bishop Museum Press, 1933.

Macdonald, Gordon, and Abbott, Agatin. *Volcanoes in the Sea*. Honolulu: University of Hawaii Press, 1970.

McGrath, Edward J.; Brewer, Kenneth M.; and Krauss, Bob. *Historic Waianae*. Norfolk Is., Australia: Island Heritage, Ltd., 1973.

Malo, David. *Hawaiian Antiquities*. Honolulu: Bishop Museum Press, 1951.

Moberly, Ralph M. *Hawaiian Beach Systems*. Honolulu: Hawaii Institute of Geophysics, University of Hawaii, 1964.

Munro, George C. *Birds of Hawaii*. Rutland, Vt.: Bridgeway Press, 1960.

Neal, Marie C. *In Gardens of Hawaii*. Honolulu: Bishop Museum Press, 1965.

Paki, Pilahi. *Legends of Hawaii; Oahu's Yesterday*. Honolulu: Victoria Publishers, 1972.

Pukui, Mary; Elbert, Samuel. *Hawaiian Dictionary*. Honolulu: University of Hawaii Press, 1971.

Pukui, Mary; Elbert, Sammuel; and Mookini, Esther. *Place Names of Hawaii*. Honolulu: The University Press of Hawaii, 1974.

Raphaelson, Rayna. *The Kamehameha Highway*. Honolulu: Percy M. Pond, 1925(?).

Schuyler, James D. and Allardt G. F. *Culture of Sugar Cane: Report on Water Supply for Irrigation on the Hononliuli and Kahuku Ranchos*. Oakland, Ca., 1889.

Scott, Edward B. *The Saga of the Sandwich Islands*. Lake Tahoe: Sierra-Tahoe Publishing Co., 1968.

Stearns, Harold T. *Geology of the Hawaiian Islands*. Honolulu: Advertiser Publishing Co., 1946.

Stejneger, Leonhard H. *The Land Reptiles of the Hawaiian Islands*. Vol. 21. Washington, D.C.: U.S. National Museum, 1899.

Sterling, Elspeth P., and Summers, Catherine C. *The Sites of Oahu*. Honolulu: Bishop Museum Press, 1962.

Stewart, Charles S. *Journal of a Residence in the Sandwich Islands*. Honolulu: University of Hawaii Press, 1970.

Thurston, Lorrin A. *Thurston's Hawaiian Guide Book*. Honolulu: Advertiser Publishing Co., 1927.

Tinker, Spencer W. *Pacific Sea Shells*. Rutland, Vt. and Tokyo: C. E. Tuttle Co., 1952.

Titcomb, Margaret. *Native Use of Fish in Hawaii*. 2nd ed. Honolulu: The University Press of Hawaii, 1972.

Whitney, Henry M. *The Hawaiian Guide Book for Travelers*. Rutland, Vt. and Tokyo: C. E. Tuttle Co., 1970.

Wright, Bank. *Surfing Hawaii*. Los Angeles: Tivoli Printing Co., 1972.

Index

190

Production Notes

This book was designed by Roger Eggers. Typesetting was done on the Unified Composing System by the design and production staff of the University of Hawaii Press.

The text typeface is Compugraphic English Times and the display typeface is Avant Garde Gothic Book.

Offset presswork and binding were done by Vail-Ballou Press, Inc. Text paper is Glatfelter Hi Brite Vellum, basis 55.